Preserving Family Recipes

Preserving Family Recipes

How to Save and Celebrate Your Food Traditions

VALERIE J. FREY

The University of Georgia Press ❖ Athens and London

Publication of this work was made possible, in part, by a generous gift from the University of Georgia Press Friends Fund

All photos are from the author's collection unless otherwise noted.

Published by the University of Georgia Press
Athens, Georgia 30602
www.ugapress.org
© 2015 by Valerie J. Frey

Designed by Erin Kirk New
Set in Archer
Printed and bound by Thomson-Shore

The paper in this book meets the guidelines for permanence and durability of the Committee on Production Guidelines for Book Longevity of the Council on Library Resources.

Most University of Georgia Press titles are available from popular e-book vendors.

Printed in the United States of America
19   18   17   16   15   P   5   4   3   2   1

Library of Congress Cataloging-in-Publication Data

Frey, Valerie J., 1969–
    Preserving family recipes : how to save and celebrate your food traditions / Valerie J. Frey.
        pages   cm
    Includes bibliographical references and index.
    ISBN 978-0-8203-3063-1 (pbk. : alk. paper) 1. Cooking—Technique.
2. Cooking—Research. 3. Families. 4. Food habits. I. Title.
    TX651.F74 2015
    641.5028—dc23   2015022630

British Library Cataloging-in-Publication Data available

This book is dedicated to my mother,

Sharon Lee Cowles Frey 1942-1993

When I came home clutching a new recipe,
she always smiled and reached for her
apron--no matter how many messes I made.

19 • 69

Sharon Frey in the kitchen
with her children, Valerie and Eric,
April 1969.

Contents

Introduction. Comfort, Revulsion, and Cultural History—Served Up in a Single Bowl   1

Chapter 1   Setting a Course   13

Chapter 2   Organizing and Protecting Your Materials   35

Chapter 3   Adjusting Recipes   65

Chapter 4   Working with Regional or World Recipes   97

Chapter 5   Interviews and Cooking Visits   109

Chapter 6   Orphaned Recipes and Conducting Research   133

Chapter 7   Sharing Family Recipes and Foodways   171

Appendix 1. Exploring a Recipe: The Quest for the Extraordinary Biscuit   187

Appendix 2. Exploring Recipe History: The Evolution of Biscuits   211

Appendix 3. Exploring a Cook's Legacy   229

Acknowledgments   253

Notes   257

Suggested Reading   271

Bibliography   277

Index   289

Preserving Family Recipes

Robert A. Frey's Squirrel Mulligan, 1990.

Comfort, Revulsion, and Cultural History—Served Up in a Single Bowl

When we pick up a certain utensil to cook a certain dish in the traditional way ...
we are enacting a ritual that binds us to the place we live and to those in our family, both living
and dead.—Bee Wilson, *Consider the Fork: A History of How We Cook and Eat* (249)

She was a bride two thousand miles from home meeting her husband's family for
the first time. Unfamiliar faces filled the room—new aunts, uncles, and cousins
galore. Because she was the guest of honor, everyone waited while her father in
law handed her the first steaming bowl of his signature stew. It was fragrant with
bacon and flecked with vegetables, served up with a wedge of cornbread. And
floating on top was a tiny skinless skull, an orb of meaty bone with empty eye
sockets staring back. Two yellow rodent teeth curled into the broth.

Newlywed Sharon Cowles
Frey. *Courtesy of Marci
Greene Severson.*

The young lady holding that bowl of soup was my mother back in 1962. My
father's people were thriving in rural Arkansas long before the Civil War, so
nobody thought to mention that Grandpa's mulligan was made with yesteryear's local favorite—squirrel meat. Or to warn my mother that the brains were
a delicacy too tender to survive being stirred in the pot, and thus the whole
skull was included. Let's just say it wasn't at all what my mother expected when
she reached out for that bowl.

In my growing-up years, I relished the "skull stew" story. Not only did I
glimpse an image of my mother as an inexperienced newlywed—so different
from the mature and competent woman I knew—but I also found empathy

The author's parents, Robert W. Frey and Sharon Cowles, on their wedding day, Rainier, Oregon, September 1962.

In the author's grandfather's home, Christmas 1967. He built the two-bedroom, one-bath home in the mid-1950s on the same spot as the family's much older dog-trot-style house. It still stands on the edge of New Edinburg, Arkansas (current population around 120).

soaked into that comedic moment. I imagined how stricken yet polite my own expression would have been if I were standing in her shoes. Thus this tale was one of the first that I recorded when I was in my early twenties, during the period of my parents' illnesses and deaths, a time when I had a crash course in no longer taking family narratives and traditions for granted. The mulligan had a starring role, and it didn't escape me how the stew I was never crazy about as a kid suddenly seemed like comfort food now that my childhood was undeniably over. I asked Grandpa Frey for the recipe.[1] Although he was willing to help, the process of preserving the instructions and creating my own mulligan was not straightforward. For starters, the recipe existed only in Grandpa's head. Luckily, he took a stab at writing it down, and a few days later I received an envelope in the mailbox with the words "Val—add a little black pepper" scribbled on the back.[2] Inside I found a recipe adapted (*whew!*) for chicken.

Even though I now had a written recipe and it was for a relatively simple dish, it was an information puzzle. I quickly sorted out the unorthodox spelling of an intelligent man whose trade as a blacksmith didn't give him much chance to expand his eighth-grade education, yet I still had a document that only hinted at a lot of know-how. Grandpa didn't realize the extent of his expertise with things like developing the flavor of broth from scratch or how to preserve homegrown vegetables at their peak. Heck, he didn't even tell me how much liquid to put into the pot. I asked a lot of follow-up questions and read many cookbook pages before my mulligan had a chance at rich flavor too. (And, yes, I now wish I'd asked him the specifics of how he made it with squirrel.)

Robert A. Frey in his kitchen, 1998.

Tasty stew aside, another part of the information puzzle was enjoying this family recipe in context. In all the years I'd heard that newlywed dinner story, I didn't stop to think about how interesting it is that my parents were both born into American farming communities and yet had vastly different experiences in many ways. In those days before cable television, routine air travel, and the Internet, there were more than a few cultural gaps between a groom from the South Arkansas flatlands and a bride who grew up in Oregon's commerce zone along the Columbia River. Perhaps nowhere were the differences more obvious than at the family dinner table. (Early in my parents' courtship, there was also a tense supper moment in Oregon. My father didn't realize his future mother-in-law was trying to please him by attempting southern cornbread, and he mistook the oddly sweet, fine-grained slice for unfrosted cake!)

My mother's people didn't make mulligan or eat squirrels. Did anybody else? A little reading taught me that famed French epicure Brillat-Savarin enjoyed a meal of squirrel simmered in Madeira during a 1794 trip to America.[3] Illustrious forefathers like Thomas Jefferson hunted (and almost surely ate) squirrels.[4] Various mainstream cookbooks in the nineteenth century included squirrel recipes, and in the 1890s, President Grover Cleveland's steward wrote a White House cookbook that included a recipe for Squirrel Soup, although I noticed that in the revised Centennial Edition it was one of the few recipes that didn't get an update.[5] In the Great Depression, the Works Progress Administration documented Squirrel Mulligan as part of America's culinary history.[6] Before more specific recipes and traditions took hold, "mulligan" started as a toss-in-the-pot-whatever-you've-got soup made by hobos during the golden age of railroading and can be considered a gastronomic cousin to popular communal one-pot dishes such as Brunswick stew, burgoo, and booyah.[7]

I started with just a funny food-related story but then tracked down and worked with a recipe. Not only does the adjusted recipe allow me a lifetime of memory-rich comfort food, but it can also be passed on to others, sharing a bit of my grandfather's know-how now that he's gone. My son can taste spoonfuls of family history he otherwise would have missed. Finally, even with an unusual recipe like Squirrel Mulligan, a little research about how this dish fits into American foodways opened a door for seeing more clearly how my family background fits into my country's culture and history. That's the beauty of family recipes.

What about your family? What recipes, stories, and food traditions are waiting to be explored?

Connections through Recipes

Since you've picked up this book, I assume you have an interest not only in cooking but also in your family's history. That intersection of interests can cast a deep spell. In my case, experiences like the one I had with the mulligan recipe turned my career path away from the field of art education and sent me back to school to become an archivist. I helped people with reference questions but also prepared collections of historical papers for future researchers. Because of my education background, I jumped at any chance to help teachers and students use primary sources (including recipes) in the classroom. I also developed presentations and workshops for the general public about historical research, oral history, and genealogy.

After researching my own family's history and helping others with theirs, I found some largely unspoken common threads that helped me realize why family recipes are so important. I believe most of us want to know more than the mere names and dates that fill out a pedigree chart. We approach the search with hopes layered by decades and generations. First, we're looking for stories and personalities, for what life was like for the ancestors we never got to meet. Second, we want to vividly remember recent family now gone, enjoying our memories while preventing loved ones' legacies from fading. And finally, we want to see our own lives in a kinship context, sharing experiences and knowledge with family members now and also creating a personal legacy as a gift for generations to come. A passion for genealogy—or even just casually poking into your family's history—is about seeking connections.

While my interest in family history grew, I was lucky enough to be related to some wonderful cooks who encouraged and worked with me. They taught me early on that family recipes are particularly valuable for nurturing connections, for highlighting and strengthening ties. Food is sensual in nature, giving family foodways and reminiscing a natural link. Much like Marcel Proust's famous madeleine cake, the same dish that satisfies hunger and pleases the senses can

>> Each food-related activity—from a simple meal at home to an elaborate public celebration—is a form of communication and communion. —Marcie Cohen Ferris, *Matzoh Ball Gumbo: Culinary Tales of the Jewish South* (9)

Sharon Cowles Frey's recipe for strawberry jam, rendered barely legible by some long-ago spill.

trigger our memories, drawing us closer to family and our cultural background.[8]

Keeping all this in mind, at work I began to include information in my public programs about how to preserve family recipes. It struck a nerve. The question-and-answer sessions grew longer and were often dominated by discussions about old recipes. I heard fond reminiscences about everything from Grandma's dumplings to Uncle's pound cake. (During my research, one elderly lady closed her eyes and fondly recalled the yeasty scent of her mother's homemade bread. Her face lit up as she spoke, although the bread had come out of the oven *nine decades* earlier.)[9] Admittedly, there were also discussions of family recipes now outdated due to health considerations or modern tastes. Yet whether now regarded as the best or the worst, recipes tell something about the families that created or used them.

When we value family foodways, it brings us joy but also makes us vulnerable to loss. Family cooking is a particularly poignant trigger for nostalgia and thus also for genealogical regret, the wish that you had captured information while those "in the know" were still alive. Recipes are often endangered. Many never reach document form, existing only as unwritten know-how that vanishes when a cook dies. Even when recipes are written down, they are sometimes inaccurate or fail to give the tips that would allow another cook to successfully replicate the dish. Finally, we often plunk Grandma's handwritten recipe card on the countertop next to the steaming pot and the spattering mixer, shortening that document's life.

There is a need, and thus this book was born.

How to Use This Book

The ideal way to go about preserving family recipes would be to hire a "dream team" of professionals to help you create a family cookbook. Chefs of varied areas of expertise and a writing coach would help you adjust recipes and add personal stories to them. You could also hire a certified genealogist, a historian or two, an oral historian, and a folklorist so that your collection of family recipes would be accompanied by fascinating family lore flawlessly documented and placed in a wider historical context. When you win the lottery, I highly recommend this approach. But this book came about for the same reason that the Georgia Archives hired me to develop educational programs—we usually have to learn to do the job ourselves. Fortunately, it is joy to do so.

An education in family recipes can be a winding road. I've always been a baker at heart and, at the same time, I'm not a big fan of meat (except for when I get a whiff of bacon or slow-cooked pit barbecue), so my kitchen skills are decidedly lopsided. Still, the more I cooked, the better I became at working with recipes. Early on, it was a disappointment that my great-aunts' recipes sometimes didn't result in the tall, glorious cakes that appeared at birthdays and family reunions. I knew that part of the problem might be a faulty memory; the lofty glory of those remembered cakes probably had something to do with my vantage point as a child just tall enough to see over the table. Nevertheless, I turned to a friend with a degree in home economics. She shook her head. "You'd have to be a pastry chef to really know what you're doing." She was right in that between ingredients and techniques, there are enough variables that even an experienced food professional can struggle with an old family recipe.

But I didn't give up.

Admittedly, sometimes it takes quite a bit of trial and error, yet I almost always come through with effective written recipes and satisfying dishes on the other side. Perhaps it was growing up as the daughter of a scientist or my

Annual Frey family reunion, Cleveland County, Arkansas, 1976.

Robert W. Frey and his cousin Sharon Atkins sharing a glorious birthday cake, ca. 1940.

Information Science master's degree peeping through, but each time I tackled adjusting a recipe as an information puzzle, I found tips, tricks, and resources that helped me successfully document and fine-tune it. That is the nucleus of this book. Then, starting with kin and moving my way outward to strangers with strong reputations, I tracked down family cookbook authors and some great cooks who shared their know-how for tweaking recipes. I read dozens of books and cookbooks. Last but not least, I visited some historical kitchens. The resulting information for gathering, adjusting, supplementing, and preserving recipes is now in your hands.

Quick Overview

Inside the seven main chapters you'll find practical, organized tips alongside sound archival principles to help you avoid pitfalls and get effective results. Depending on your needs and interests, you may not use every chapter or section, so bolded headings can help you find your way or can be used as project checklists.

- *Chapter 1: Setting a Course.* Getting started is often the hardest part of a project, and this chapter will help you figure out a scope and approach that work best for you.
- *Chapter 2: Organizing and Protecting Your Materials.* Setting up an effective workflow will help you preserve recipes and may even streamline your everyday cooking. You'll also learn how to think like an archivist, safely preserving heirloom materials for future generations.
- *Chapter 3: Adjusting Recipes.* An inaccurate or sketchy recipe can lead more often to frustration than to a tasty dish. Here you'll learn to record and fine-tune recipes so that they can be used successfully time and again by yourself or others.
- *Chapter 4: Working with Regional or World Recipes.* Tips from cooks who bridge cultures in their kitchens can help you with family recipes that originated in another region or country. This chapter also gives ideas for tracking down hard-to-find ingredients.
- *Chapter 5: Interviews and Cooking Visits.* Successfully collecting information from others takes organization and people skills. This chapter offers practical guidance.

- *Chapter 6: Orphaned Recipes and Conducting Research.* Finding and learning more about family recipes may turn you into a historical research sleuth. This chapter explores ways to find lost recipes but also how to examine family papers with a historian's eye.
- *Chapter 7: Sharing Family Recipes and Foodways.* If you aim to create a family cookbook, you'll find many tips and ideas in this chapter. There are also ideas for sharing family recipes and history in new ways.

The longer I am involved in education, the more I am convinced that concrete examples are a crucial part of the learning process. Thus I have created appendixes that showcase explorations you may find with your family recipes and foodways.

- *Appendix 1.* This in-depth look at perfecting a single recipe through adjusting ingredients and methods explores how to develop an extraordinary biscuit.
- *Appendix 2.* The same biscuit-related quest teaches by example how to research the history behind a dish.
- *Appendix 3.* Preserving the know-how of a deceased master cook is challenging, but this themed biography thoughtfully explores the task and may also help you sort out your own cooking legacy.

Any new project can be daunting, but know that there is a sort of magic in practicing a family recipe. When you focus on scents and flavors, both departed family members and moments long gone come into sharper focus. Slowing down to ask questions, to listen, to replicate a dish with your own hands connects your present life with the past through a satisfying sensory puzzle. And once you record what you have learned, creating a well-written recipe that also preserves family lore, you now have a family treasure for future days.

⊰⊱ A word about the recipes in this book: Owing to space limitations, not every recipe mentioned in the text could be included, let alone all of the notes that might accompany them. Additional recipes and information are available via www.valeriejfrey.com. Please note that recipes from other cooks are written just as they shared them and thus may not be in the format recommended by this book. Finally, recipes often travel from cook to cook without background information. I made every effort to check each recipe to see if it was previously printed or if there was a known creator who should receive credit.

We tend to think of family recipes as fixed and static, but in actuality Grandpa's Mulligan didn't taste exactly the same from batch to batch. He adjusted the recipe as he stood at the stove each time, working around how strong or "gamey" the squirrels tasted, how juicy the tomatoes were, or how much of the liquid boiled off while he was busy with other kitchen tasks. Still, I think I could always have picked his mulligan out from similar pots at a church covered-dish supper. The basic flavors were always present, and he always achieved something akin to creaminess thanks to the starch from the corn and softening noodles.

Robert Alvin Frey's Chicken Mulligan

(Adjusted by his granddaughter Valerie J. Frey in 1993 with updates in 2014.)

1 medium-sized chicken (about 4 pounds), cut into pieces

1 large potato (around 1 pound), cut into half-inch cubes

1 large onion, diced

6 pieces unsmoked bacon or pork belly (about 6 ounces), cut into pieces

1½ teaspoons kosher salt, or to taste

1 to 4 cups chicken stock (only as needed)

1 (14.5-ounce) can diced tomatoes, or about 1 pound fresh tomatoes, blanched, peeled, and diced

8 ounces thin spaghetti, broken into 1-inch pieces, or elbow macaroni

¼ teaspoon black pepper, or to taste

1 (14.75-ounce) can of cream-style corn, or fresh creamed corn

1. Put chicken, potato, onion, bacon/pork belly, and salt into an 8-quart stockpot. Add enough cold water to just cover the ingredients and place on the stove over medium heat.
2. When the water is hot, reduce heat and simmer covered until the chicken is tender and falling off the bone (about 45 to 90 minutes, depending on your chicken and stove setting).
3. Skim off the froth across the top and discard. Lift chicken from pot, cool slightly, and pull meat from the bones in small pieces. Discard skin/bones and place meat back in stew. Remove pork and discard.
4. If at this point much of the liquid has steamed off, add chicken stock so there is enough liquid to fully cook the pasta. Add tomatoes, noodles, and pepper.
5. Increase heat until mulligan is bubbling gently. Cook until noodles are soft. Add corn and stir periodically for about ten minutes. If bottom begins to scorch, reduce heat slightly and stir more often. Noodles should be soft and beginning to break down so they add to the creaminess.
6. Serve hot, preferably in a large bowl with a piece of fresh cornbread.

Robert A. Frey in his kitchen, 2005.

I truly see the generation gap in this recipe. Grandpa Frey's "spice rack" was just salt and pepper—no kidding. The flavor for this dish came mostly from his garden's fresh or home-preserved vegetables, but also from selecting the right meat. Long ago if Grandpa used this recipe with chicken, the old yard biddy was tougher and needed to cook longer, but also had better flavor because of its age and diet. And Grandpa was able to get local dry-cured bacon. I find using farmers' market veggies and organic meat helps, yet my contemporary palate is simply used to more seasoning. I build additional flavor with root vegetables, celery, and garlic but also spices and herbs like turmeric, oregano, thyme, and basil. Recipe tester John Preston suggested rendering the bacon and browning the chicken first for additional flavor.

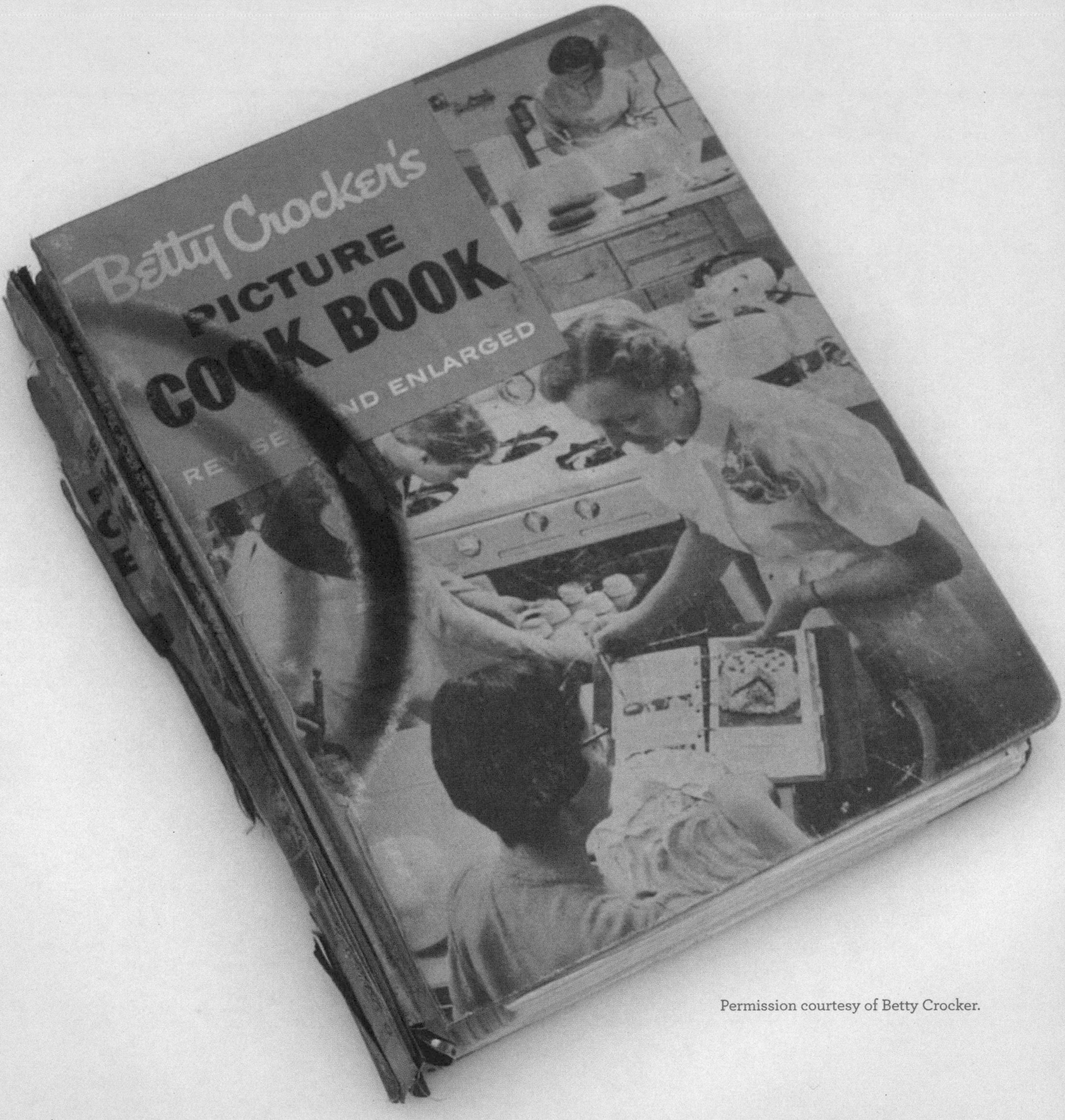

Permission courtesy of Betty Crocker.

Chapter One

Setting a Course

Our original family home no longer stands. The old wood-burning cookstove has rusted into pieces. . . . But precious recipes are still intact, and the tastes and smells of the foods of my childhood let me know that I can go back again.—Dori Sanders, *Dori Sanders' Country Cooking: Recipes and Stories from the Family Farm Stand* (xv)

If someone asked you to pull out your current collection of heirloom recipes and place it on the kitchen table, what would it look like? For some of us, there would be nothing to see—ideas and memories but zilch written down. Others may have an old recipe box or a stash of papers. Since you've picked up this book, perhaps the more important question is, what do you hope your heirloom recipe collection will look like after you've worked with it?

- Will it contain recipes from past generations, current family favorites, or a blend?
- Will it be made up of recipes from other family members, just your own signature dishes to share as a personal legacy, or a combination of the two?
- For older recipes, will they be saved solely in their original form or adjusted to be more authentic and/or pleasing?
- What will your end product look like? Do you want to create a tidy stack of computer printouts for your kitchen drawer, organized and ready for

making special meals? A leaflet of recipes to share at the family reunion? Perhaps you daydream about a bound cookbook with copies to give as gifts to the ones you love.

This book can help you transform your heirloom recipe collection, and the end result will first and foremost depend on your preferences. If your goal is simply to master a couple of recipes already in hand, then the next chapter will help you plunge right in, and you may only need chapters 2 through 5. Please feel free to skip around within this book, using the section and paragraph headings to guide you to the specific information you need.

Perhaps, however, you have a glimmer of a somewhat larger project. The ultimate shape and depth of your heirloom recipe collection will then depend on your enthusiasm and persistence, but also on your resources. Some families have a wealth of food traditions, old recipes, and noteworthy cooks. Others do not. Maybe you're hoping this book will point you in the direction of resources you hadn't thought about. (It can.) Perhaps you'd like to explore possibilities for connecting recipes with family lore, creating a polished cookbook, or developing a foodways project that draws kin together in the effort. This chapter is your gateway.

An Appeal for Supplemental Materials

Most cookbooks are considered complete with cooking instructions alone, so why add supplemental materials—genealogical notes, stories, anecdotes, photographs, and the like—to a family recipe collection? And why think about it now, at the beginning of your project?

The last question is the easiest to answer. It is usually far more efficient to collect supplemental materials at the same time that you're working with a recipe. Your memories are flowing, perhaps you're already in contact with family members who can help, and you have time to mull over what you've gathered.

As for the question of *why* to collect supplemental materials, it has to do with those connections discussed in the introduction. If you are a history buff, the value of old pictures, documents, and stories may seem obvious. Mulling it over, however, brings clarity to your project. Sometimes that clarity is needed in a pinch. A few years back, after finally getting a stodgy elderly cousin on the phone, I had one shot to convince him not to toss out his late wife's "old stuff." I even had to convince him that it was worth his time and effort to mail it hundreds of miles to me. This brief section offers you some food for thought (as well as some words to say) should you find yourself needing help from a curmudgeon.

In my archives workshops, I often touched on the fact that the personal study of genealogy and the formal field of history are part and parcel of the same quest for knowledge. That common-sense connection is much stronger than some non–history buffs realize. Learning about our roots at a family level gives us a clan-like sense of belonging but also links us to the larger community and culture. Whether at a family, local, or national level, studying the past helps us better understand the zigzagging progress of civilization and learn from both the mistakes and achievements of those who came before us.

My grumbling cousin pointed out that his wife's scrapbook materials were just snapshots and ticket stubs, so what value could they really have? First of all, what seems commonplace to us may very well be rare, fascinating, or useful to future generations. Value may also be cumulative, as supplemental materials add small clues to build a larger understanding. Even with a blurry snapshot, we can look at expressions, body language, clothing, and setting to help piece together what people, places, and periods were like. Finally, the value of supplemental materials may be in their ability to stir our emotions and build connections.

Cousin Curmudgeon kindly plucked the scrapbooks out of the trash and mailed them, even though I could tell he wasn't really sold on their importance. I wondered if he might have felt differently had he ever had a "brush" with a distant ancestor previously known only as a name. Cookbook scholar Janet Theophano refers to this as an "imaginative leap" that allows us to "cross divides of time, space, and self."[1] Have you had such an experience? Perhaps you tracked down a person's final resting place, walked old family land for the first time, or held an heirloom object a forebear owned. It is captivating emotionally—that eerie sensation of overlapping experiences, of sharing something with an ancestor across the years. A recipe can provide just such an encounter.

Even though we learn from those "brush" experiences and they help us connect with a person that would have otherwise just been a name on a pedigree chart, most of us crave more. Questions bubble up. There is a tinge of frustration at the very muteness of that tombstone, that landscape, that artifact because, taken alone, they have only so much to teach us. It seems to be a human reaction that a sense of connection leads to a craving for still greater understanding.

In the same vein, it is wonderful to experience food just like that from our forefathers' and foremothers' kitchens. Foods and foodways give clues about what life was like for family members in yesteryear and allow us to share a sensory experience. Still, recipes can be as mute as a tombstone, landscape, or artifact when they exist alone. Notes, stories, and visuals give additional clues and context, allow recipe users a chance to connect on a deeper level.

Right now you have the chance to net what is currently available, gathering the anecdotes and details that future generations will yearn for but may no longer be able to collect themselves. As time marches on and firsthand memories of original cooks and shared meals fall away, supplemental materials help descendants feel a given recipe is relevant to their lives and part of their own history. Even readers or cooks unrelated to you will likely care more about a recipe when it has context in the form of a story, anecdote, or image. In fact, some future folklorist or food historian may be thrilled to come across recipes and foodways with your helpful documentation.

General Recipe Project Tips

We've touched on what recipes you have now and what you might like to add to them. Let's now turn to practical matters about starting a project. Since embarking on this book, I have loved hearing success stories of recipes saved and brought back into use. Still, I wish I had a nickel for every person who sighed and said something like "Well, I started to gather my grandmother's recipes, but . . ." When there is great interest in developing an heirloom recipe collection, why would it remain untouched?

The pitfalls that manage to undermine a whole project are often surprisingly basic. People sometimes feel a disconnect between their hopes for a project and their confidence. ("I'm just not much of a writer." "Organizing isn't my strong suit.") As I worked and researched, I began to keep track of the common pitfalls. In order to make sure this guide is truly useful, I would be remiss if I didn't address them—especially when there are solutions.

Roadblocks are personal; what causes another person's project to grind to a halt may not slow you down at all. I leave it up to you to decide which solutions, if any, are relevant. If you're feeling confident, please feel free to bypass this section of the chapter and move on to the "Working Solo versus Working with Family" discussion.

Start Small. We've all done it. We've all started a project so complex that it couldn't get off the ground. Right here at the beginning, it bears mentioning that it is better to create a humble family recipe collection than to stall out on an elaborate one. Once you have a basic collection, your satisfaction as well as the enthusiasm of your family may inspire you to add more recipes and turn up the creativity level.

Starting small is not just a way to keep yourself from stalling out. Particularly if you plan to create some sort of cookbook for family members who don't cook often and who aren't genealogy buffs, too much information can overwhelm. Think about offering enough recipes to interest various palates and suit various cooking needs. Add a few family facts, photos, or brief, compelling family stories to spark interest and you're done. Then you can start working on the enlarged edition or volume number 2.

Pave the Way with Cooking Notes. Even if your family recipe project is years down the road, you can make it easier for yourself by taking a few extra minutes now. When you cook with recipes, add notes—where a recipe came from, the date you acquired it, and noteworthy occasions when it was used. Also note cooking tips, your adjustments, and serving suggestions. Not only will this practice help you remember the finer details of the recipe, but you've already left valuable information for the next generation.

Put Your Ideas in Writing. Going "from zero to sixty" on a project can drain momentum. What recipes and stories do you want to include? How would you like to organize the project? What will the finished product look like? Writing down ideas can clarify your thoughts and keep you on track, especially if the project takes some time to complete.

What form should your notes take? It could be anything from a word processing document on your computer to a note-taking app on your smart phone to paper slipped into the front of your recipe file. Personally, I create idea folders for various projects on my computer, but when it comes to capturing "pop-up" ideas while away from my desk, I am addicted to low-tech index cards. They are cheap and small enough to carry around easily. A handful fits in my purse, my bedside table, and the glove box of the car, allowing me to catch ideas anytime. They are also stiff, so I can write in the palm of my hand while waiting in line at the grocery store. Periodically, I look through the cards to see how various projects in my life are taking shape. Sitting on the floor, I process my ideas by shuffling and sorting, which gives me clues on how to proceed.

≫ What is the value of adding notes to a recipe? Because my mother had the habit of recipe note-scribbling, our family's traditional (and beloved) Chess Tarts taste just like hers even decades after her death. And I not only smile when I come across a recipe with a date from early in my parents' marriage with "Bob likes!" written across the top, but I also know my father-in-law will probably like the recipe, because his preferences are similar to my father's. If I hadn't written in my own cookbooks, I would long since have forgotten that I made Silver White Cake to celebrate the birth of my oldest nephew, an isolated use of a recipe that can become a tradition if it is remembered and repeated.

Sharon Cowles Frey's favorite cookbook, *Betty Crocker's Picture Cook Book* from the mid-1950s, contains many handwritten notes including those for the family's beloved Chess Tarts. Although the original recipe works flawlessly, the notes show how she modified it so that these delicate tarts traveled well for family visits. The exterior of the cookbook bears the scars of being accidentally placed on the hot eye of an electric stove. *Photo by the author; permission courtesy of Betty Crocker.*

Sharon Frey's recipe for Cheese Straws, February 1967.
"Oleo" refers to oleomargarine.

Gather Supplemental Materials as You Go. We've already discussed not putting off finding supplemental materials, but here are some additional tips. Working intensely on your project over a holiday visit with family sounds ideal, but it is usually hard to find everything you need within a short period. Working a little at a time may be a more effective mind-set and allows family members more time to respond. I use a calendar to keep track of requests and find that giving people a reasonable but concrete deadline for when I need items gets better results. With this type of system, there's a lot less to track down when it comes time to put the final collection together.

Collecting Stories and Family Lore

If you know you want to go beyond facts and anecdotes to add full stories to your recipes, you may be able to find excerpts from family letters or diaries that would work well. You may also find family members willing to write down memories for you. Your own memories and stories, however, will need to come from you. Writing them down is satisfying and even cathartic. If you're not in the habit of writing, however, the task may seem daunting at first. Luckily, there are many ways to keep this hesitance from becoming a pitfall.

Think Memoir Rather Than Autobiography. Mary Jane Moffat, author of *The Time of Our Lives: A Guide to Writing Autobiography and Memoir*, makes a distinction between autobiographies and memoirs that is also valuable when applied to family histories. "The task of setting down a whole lifetime in an artful and honest form may seem too overwhelming to some of us. In this case, writing memoirs may be an appealing alternative. The memoir offers a more restricted view, focusing perhaps on one section of the life—for instance, childhood, or one's career."[2]

Similarly, in her work *You Can Write a Memoir*, Susan Carol Hauser notes that a memoir "is not necessarily concerned with the chronology of things nor does it have to move from date to date. Rather, it might be concerned with themes that recur within a chronology, such as a memoir about birthdays throughout one person's life. Or it might be concerned with a place, or another person, or any subject chosen by the writer."[3] Collecting favorite family recipes and then simply adding stories that occur to you about each one is a great way to create a manageable family memoir.

Look for Shorter Supplements as Well as Full Stories. Keep in mind that sometimes the best "stories" don't have a plot but are simply brief details related to mealtimes or recipes that can make a family cookbook more endearing. For example, interviewee John Ihrie of North Carolina told me about dining at his future in-laws' house. "I don't know what the recipe was and I don't know anybody who has a recipe for baked crow, but it was the first meal I ate at Mrs. O'Neal's house. She always told the boys, 'Anything you kill, if you clean it, I'll cook it.' And Fernie had killed a crow."

For a light touch in a family cookbook, add a "non-recipe" that is easy to write but nevertheless shares family foodways:

Eric's Four-Wheeling Spaghetti

1 Jeep
1 metal storage box
1 blowtorch
Baling wire, as needed
1 can spaghetti, any brand

Open hood of Jeep. Weld metal box inside engine compartment. Add unopened can of spaghetti and use wire to securely fasten the box shut. Go four-wheeling in remote locations for several hours during wintertime. Stop Jeep. Retrieve and open can.* Dig into hot, prestirred pasta with a spoon while watching four-wheeling buddies eat cold sandwiches.

*Do not forget to bring a can opener and spoon along with you to remote location.[4]

Family foodways include cooking ideas that are short and easy to write. Here's an example: My mother has been gone many years now, but sometimes I quietly celebrate her birthday by making cookies or a cake decorated with gumdrops in the shape of orange slices. One summer Mom craved those candies and called to have them added to our food order when we lived on remote Sapelo Island off the coast of Georgia. Bluestein's Grocery on the mainland boat-delivered fresh oranges instead. She tried again the following week and found just a can of mandarin orange slices in our order. Next? A bag of gumdrops. She never did get the exact thing she wanted, but it became a running family joke unique to island life. Despite neither being a full story nor being attached to a specific recipe, this anecdote connects well as a dessert decorating idea in a family cookbook, preserving family memories.

Write a Little at a Time. If you plan to write elaborate stories to go with your recipes, starting from point A and writing to point Z on a project often requires a type of discipline easily sapped by the pressures of daily life. Writer Glenda Major had an advantage in this respect when she began to put together her family cookbook; she had some written pieces already tucked away in her files. She organized the recipes into categories, fit them with her previously written material, and then filled in the gaps to create *Hollyhocks and Old Maid Aunts: A Book of Memories, Favorite Poems, Amusing Quotes, and Family Recipes.*

Even if you don't have anything on paper (or computer file) yet, the concept of writing a little at a time may be quite helpful. William Zinsser, author of *Writing About Your Life: A Journey into the Past*, suggests, "Go to your desk on Monday morning and write about some event that's still vivid in your memory.

What you write doesn't have to be long—three pages, five pages—but it should have a beginning and an end. Put that episode in a folder and get on with your life. On Tuesday morning, do the same thing."[5] Zinsser states that the pieces written on separate days do not need to be on related topics; the important thing is simply to keep writing.

Not only will this process give you writing practice, but it also results in written pieces that can be pinned together. Zinsser suggests pulling out the written pieces and sorting through them to discover natural themes. "You'll begin to glimpse your story's narrative shape and the road you want to take."[6]

Take a Natural Approach. Above all, choose recipes and stories for your cookbook by what is compelling, interesting, and useful. While consistency from page to page and section to section throughout a cookbook helps the reader make sense of the whole, it doesn't mean the recipes or stories must all be the same length or tone. Every recipe doesn't have to have a story and vice versa. Images or copies of documents should earn their place by drawing the reader's interest and helping to tell your family's history.

Find Ways to Maintain Momentum. Interviewee Paula Eubanks benefited from a monthly writers' group while creating her family cookbook. She received feedback on her recipe-story combinations, plus the monthly deadline helped her establish a project pace.[7] If you know of others working on cookbooks or similar creative projects, swap proofreading or simply touch base regularly. If meeting in person is too difficult, technology may help. Creating a cooking blog with a promised weekly or monthly posting schedule is one idea. An online writers' group with communication via e-mail is another. Phones and old-fashioned snail mail do a fine job as well.

Finding Your Writing Voice

Practice and Edit. Writing down family stories gets easier with practice, a process of increasing your powers of observation and your writing skills. In the beginning, let yourself write without worrying about proper grammar or what a reader will think. Just write. When you're done, tuck the writing away for a little while so you can come back to it with a fresh eye. Rewriting is a crucial part of the process, so don't feel bad if you need to edit heavily later. If you need outside help with editing, finding a friend to proofread is fine too.

Pound Cake for Breakfast

Remembrance and Recipes from Jean J. Rowe of Decatur, Georgia

When I was a kid, our family left the dripping heat of Columbia for North Litchfield Beach, South Carolina. The Duffs came, too. Patty, one of Mama's college roommates, had children about the same age as my sister, brother, and me. Family rules relaxed, but one beach rule was we could eat whatever we wanted for breakfast, and, trust me, not just any breakfast could carry a kid through all the adventures we found there. Mama prepared food well in advance. I remember best a chocolate pound cake and a French pound cake.

When we weren't digging up sand crabs just to watch them return right back into the mucky ocean floor, we walked down to Huntington Castle to stand on the cold stone floors where Anna Huntington had sculpted exotic animals. We searched on cloudy days at Pawley's Island for the Gray Man, a "good" ghost who warned of terrible storms. After dark, we scared ourselves into giggling fits placing pull tops from aluminum cans on Alice's grave at All Saints Church to see if Alice would return to reclaim her stolen diamond. Our families watched the 1976 Olympics together. The beat-up table over which we broke bread transformed to a card-playing battlefield where Spoons reigned. Patty dove across the table during one game, grabbed a spoon out of my brother's hands, and knocked him clean out of his chair.

One morning, I threw back the sheets, sunburn pulling at my skin, the room too bright to sleep.

At breakfast, Daddy read the newspaper. He wore a white tee shirt, long dress pants, had bare feet and was smoking a non-filtered Chesterfield King. Armed with a frying pan and spatula, Mama eagerly asked, "What would you like for breakfast, Sugar Lump?"

Feet swinging under my chair, I announced, "I'll have a slice of chocolate pound cake and a slice of French pound cake. Please." Wanting a good outcome, that *please* was highlighted.

"Baby, you can't have pound cake for breakfast." Mama chuckled and then asked, "Now come on, what'll it be?"

I argued my point. "You said that when we came to the beach, we could eat whatever we wanted to for breakfast. So, I'd like a slice of each. Please."

Mama opened her mouth to protest again. Just then, the corner of Daddy's paper turned inward, toward him. "You did say that, Billie," he said.

To my delight, my mother, without another word, took out both cakes from the fridge. She removed a layer of aluminum foil, peeled away a plastic wrap layer, and, as a wax paper layer unfolded, I was at Mama's side, excited and hungry. During that one magical week, I enjoyed both pound cakes for breakfast.

Many days concluded with a nighttime walk on the beach, with the tide way out. I would hold hands with my parents awhile and then tear off running to nowhere. Just because I could.

Chocolate Pound Cake

1 pound unsalted butter
3 cups granulated sugar
5 large eggs
1 teaspoon vanilla extract
3 cups all-purpose flour

4 tablespoons unsweetened
  or Dutch-process cocoa
  powder*
½ teaspoon salt
½ teaspoon baking powder
1 cup whole milk**

Preheat oven to 325°F. Grease and flour a 9–10-inch tube pan; set aside.

Cream together butter, sugar, and eggs. Add vanilla extract. Sift dry ingredients together. Add alternately with milk to creamed mixture. Bake in prepared tube pan for 80 minutes. Invert on rack to cool. This cake is delicious with or without the icing.

* Cocoa powder can be left out if desired; just add 4 more tablespoons of flour to sift.
** Substituting soy milk is fine and yields a moist, tasty result.

Chocolate Pound Cake Icing

¼ cup butter
2 (one-ounce) squares of
  unsweetened baking
  chocolate

1 (one-pound) box confectioner's sugar
1 teaspoon vanilla extract
Cream (as needed)

Melt butter and chocolate together in a medium saucepan. Add vanilla extract. Using an electric mixer on low speed, slowly alternate sugar with a little cream for smoothness. Depending on how much cream you add, you can spread the icing with a knife or offset spatula or drizzle the icing.

French Pound Cake

The double cream called for in this recipe is difficult to find in the United States. It is pasteurized but not ultra-pasteurized and has a high percentage of butterfat (almost 50%). Heavy cream or heavy whipping cream is probably as close as you'll find.

1½ cups self-rising flour
1½ cups granulated sugar
4 large eggs

1 cup (½ pint) double
  cream
½ teaspoon vanilla extract

Preheat oven to 350°F. Grease and flour a 9–10-inch tube pan; set aside.

Combine all ingredients and mix until smooth. Bake in prepared tube pan for 40–50 minutes. Invert on rack to cool slightly, then remove from pan.

Citrus Glaze for French Pound Cake

About 1 cup confectioner's sugar
¼ cup lemon juice
1 teaspoon vanilla extract

Mix all glaze ingredients together. Use a toothpick to poke some holes in the top of the pound cake and pour the glaze over the top. After pouring glaze over the top and the cake has cooled, refrigerate.

Write Naturally. When it comes to the tone of your writing, be yourself. In the mid-1990s, Grandpa Frey surprised me by taking on his community's column for the county newspaper.[8] When he was a child, family needs kept him from finishing high school, so both his spelling and his grammar were, um, *original*. While the most distracting errors were fixed by an editor, Grandpa's newspaper pieces followed his natural storytelling style, blending reverent reminiscences with everyday neighborly news or even jokes about the dead skunk on the highway upwind from the grocery store. If those columns were polished to perfection, chances are that his personality and sense of humor wouldn't shine through so clearly. Years later, I am grateful that nobody (including Grandpa himself) edited away that homespun charm.

Try Writing Guides. If putting pen to paper is an exciting yet daunting task for you, there are many writers who have created instructional and inspirational guides about the process. My personal favorites are Natalie Goldberg, Anne Lamott, Steven Pressfield, and William Zinsser. Works by these and others can be found at your local library or bookstore.

Your Story as a Cook

When I began interviewing various master cooks for this book, my intention was to learn how they preserved and adapted recipes. I soon learned, however, that their stories as cooks were often fascinating, revealing much about their lives and family histories. They often described family members who taught or influenced them, and they also discussed how cooking has changed through their lifetimes, reflecting advances in technology and shifts in society as a whole. This type of memoir is a wonderful legacy to future generations. If you don't know where to start with adding family information and stories to recipes, your own story as a cook can be a wonderful place to begin. Here are a few questions to help you:

- How did you learn to cook?
- Who taught you to cook or inspired you?
- What were your experiences making some of your first dishes?
- What are some important kitchen lessons you have learned?
- What cooking triumphs (or disasters) stand out in your memory?
- How has cooking changed for you over the years?

Working Solo versus Working with Family

We've looked at some ideas for shaping up a recipe collection project and also adding family lore. Another important aspect to consider in the beginning is how much you want to involve others in the task itself—a decision that can greatly affect the size, breadth, and feel of your finished project. Since it is helpful to explore the ways others have approached collecting recipes, we'll start with a family cookbook author who accomplished most of the tasks herself. Later we'll look at a couple of examples of community cookbooks put together by committees that can help you envision ways to involve family members.

A Single Editor

I spoke with many people who created cookbooks by themselves, but Georgia native Tamara Patridge was particularly articulate about the process and found a system that worked well. Her nearly 150-recipe cookbook titled *Collard Greens and Sushi* focuses on her family's diverse culinary background ranging from home-style southern cooking (reflecting both European American and African American ancestry) to dishes from her mother's homeland of Japan.

To begin, she selected a printing company that offered cookbook templates (see chapter 7). Next, she wrote a letter to potential contributors explaining the project, pointing out the value of saving recipes for posterity, and requesting a few favorites from each branch of the family. The letter included a template from the printing company so contributors would be more likely to send recipes back in a functional format. In addition, Tamara's letter set a deadline of around two months—not so long that family members would forget but long enough for them to thoughtfully gather recipes.

As the project progressed, if Tamara didn't receive a contribution from someone she expected to hear from, she followed up with an e-mail or call. She typed the contributions into her computer using software provided by the publisher. (Many cookbook printing companies give customers a password to an online form where contributors can enter recipes themselves.)

Patridge's cookbook is a testament to the fact that families scattered geographically can come together for a project. It contains recipes from more than thirty individuals in eleven Georgia towns as well as eight states. Family members reported being impressed and pleased with the finished product.

With a family cookbook project, there is real value to testing and editing recipes submitted by others, making sure they are accurate and work well. Other considerations, however, are that the testing/editing process can take considerable time, may offend some contributors, and can erase some of the original recipe writer's unique voice. Although she spot-tested recipes, Tamara said, "This book was about saving the recipes, but it was really more about story. I didn't want to say, 'Okay, this is *precisely* how the recipe should be.' Just tell me. If we were going to talk about this recipe, as if we were sitting side by side, I want to hear it from you." The instructions in her request letter even warned contributors that she would correct misspellings but otherwise would type up the recipes just as they were.

The Patridge family, enjoying a holiday feast in Atlanta, Georgia, 1940s. *Photo courtesy of Tamara Welborn Patridge.*

Three generations of the Welborn family making spring rolls: mother Masako, Tamara, and niece Ashlyn. *Photo courtesy of Tamara Welborn Patridge.*

The response rate for stories or anecdotes with recipes was about 25 percent. She had trouble fitting the stories and notes into the software template required by the publisher, so some supplemental material had to be edited. Still, the cookbook contains significant family information as well as cooking tips.

Thinking back on how the finished project brought her family closer, Tamara said, "I almost feel, as corny as this sounds, that now I'll always have a little piece of them. When they sit down and write this recipe, they may be a million miles away. Later, I'm making the same recipe. I feel connected."

Sharing the Workload

Tamara's cookbook was largely a solo project. There are significant benefits to creating a family collection this way, such as the ability to work at your own pace, the independence to create something that satisfies your specific needs, and the assurance that the work will be completed. An alternative method is to enlist the help of others.

For many families, life patterns are quite different than they were a few generations ago, and this impacts family foodways.[9] Nowadays, when adult generations more commonly live in separate houses—and indeed are often distanced from family by hundreds of miles—it's harder to learn from watching others' hands or by asking questions in the middle of the cooking process. When trying to remember the way a family member cooks, it isn't easy to recall processes you haven't seen time after time.

The dispersal of family means that learning and preserving family foodways is more difficult, yet it also means a rich body of knowledge and varied recipes are just waiting to be explored. Embarking on a cookbook that is not just *for* family but involves the *participation* of the family is one way to preserve knowledge and celebrate foodways while emotionally drawing scattered family members together in the process.

Those new to the task of learning from other family cooks will find that it is often a straightforward process, yet there are times when it becomes strangely complicated because the relationship between one family cook and another is just that—a relationship. Effectively collecting family recipes and lore ultimately comes down not just to cooking and writing skills but also to people skills. Interview techniques and recipe-related etiquette can make all the difference in the quality and quantity of what you are able to collect.

We'll cover several aspects of such working relationships throughout the next chapters, but at the outset it is helpful to look at recipes as a legacy.

"Passing the torch" from one generation to the next is sometimes effortless. At other times it is awkward or downright frustrating. When I asked one elderly interviewee about sharing her substantial kitchen knowledge with her children, she replied, "They say, 'Please write us some recipes down so when you're gone we'll know how to do it.' I say, 'Well, y'all better learn *now*." She smiled and shrugged. Although her response was good natured, there was a definite edge of annoyance and disappointment. They were asking her to do all the work by herself.

Helen Q. Kivnick, a professor in the School of Social Work at the University of Minnesota, studies the way elders pass on what they know. When older citizens sort through their life knowledge and effectively pass it down to younger generations, it becomes a "reciprocal process of legacy" that allows both giver and receiver to feel useful and valued.[10] We may think of collecting recipes as "asking favors" but, as Kivnick suggests, you may provide a life-affirming service to those ready to be asked. "Please write us some recipes down," however, probably won't be enough. By taking the time to listen carefully, recording and discussing what you experience, you stand to gain not just the recipes and stories but also, says Kivnick, "an enduring bond."[11]

Working with a particular cook and that cook's recipes has its rewards. Enlisting the help of others with the entire collection process can have benefits as well. On a practical level, if you find creative family members to work with, they may come up with ideas for the project you hadn't thought about. Those family members may also know recipes, stories, or contacts that you don't. Finally, it helps the venture become a true family project.

Cookbooks by a Group

Especially if you are interested in collecting recipes and stories from extended family, it is helpful to turn to some examples of collecting from a large group. As you read the section below about collecting recipes by a committee, think about how members of your family might accomplish the same tasks.

During the early days of my archives career, I served as a junior fellow in the Manuscripts Division at the Library of Congress. During that assignment, I volunteered on a committee working toward an institution cookbook—a celebration of the Library's bicentennial in 2000. The project was organized

> Jan Harold Brunvand's *American Folklore: An Encyclopedia* calls foodways "the intersection of food and culture" (299). Thomas A. Green's *Folklore: An Encyclopedia of Beliefs, Customs, Tales, Music, and Art* defines the term this way: "Foodways means nothing less than the full consideration of how food and culture intersect—what food says about the people who prepare and consume it and how culture shapes the dietary choices people make" (367). Take that to a personal level. Foodways are about how food and your family interconnect—what food says about your family members who prepare and eat it, as well as how the behavior patterns and beliefs of your family shape the food choices you and your family make.

by a committee chair who posted meeting reminders and periodically sent out requests for specific types of recipes not yet well represented.

The committee of around twelve employees from various divisions met weekly and were each assigned one or more new recipes to test from the pool of submissions. Since meetings were during lunchtime, we shared a potluck meal of dishes we made using the previous week's assigned recipes. This system allowed us to test every recipe and gave everyone on the committee a chance to offer feedback. Because the institution is quite large, contributions were plentiful and weeding was essential. Some recipes were accepted, a number were returned to the contributor with suggested changes, and others were turned down as gracefully as possible—usually because they were too similar to recipes already accepted.

Although I was unable to see the cookbook project through to completion because my assignment was short term, I quickly saw the value of participation and teamwork in a recipe-collecting process. With that in mind, I was glad to have a chance to speak with Savannah medical librarian Jane Bridges about her experiences working with a group to create a community cookbook for the Southern Chapter of the Medical Library Association (SCMLA). *You Say Cuisine; I Say Vittles: The Southern Chapter Compendium of Recipes and Reminiscences* began as a fund-raising project proposal to the chapter's executive board.[12]

I spoke with several people who had experience working with community cookbooks, but SCMLA seemed to have the process down to an art. First, they selected an editor in chief to provide a final say in decisions and serve as a ringmaster for moving the various parts of the project along. Supporters then formed two groups—an eight-person editorial board handling the business end of the project and a group of thirteen section editors, longtime members and experienced cooks in charge of soliciting recipes from the membership. (Five people, including Jane, served in both groups.)

Sections had one to three editors. Jane was one of three working on "Meats & Main Dishes" and was in charge of the seafood recipes. It was up to each editor to "beat the bushes" for contributions or come up with their own recipes to fill in gaps. Jane volunteered for her section because it was a favorite; she knew she had many recipes but felt she knew enough good cooks that she could get more. She pointed out that going to someone directly is much more effective than putting out a general call. "If you buttonhole somebody," she said with a laugh, "they feel like they have to answer."

The committee did not test recipes but instead depended on the cooking experience of each editor to weed out recipes or work with contributors on problems. Two members of the editorial board were in charge of typing the recipes into the format required by the chosen printing company. As for garnering support for the project and selling the finished cookbook, during organization gatherings the editorial board put up a booth for publicity and cookbook committee members would circulate offering trays of finger foods from the cookbook.

In our interview discussion following her description of the cookbook project, Jane immediately thought the *Vittles* process could be modified to work well for families—especially when there are gatherings such as reunions and holiday get-togethers. She recommended appointing family scribes (who could perhaps also serve as section editors) to circulate and poll everyone about favorite family recipes. These scribes, after comparing notes, could then approach the cooks who had been named and ask them for recipes, following through to obtain cooking tips as well as stories and other supplemental materials. Jane mentioned that most people are interested in sharing their food successes and helping with a group goal, but motivation and perseverance are needed—often in the form of reminders.

Getting Started on a Group Project

Poll Your Family. Making a list in advance is a helpful way to start collecting family recipes. Jot down what recipes and stories you hope to preserve and then find out what other family members think should be included. This helps generate enthusiasm, and many heads are better than one when it comes to remembering the past, especially if you want multiple viewpoints. (Chapter 7 can give you some ideas.)

You want to consider favorite dishes, exemplary cooks, unusual foodways, and the most compelling family stories. Although you can approach a recipe collection any way that makes the most sense to you, consider seeking out a variety of dishes representing each branch of the family and reflecting important stages in your family's history. Collecting widely is the best idea; even if some materials don't work for this particular collection or cookbook, they will be preserved and can always be used for another volume. If you take this approach, let family know in advance so they will not be disappointed if everything they contribute does not appear in the first shared collection.

Collect from a Distance. Because of expense and time constraints, sometimes the only real option is to collect family materials from a distance. Phone calls and letters are certainly good methods, especially for letting people know about the project as it launches. E-mail may be better later in the project, as it allows you to more easily keep track of conversation threads. Computers have revolutionized genealogy in the last few decades, and social media sites are wonderful for outreach or maintaining family connections. I created Facebook groups for various clans of cousins. Sharing old photos or recipes this way can create instant enthusiasm for your project, and the discussions that follow can jog people's memories and turn up valuable information.

Be as Mobile as Possible. For a richer experience that will build family memories and to have the best chance to collect what you need, travel as much as you are able. Many family members will be best motivated to help you in person, plus face-to-face contact is often most efficient and helps to avoid misunderstandings.

Family members may be willing to help but find the idea of writing down what they know too daunting or too time consuming. Therefore, on-site interviews and cooking visits are often the most effective way to gain rich information. If you let family members know well in advance that you are coming and what specific recipes or family materials you are looking for, you'll have the best results. (See chapter 5.)

Delegate. Spreading recipe collection or cookbook tasks across family members lightens your workload and gives you wider access not only to

If you want to create a family cookbook that includes images of the finished dishes, you can develop the necessary skills. For compelling, inspiring cookbook illustrations, food stylists employ quite a few tricks to make edibles look perfect for the camera. There are websites and books dedicated to this art if you want to learn more. You may find, however, that looking at cooking blogs or image banks such as Pinterest can give you pleasing ideas that are not too hard to recreate. In addition, author Heidi Adnum created *The Crafter's Guide to Taking Great Photos.* Her practical tips make *The Crafter's Guide* one of the most helpful sources I've found for taking quality photographs of objects—which for your project may include ingredients, finished dishes, and family kitchen artifacts. Many of the still-life-type photos in this book (including the cover) were created using a light tent built according to Adnum's instructions.

ideas but also to recipes, stories, family documents, and photographs. Those working with you develop "sweat equity" in the project and usually become more interested in the family history. If you know of family members who are particularly interested in cooking or genealogy, it makes sense to approach them first, because the project will be an easy sell. Also keep in mind that the senior members of the family may have more clout when it comes to making requests and will also draw from a larger pool of memories. When approaching family members with requests for help, try to find a task that plays to their strengths:

- The cousin with the annoyingly organized house may be just the person to help you methodically set up the project.
- The most dependable (and well-liked) members of the family are prime candidates for help collecting recipes and supplemental materials.
- Experienced cooks can test or proofread recipes as well as accompany you on cooking visits.
- Anyone with good listening skills can be an asset for a collecting visit, taking notes or providing a sounding board for your findings.
- The technically savvy can help with video recordings of cooking visits, scan family materials, or create a family recipe website to unite relatives near and far.
- Photography buffs may be willing to capture images for you—pictures of finished dishes, portraits of cooks, landscapes of old home places, still-life images inside family kitchens.
- Artistic family members (children or adults) can design covers or cookbook section dividers.
- Those who read a lot may be good at proofreading or editing.

Include Young and New Family Members. Asking for help from young or new-by-marriage family members may draw them more deeply into the family and help them feel more vested in shared history. You may be surprised, too, at the benefits you receive in return. Many young ones are adept in technology and eager to show off their skills. Taking well-behaved older children with you on short visits to collect recipes and stories sometimes results in family members who enjoy kids being more willing to share. Those same family members may also do a better job giving background information and explaining details because they know they are addressing a less knowledgeable audience. When it comes to testing recipes, working with young or inexperienced cooks can help you detect confusing parts of a recipe.

Create a Comfortable Group Timeline. Allowing plenty of time for family members to contribute recipes or help is important, even though it will probably work best to set a concrete deadline. Many of the family cookbook authors I talked to found that everyday life gets in the way of the best of intentions, and reminders are often needed. Sometimes, too, what we ask for is larger than we imagine. Once when visiting Arkansas with my laptop computer and scanner in tow, I asked a cousin if I could make copies of her oldest family papers and photographs. She cheerfully led me to a back bedroom where she began pulling tidy box after tidy box from under the bed. She was willing to share, but didn't remember where the items might be in those boxes. As an experienced archivist, I knew the hours of work I was looking at and realized it had to be a project for another visit. Similarly, Grandma's recipe box may be buried deep in Dad's closet, unseen for years—and perhaps surrounded by memories that he isn't sure he'd like to deal with at present. Be ready to offer patience, understanding, and perseverance.

Be Prepared. As I began collecting family recipes, I quickly discovered that even casual visits with family can suddenly become opportunities to catch recipes and stories. I got in the habit of carrying blank note cards, a pencil, a digital camera with a video feature, and my digital audio recorder whenever I visit extended family. Luckily, in today's modern world, these items are quite small and lightweight; I carry mine tucked in a padded camera case not much bigger than a sandwich. In fact, the tools you need might be as close as your smartphone or computer tablet. If so, charge it up fully before visits with family.

Be Realistic. The larger your project, the more likely it is that someone along the way will turn down your requests. The ups and downs of daily life will get in the way of your deadlines. There will be precious recipes that are lost to the ages. In addition, family cookbook author Glenda Major observed that people are afraid when writing down recipes and stories that they'll forget and leave something out. "You will," she said with a wry smile.

These are the sorts of pitfalls that hinder some family recipe enthusiasts. Yet the great news is that whatever you collect will be more than what you had before, and your efforts will promote your family's history regardless of how well your finished cookbook matches what you envisioned. Don't give up!

Lydias

Fruit Cookies. 4 Egg.
1 Cup Butter
2 " " Sugar
1 " " sour Milk. 1
Soda, 1 Cup Raisins
Cinnamon, Nutmeg,
Cloves to taste. fl
to make stiff doug
Miss Augusta M

Devils Food Cak
1/2 Cup Butter. 2
1/2 Cup Sour Milk.
soda dissolved in
1/2 Cup if Chocol
in 1/2 Cup of b
(use when cool)
2 Eggs. 2 Cup
Mothers
Sponge

Chapter Two

Organizing and Protecting Your Materials

Among the millions of things that torment you when someone you love dies is not being able to ask them how they made something. Or where they hid a recipe.—Gesine Bullock-Prado, *Confections of a Closet Master Baker* (62)

Reference archivists frequently advise budding genealogists, "Start with yourself. Begin with the information you already know." Similarly, when gathering family recipes, you will most likely wish to begin with your cooking repertoire and/or the family recipes you already have. This chapter helps you get a handle on your current collection, but also sets you up for successfully organizing the recipes you soon may gather. An added benefit is that you'll learn how to safeguard all sorts of heirloom papers, photographs, and artifacts.

Organizing Recipes

In these modern times, our recipes are no longer a homey handful, but more reminiscent of cattle. Most cooks have vast herds, and those recipes seem to amble anyplace they please unless you fence them in. A few stay put on the pages of cookbooks—if you can remember which cookbook. Others have settled into a kitchen drawer but, then again, are they in that pile of papers atop the

Wooden recipe box, a premium from Gold Medal brand flour, ca. 1926.

microwave? To have a truly useful collection, you've got to corral recipes and even thin the herd.

It may seem odd to address organizing schemes in a book about family recipes, but it was painfully obvious during the dozens of interviews I conducted that many cooks are hobbled by recipe chaos. In the last chapter we discussed project pitfalls, but this is by far the most common one. (If your recipes are organized to your satisfaction already, then please move on to the "Identifying Heirloom Recipes" section later in this chapter.)

The good news is that even a little more order can revolutionize the way you cook and share recipes. Personally, as I began to take stock of my collection and thoughtfully arrange it, recipes from my mother, grandmothers, and cousins were no longer stagnant pieces of paper in my genealogy stash. Copies of family recipes integrated with my now-organized personal recipes mean that I cook with them and enjoy them much more often. (Never underestimate the appeal of nostalgia! Whether at the school picnic or a work

>> Organization isn't one-size-fits-all, so mull over your own needs and habits. Here are some considerations:

- How many recipes do you have, and how quickly do you expect the collection to grow?
- Will you often need to add, shift, or remove recipes?
- Will you need to share recipes frequently?
- What physical considerations are important to you? For example, do you need large print, or will a large binder be too heavy?
- Is portability important?
- Are you willing to type up or photocopy recipes?
- If your recipes are mostly electronic, do you need them to be available on all your devices?
- For keeping track of favorite recipes in cookbooks, would you rather mark, list, index, or copy them?
- How will you access specific recipes in your collection? In other words, is making sections like "Vegetables" and "Breads" enough, or will you want to make an index? Do you want the collection to be on your computer, so you can search your recipes by keyword?

luncheon, Great-Aunt Avis's Cherry Bubble Cake or Grandma's Karo Nut Pie are pleasingly old-fashioned standouts.)

When reorganizing, it is inspiring to see how form follows function. In the past, the bound notebook was probably the most common format for home recipe collections. When paper was expensive and books rare, handwritten recipes often shared pages with business logs or diaries. (A favorite example is an Arkansas undertaker who interspersed coffin sketches with recipes for everything from wood stain to pickles made from cabbage, cantaloupe, and green tomatoes.)[1] In my career as an archivist, I've seen mail order catalogs and outdated almanacs pasted over scrapbook-style with handwritten or clipped recipes.

There are many people who still prefer a bound recipe notebook, but when recipe boxes became popular in the late nineteenth century, they offered several improvements. The cook pulls out a recipe card to use, keeping the remainder safely out of the way. Unlike bound recipe books, cards make reorganization, interfiling, and thinning easy. Food companies quickly got into the swing, offering printed recipe cards touting their products.

Recipe boxes and cards are certainly still used today. Still, after asking many cooks to tell me about how they store and organize their recipes, it seems that times—and needs—have largely changed. In these days of computers and copy machines, few want to write recipes by hand or fit them onto a small, pictureless card.

On the right, the box the author's mother received after her marriage in 1962 and used all her life.

A Sample Filing System

After years of experience both organizing papers in archives and working with family recipes, I've developed my system. Perhaps some or all of it will work for you as well.

First, I've become hard-hearted about cookbooks. I admittedly have several shelves full, but they are ones that have earned their keep. If I get a new cookbook and don't use it much or am not inspired by it, I send it on to a charity sale. Once upon a time I kept various cookbooks for "just in case," but now if I need to find a new recipe for a particular dish, I turn to the Internet or the library rather than clutter my bookshelves. Even if it feels a little wicked for someone with a library degree, I pencil notes in my permanent cookbooks to mark my favorites recipes and explain any changes I make when I use them.

I find I cook most often from loose recipes—those shared by friends, printed from websites, or clipped from magazines. With ones that prove their worth, I add information about the source of the recipe and my cooking notes before sliding them into clear plastic sleeves (also called sheet protectors) in three-ring binders grouped by type of dish (vegetables, grains, breads, and so forth). I lift the sleeved recipes out when I cook from them, often hanging them on the refrigerator with a magnet so they are visible but out of harm's way. The sleeves can be wiped with a damp cloth in case of accidental spatters, and they easily hold recipes from a tiny clipping to a full page. Many folks like to cook directly from their laptop or computer tablet, and there are various holders on the market to keep these electronic devices safe in the kitchen, but I prefer paper so I can always slide out a recipe, add notes with messy fingers, and then reprint a fresh, updated copy later.

When it comes to office supplies, I purchase plastic sleeves and binders labeled "nonstick" and "archival quality" not because I expect them to truly stand the test of decades but because they are less likely to soften and lift inks. Most of the plasticizers that cause this problem have a distinctive smell, so I let my nose guide me and buy supplies that don't have a smell at all.

When I realize that a recipe has become a favorite, I type it into my computer complete with a brief history plus cooking notes. That five- to ten-minute task is worth it. First of all, I now have access to the recipe everywhere I travel with my laptop or other devices linked to it. Second, the keyword search function is helpful for finding specific recipes by title or ingredient. Third, a digitized version makes it easy to share the recipe via printing or e-mailing. Last but

Berry - Marble Cobbler
1. Sift together in bowl:
   ½ c. sugar
   1 c flour
   2 tsp. baking powder
   ¼ tsp. salt.
2. Stir in:
   ½ c milk
   ½ tsp. vanilla
   1 Tbsp. melted butter
                    over

Spread batter in buttered 10 x 6 x 2"
baking dish.   (8" square)
3. Scatter 1 cup fruit or berries over
   the batter. Sprinkle ½ c. sugar over
   berries. Pour ¾ c boiling H₂O over
   all. Bake at 325 (Mod) for 25-30 min
   or until well browned + done.

[Marjorie Greene Cowles]

Makes enough for 2 people

Recipe from the author's maternal grandmother. Some inks
are less permanent than others, migrating with alarming
ease when re-wetted by a kitchen spill. Unlike ballpoint pens,
fountain pens and felt-tip pens don't even leave indentations in
paper, so it is possible for words written with these implements
to literally vanish without a trace.

Three generations of the author's family berry
picking on Mount St. Helens, Washington, in
the late 1940s: Judy Cowles, Marjorie Greene
Cowles, Dessie Greene, and Sharon Cowles.

certainly not least, once a recipe is an electronic file, I can back it up to prevent
loss. So that all those recipes stay organized, the titles of the recipe folders on
my computer match the sections in my three-ring binders.

My untried loose recipes are in file folders in a cabinet, waiting until I'm
in an adventurous mood. I have a similar electronic folder on my computer
for downloaded recipes I haven't tried yet. Since I mark these files as unused
and keep them separate from my personal recipe collection, after I am gone
anybody searching for my familiar recipes will not have to sift through them.

Similarly, the recipes I try that aren't worth messing with again immediately go into the recycling bin. (So liberating!)

Finally, there are the heirloom recipes. I used to cook directly from handwritten family recipes, not thinking about the fact that they are exposed to food spatters, steam, and other dangers. After my parents and grandparents died, however, I realized their handwritten recipes are now irreplaceable documents preserving know-how and memories, and I treat them accordingly. My heirloom recipes are now gathered in acid-free folders and filed with the rest of the family genealogy materials. My mother's painted steel recipe box is safe for her cards, so I keep her collection intact but in my home office rather than the steamy kitchen. As a final step, all of the recipes passed down to me from previous generations have been scanned and backed up electronically.

Family recipes stowed in a home office are safer than in the kitchen, yet they aren't handy for cooking. In time (and hopefully thanks to this book), you may have a working copy of a family cookbook for your kitchen. In the meantime, you may wish to merge copies of heirloom recipes with your personal recipe collection. As mentioned, when I started doing this, I found myself using older recipes far more than I did before. I type my favorite heirloom recipes into my computer (complete with history and cooking notes) and print working copies to place in my regular recipe binders. Some of my heirloom recipes are straightforward and well written, so with these I simply printed out a copy of the scan, enjoying the handwritten look of the original when I use them.

Whether typed or scanned, copies take a few moments to create, yet an heirloom recipe can be lost as quickly as a pot can bubble over. Your care and thoughtfulness now means future generations can enjoy a cooking legacy.

Alternate Ways to Organize

No single system will work for everyone. Here are a few suggestions that may prove useful to you.

Portfolios. Bookstores and office supply stores sell binders, accordion folders, or other portfolios designed to organize loose recipes. Features may include plastic sleeves, section dividers, and notes pages. Some offer indexes where a cook can record cookbook titles, recipe names, and page numbers that help them find their favorites within large cookbook collections. Although portfolios may be a good solution for small collections, keep in mind that a paper-only system can't be backed up the way electronic files can. Stow or share duplicates with a friend or relative. If a house fire occurs (and many start in the kitchen), you'll be very glad you did.

Computerized Recipes. There are new-fangled solutions to the age-old problem of organizing recipes. Interviewee Willene O'Neal uses recipe software on her computer to manage her collection and is pleased with the results.[2] She types her recipes into a form that includes ingredients, methods, and notes. Recipes can be printed, shared via e-mail, and backed up. Software features vary but may include a recipe compendium preloaded by the software company, menu planning, nutritional analysis, tips from chefs (sometimes with video clips to teach techniques), rescaling of recipes for more or fewer servings, varied printing options including recipe cards, and shopping lists.

Many cooks embrace digital recipe collections. In this age of linked data, it means that your recipes can be available on your desktop computer, on the tablet computer propped up on your kitchen countertop, and on your cell phone where the ingredients list is handy at the grocery store. Whether using a fully developed software program, the newest free recipe app, or just word processing software, there are some important considerations to keep in mind. Eventually you will need to purchase a new computer (or handheld device) and your software will need upgrades, possibly causing compatibility problems. Making sure you don't wait too long to upgrade should help; the more versions of hardware and software you skip over, the more likely there could be glitches. Be aware that upgrades of the software may have different features than your original version. Finally, it is possible for the software creator to stop updating your particular electronic product. A combination of backing up your files and printing your recipes is important to safeguard against loss.

Quick Filing. If you're dreading a major recipe collection overhaul, a quick way to organize loose printed recipes is to make folders for different types (desserts, vegetables, et cetera) and stow them in a file box. When you get ready to cook with a recipe, you can temporarily slide it into a plastic sleeve to protect it.

Identifying Heirloom Recipes

Now that your recipe collection is in better order, look over it with a genealogist's eye. If there are just a few recipes, then your selection process is probably done. If the collection is large, however, you may not consider them all "heirloom worthy." Which recipes go into your genealogy files or become part of a family cookbook?

I spoke with many authors of family cookbooks, asking them how they decided which recipes were significant. Professional baker Karen Vessels of Chattanooga created a cookbook for her adult children, picking the recipes "that you go back to time after time after time over the years." An interviewee who created a recipe collection for her niece spoke of "sure-fire hits."[3]

Perhaps the best advice is to start with the dishes that would haunt you the most if you never tasted them again. But there are additional considerations. Do your files contain recipes passed down from previous generations? Are there recipes that represent particular people, events, periods, or places for your family? (Chapter 7 will give you additional suggestions.)

Consider your audience. Think about specific family members and the dishes they often request or reach for first. In terms of pleasing younger generations, kids are notorious for preferring dessert or comfort-food dishes. Also consider including recipes with a small number of steps so that children and new cooks can use your collection, developing enthusiasm for it.

You may decide to go in search of missing recipes, but a cookbook can come solely from your present collection. Family cookbook author Glenda Major found that her project moved along quickly because she used this approach. One downside, however, is that some important people in her life were not represented in the finished book. Her solution may be one that is useful to you as well. "I had to put a disclaimer in the back," she said. It states: "Many wonderful friends and family members will not find their names herein—I didn't intentionally leave you out, I just didn't have a recipe from you. I hope this will not dampen your enthusiasm for reading this book and using the recipes included."[4]

If you've been cooking for a long time, selecting recipes that tell the stories of your life may mean pulling out recipes you don't use often anymore. Or you may have developed multiple versions of a recipe over time as traveling taught you to love new spices or as you became more health conscious. Which recipes or versions truly represent your life or your family's history? All of them. The recipes that come and go as well as the alterations we make to recipes over time reflect the patterns of our lives. Adding notes to explain changes will help future cooks understand how these dishes fit into your life and the family's evolution.

A final consideration when selecting heirloom recipes is being inclusive. It is generous to share your food traditions, but you don't want it to be one-sided.

Depending on the type of family cookbook you're working on, consider asking a family member's new spouse or older stepchildren whether they have recipes they would like to contribute to the project and also serve at family gatherings. Your thoughtfulness may be rewarded with yummy dishes but also closer relationships and fun new traditions.

Expanding Your Circle of Recipes

Working with family recipes will most likely begin with your existing files, but it could quickly lead into tracking down and organizing recipes from other family members. Interviewee Paula Eubanks invited me to join her at a "family cookbook building session" with Martha Eubanks, a cousin by marriage and one of the family's most experienced cooks.[5] A look at their work process may be helpful to those who have family materials available yet don't know how to begin working with them.

The two sat down in Martha's living room in Macon, Georgia, surrounded by boxes of loose recipes as well as old cookbooks—items gathered from their two households but also borrowed from other cousins. Some of these materials represented Paula's and Martha's cooking repertoires, while some were left behind by previous generations. The two agreed that they wanted to focus primarily on Dot, the most legendary cook of the family. She was Martha's mother-in-law and Paula's aunt.[6]

Discussing family dinners of yesteryear as well as using gathered materials as memory prompts, the two brainstormed a list of "must have" dishes and then set about finding recipes for each. Multiple versions existed for several of the recipes—a clue that these dishes were important to the family. At the same time, multiple versions made it difficult to pick a definitive recipe. They often debated whether to automatically pick the one in Dot's handwriting even if it wasn't very detailed or to choose the one annotated by a family member who tried "getting it right" longer than anyone else. Both cooks were experienced enough to read the recipes and decide how closely they matched the dishes they remembered. In the end, by talking through the process (and sometimes contacting other cousins for their input), they pulled together a body of written recipes they felt were the most important and the most authentic from the generations before them. Whether you work alone or with family, your gathering and selection process may be similar.

Recipe Feast or Famine

The Eubanks family has a rich collection of recipes to draw upon for their family cookbook project. They noticed a fact that holds true for many families across the last century—each generation amassed more recipes than the one before. If this is the pattern your family also falls into, recipes from recent generations will require thinning for a family cookbook. You'll most likely need to sort out the used recipes from the untried ones and the noteworthy recipes from those that are run of the mill. As with the Eubanks family, working with other cooks in your family can help with those decisions.

On the other hand, gathering recipes from long-ago family members is most likely a task of "shaking the branches of the family tree," finding out what other members may have inherited and conducting research. For older generations that left fewer recipes, you may find yourself collecting everything you can find rather than seeking the "sure-fire hits." (See chapter 6 for help.)

Recipe Origins

Another consideration when selecting recipes for an heirloom family collection is where the recipes came from. Many of my long-time-favorite recipes were passed down from my mother. And before that? My mother was particularly good about making notes, so thankfully I have some clues. Leafing through the card box she left behind, I find that many of the recipes so familiar from the dinner table during my childhood—dishes that I think of as "Mom's cooking"—actually came from my grandmothers, my aunts, neighbors, or my mother's friends. A few were clipped from newspapers and magazines. But before that . . . ?

If one could somehow permanently tag recipes from the start, banding them like wild birds, it would be fascinating to see how far and wide they fly. There are two basic origins of recipes. First, there have always been and will always be cooks who come up with new recipes—either for a one-time creation to suit the moment's need or for a carefully developed dish. When these recipes are written down, they can be particularly compelling for recipe collectors because of their unique nature. Recipes from this type of source may reveal considerable creativity and cooking sensibilities. Second, there are recipes that developed as folk traditions and harbor the know-how of many hands. They may change slightly with each cook, but for the most part they pass along the same cooking knowledge. At least until the early twentieth century, most cooks learned recipes primarily by watching or talking with other cooks. By and large, word of mouth and shared tips brought new cooking knowledge into the kitchen more often than cookbooks or periodicals did. Some of these recipes were eventually written down. These are the recipes that perhaps have the most to teach us about history and folkways.

As literacy rates rose and printing press materials became more affordable, written recipes of both origins began to find their way into manuscript recipe collections and published sources. It also became more common for written copies—often without attribution—to circulate between family members, friends, and neighbors. Sometimes when recipes are shared, they are adjusted and rewritten, blurring lines between what can be considered old and new, traditional and original. Nowadays we have access to thousands upon thousands of written recipes, and globalization means opportunities to taste a world of dishes. Owning recipes from widely scattered sources is normal for cooks of our time. Regardless of how far or wide those recipes flew in the past, the ones we cook with often or cherish the most we tend to think of as "my recipes."

Your hungry family gathered at the table may not care at that moment where a dish originated. When you are selecting which recipes to include in a family collection, however, it does matter. The origin of each recipe helps tell the story of your life and your family, gives thoughtful cooks cues or ideas to tweak the recipes so the dishes can further evolve, and leaves a record for historians and folklorists studying foodways.[7]

Informally, acknowledging where you got each recipe shows respect to those who were considerate enough to share their knowledge. You can then add your own notes, crediting yourself for adaptations. But there is a formal level as well. Copyright—the protections afforded to creators of intellectual works—can come into play, depending on such considerations as where your recipes originated, how much you changed them, how you decide to distribute or present them, and whether you use them for financial gain. If you are planning to create an elaborate or widely distributed family cookbook, please do not let the idea of recipe ownership discourage you. It is simply a matter of educating yourself about the guidelines and asking for permission whenever necessary.

Food writer Corby Kummer published an essay on the topic of recipes as intellectual property in the *Atlantic* magazine. "How to protect a creation that can take weeks or years to perfect? This has ever bedeviled inventors, but has been particularly vexing for people who try to make their living by cooking. Recipes are practically impossible to copyright," he laments.[8] Barbara Gibbs Ostmann and Jane L. Baker, authors of *The Recipe Writer's Handbook*, state that nowadays food professionals often speak up when they find their work reproduced without permission and particularly without attribution. They note, "The general rule of thumb is that three major changes are required to make a recipe 'yours.' However, even if you make such changes, it is a professional courtesy to acknowledge the source of or inspiration for the recipe."[9]

There are several steps you can take to be fair and to stay away from potential recipe ownership problems. First and foremost, give credit where credit is due. Second, explore the origins of your recipes. Asking for more details from the persons who gave you the recipes is probably the easiest and most effective way. What if that isn't possible or doesn't provide any usable clues? For recipes from cooks who are now gone, if you can find out which cookbooks they preferred, try checking those sources. Also, it is sometimes possible to uncover the recipe origin by conducting searches on the Internet (and in library databases) using a combination of recipe title, the most unusual ingredients, or snippets of recipe text placed in quotation marks. Recipes from newspapers, magazines, or product labels can sometimes be found this way, and even those from older cookbooks that have been digitized. Third, when you create a family cookbook, steer clear of published recipes unless you are simply going to use them in your own kitchen, have adapted the recipe considerably, or thoroughly understand the copyright laws pertaining to fair use (see the next paragraphs). Fourth, if you are in any doubt about using a particular recipe in your own cookbook, ask for permission from the individual you received it from (loose recipe), publisher (cookbook/periodical/website recipe), or ingredient manufacturer (product label recipe).

What falls under the rules of "fair use" is ultimately determined on a case-by-case basis, so it is impossible to outline all the considerations here. The United States Copyright Office maintains a website to explain the basics of current laws, and this is an excellent place to learn more. A search for "recipes" on this website results in publication FL-122. Check the website for the most current revision.

> Copyright law does not protect recipes that are mere listings of ingredients. Nor does it protect other mere listings of ingredients such as those found in formulas, compounds, or prescriptions. Copyright protection may, however, extend to

substantial literary expression—a description, explanation, or illustration, for example—that accompanies a recipe or formula or to a combination of recipes, as in a cookbook.[10]

Other publications found on the website such as "Copyright Basics" may be helpful as well. A guide to copyright for unpublished material is available on the Society of American Archivists website.[11]

Recipe Sharing Etiquette

Even if you give credit where credit is due, there are some additional points about recipe sharing to consider. There are cooks who regard imitation as the sincerest form of flattery and react with delight when asked for their recipes. Other cooks share recipes as a matter of course, never wondering where those recipes may go next. Still other cooks keep a tight rein on their recipes and mind a great deal who else uses them.

Interviewee Connie Carter told me about acquiring her friend's tomato aspic recipe and subsequently sharing it. "I called him one day to cheer him up and I said, 'Oh, you'll be so pleased that your tomato aspic is being served in Portland, Maine, in Eugene, Oregon, and in Beaufort, North Carolina, today!' He spluttered and said, 'Connie, I gave that family recipe to you and to you alone! That was not for you to give away!'" Connie still looked a little shaken by his reaction. She spread her hands in a gesture of bafflement and added, "I'm so thrilled when somebody wants anything of mine!"

Amy Sutherland's book *Cookoff: Recipe Fever in America* is eye-opening if you've never given recipe exclusivity much thought. Winning a recipe competition can mean anything from a few free kitchen utensils to the million-dollar prize for the coveted Pillsbury Bake-Off. But if you want to win, your recipe must be original.

Sutherland briefly examines American history as it pertains to recipe exclusivity. Massachusetts native Elkanah Watson, a well-to-do sheep farmer, started the American agricultural fair movement in the early 1800s. As the idea of the state or local fair caught on, ordinary citizens had the chance to show off success in aspects of their everyday lives. For women, who were largely denied leadership roles, fairs offered a rare way to excel publicly. A woman could rise to prominence by making jam or baking a pie—but she had to make the *best* jam or the *best* pie. To stay on top, she wasn't about to let the competition

Food preservation ribbon winners at the Georgia National Fair in Perry, 2014.

know her secrets. For many cooks, the spirit of the fair is alive and well in their kitchens; they merely swap blue ribbons for praise. Below are a few tips to make sure you don't run afoul of recipe hoarders.

Ask Before You Share. This step is the only way to be sure another cook doesn't mind you including a recipe in your project or sharing it with others. If you think that the person's direct descendants may protest and you hope to publish a cookbook, it may be wise to have the person's consent in writing.

Give Credit. Always include the origin of the recipe to give proper credit if you put it in a cookbook or pass it along. With old family recipes, I usually put the original cook's name in the title of the recipe, and I add notes with basic genealogy information as well.

Acknowledge Changes and Maintain Quality. If you adjust someone else's recipe, add notes explaining your changes. Several of the cooks I interviewed mentioned not wanting to share recipes because the next cook might use poor ingredients or otherwise alter a signature recipe into one of dubious renown. I have to admit that someone proudly proclaiming she was serving Valerie's Cinnamon Toast Salute Cookies but then passing around samples that were overbaked or bland would make me want to leap out of my chair with disclaimers. (Please see chapter 6.)

Honor Signature Dishes. It is gratifying to be known for a particularly good or distinctive recipe. If other cooks are kind enough to give me recipes for their signature dishes, I let them continue to be known for their masterworks. If I am cooking for a gathering where they could be present or that is within their social circles, I don't upstage them by using their signature recipes.

Think about Distribution. A friend may be glad to have you use her mother's recipe for an appetizing supper for your family and wouldn't bat an eye if you shared it with your next-door neighbor. Would she feel the same if you published it in a cookbook that suddenly became popular in your community? If in doubt, ask before including a recipe in a cookbook that may possibly enjoy wide distribution.

Consider a Release Form. Especially if you think your family recipe collection and/or the supplemental materials you collect might be widely distributed or someday donated to an archives, a simple release form for contributors may solve problems with permissions. Write a brief description of the project including details about how it will be promoted or archived, and then you or your contributors can list what they are sharing—recipes, stories, photos, and more. If they have any stipulations about their gifts, they can add details. They sign and date the documents for your records.

Handling Family Materials

Hopefully now your recipes are organized, selected, and credited. But before we move into the kitchen and work with those recipes, you want to make sure they are safe from loss. For a moment, take off your collector's hat and put on an archivist's cap.

As you begin your family recipe project, anticipate that you'll collect recipes but also items such as newspaper clippings, photographs, and documents. Your filing cabinet may soon grow fat, and your computer may become a treasure trove of notes, stories, scans, digital pictures, and recordings. How can you make sure all these materials last for future generations? Read on.

Limiting Cumulative Damage

Working with recipes often means using old papers and cookbooks, but also vintage photographs and other aging materials. With heirloom objects like these, casual care is not enough. You have to think about cumulative damage—the buildup of residue and physical wear across many years and users. Here are some simple ways to ensure that recipes and other family materials last as long as possible.[12]

Clean Your Hands. We all have natural oils in our skin, and our hands may also have residue from food or personal care products, or dust from surfaces we've touched. Thoroughly wash and dry your hands each time before handling family materials. A pair of thin cotton gloves is a good idea if you are working with photographs, as these thick-paper items have an emulsion surface that is easily smudged.[13] Despite what you may see on television, however, gloves are generally not recommended for documents, because they reduce your ability to carefully handle paper thinner than photographs. Fumbling while in gloves could mean torn pages. Clean, dry hands are best with most documents.

All it takes is getting caught in a kitchen drawer or sliding beneath a stack of cookbooks for a recipe to be damaged, sometimes forever losing information. Working with copies rather than originals can keep family recipes safe.

Chow

Cabbage Chopped
Cucumbers   "
+ green tomatoes Chopped
½ C. green peppers
1½ cup sugar
1 Tblsp Mustard seed
1 tblsp. allspice
½ C. salt

Mix +
Drain + Press Out liquids.
Mix Vinegar, Sugar Spices
Simmer 10 Min. add
Vegetables Cook Until
hot + well seasoned –
(Put in jars).

Create Working Copies. Well-meaning history buffs may celebrate old family documents and photos by passing them around at the family reunion. Unfortunately, this results in unnecessary wear on these items. Similarly, framing original documents and photos causes long-term exposure to air and light that shortens their life. Make a quality copy to share or frame instead, so that the original can remain safely with your family files. This is especially important for recipes that could be used around damaging food substances and heat sources.

Although a scan briefly subjects a photo or document to bright light, it is almost always worth it. (If you have a particularly fragile or important item, consult an archivist or conservator before proceeding.) A scan is usually higher quality than a photocopy, becomes available on electronic screens for close viewing, and can be printed out as many times as needed. If you don't have access to a scanner, you may want to consider getting one. Prices have fallen drastically in recent years, with previous models often at a discount or available used. Or check local copy or photography shops for scanning services. Please note that for heirloom documents and photos, you'll want a flatbed scanner; feeder scanners that pull the paper through a slot could damage your one-of-a-kind materials.

Keep Your Workspace Clean. Find a work area that pets or children cannot reach and where materials are safe from air currents. Before beginning to work, take a moment to clean your work surface. If you use a spray surface cleaner, follow this by wiping down the table or desktop with plain water to remove chemical residues and then thoroughly dry the surface afterwards. Don't bring food or drinks—even water—to your workspace.

Limit Pressure on Papers. We are so used to thinking of paper as soft and flexible that we may accidentally abuse the weak, brittle fibers of old documents. I used to tell researchers in the archives reading room, "Pretend old papers are sheets of very thin glass."

- Handle heirloom materials slowly and gently.
- Properly support old papers when you carry them by using a folder, and leave papers flat on the table while you read them.
- As you work with old papers, position them so that you won't accidentally lean on them with elbows or hands.
- Make sure old papers never hang off the table edge.
- Be aware that "chipped" edges or yellowing may be signs that the whole paper has become dangerously fragile.

Take Care with Folds. When you bend paper backward to flatten a fold, you are actually breaking the fibers of the paper and making it much more susceptible to tears. To treat a document that is stubbornly folded or curled, place the document between sheets of plain white copy/printer paper, gently flatten with your clean hands, and then place a light weight larger than the document, such as a book, on top for several days in a safe place. This treatment will work best on humid days, which better allow the fibers of the paper to relax. For severely bent or tenaciously rolled documents, it is possible to build a homemade humidification chamber. A web search for "how to flatten documents" or "build a humidification chamber" will turn up instructions from various reputable archives and museums.

These days most copy or printer paper is acid free and therefore safe for prolonged contact with heirloom documents. Later in this section we will discuss testing materials for damaging acid content.

Clean Carefully. Use a clean, soft, natural-fiber paintbrush to lift food residue from old recipes. If a recipe has a grease spot, slide the recipe between sheets of plain white copy paper and place a light weight larger than the recipe, such as a book, on top of it for several days. Repeat as necessary until the blotting paper comes away clean.

For food stains, it may be tempting to try water to remove them, but this treatment can easily spread debris, dissolve inks, and buckle the paper. Taking the document to a reputable paper conservator is a better idea. Ask an archivist, museum professional, or rare book dealer if they can help you find one with who has proper credentials and solid references.

Avoid "Sticky Notes." Small memo pads with a light adhesive strip along the back of each page leave chemical residues and should not be used with heirloom materials.

Safeguarding Materials

With the heirloom materials in our care, it is important not to alter them in ways that might erase valuable information, decrease their longevity, or affect their value.

Preserve Original Order. If you inherit someone else's photo albums, scrapbooks, recipe collections, or similar groups of materials, preserve them intact if at all possible. The original order of the items often holds clues about how they were created or used. Make copies to share or use, but avoid shuffling or removing parts of the original collection.

Preserve Provenance. Provenance is the story of heirloom materials—who created them, who owned them, and how they traveled or were altered over time. Take time now to write detailed notes about heirloom materials and collect additional information from others if need be. Be very hesitant to get rid of old envelopes, containers, or wrappings. At the very least, make sure these don't have ownership labels, addresses, postal marks, or other clues that add information or value.

Beware Repairs. One of the basic rules of archives is, don't do anything to documents, photographs, and artifacts that can't easily be undone. Adhesive tape, heat-set lamination (putting paper through hot rollers to seal it in clear plastic sheets), and cold lamination (sealing between layers of clear adhesive film) may seem like good ways to repair torn items or make them less fragile. Unfortunately, these treatments cannot be removed and usually contain chemicals that ruin paper over time. If it is too late and your documents have already been taped or laminated, your best bet is to scan the document now before the plastics/adhesives become yellowed or cloudy. For laminated items, take care that the plastic film doesn't become scratched, as this reduces legibility.

Repairs are usually not necessary. I have several family documents that are in poor shape, and I carefully scanned these documents. With the ones that were in fragments, I pieced them together on the scanner bed using stacked checkers swiped from the family game cabinet to gently and safely weight the scraps down. The finished scan of the document is easy to use, while the original, still in multiple pieces, went into an acid-free folder in my family files. If you feel strongly that a document or artifact needs repair, find a reputable conservator.

Beware Glue and Other Adhesives. Here's a prime example of adhesive damage. My mother wrote in a family letter, "Since we've been married I have never made peanut butter cookies because Bob doesn't care for them. So I decided long ago, if I wanted any, I'd have to train our kids to eat them." She added that my brother, a toddler at the time, "could poke in those cookies as fast as I could take them out of the oven and cool them."[14] On the recipe card for the cookies, my mother noted, "Very good!" Sometime afterwards my father penciled in "Ugh!"

This family story backed up by documents admittedly isn't one of earth-shattering importance. Still, it is warm and funny, nicely illustrating the tone of my parents' marriage and giving an early portrait of my brother. Because we lost our parents relatively early in life, I think my brother and I are always craving remembrances and also wishing to help our children get a sense of the grandparents they never had the chance to meet. Thus I wanted to frame copies for my brother's kitchen as a gift, but I soon discovered the rubber cement used on the original recipe card has turned it almost illegible in the last few years. Should you decide to put together a family cookbook scrapbook-style, it is worth a little research to make sure you can create it without problem

Adhesive damaged Sharon Cowles Frey's undated recipe for peanut butter cookies. She attached the thin paper to cardstock using rubber cement.

adhesives or other short-lived materials. If you find severe adhesive problems in an existing family recipe collection or scrapbook, your best bet is to scan or photograph the materials before the problem gets more severe with time. You may also wish to seek help from an archivist or conservator.

Practice Scrapbooking with Care. Many archivists have love/hate feelings about the scrapbooking industry. On the positive side, it is heartwarming to see people preserving family stories for future generations. The industry publicizes the danger of acids in paper as well as the value of adding stories and information to family materials. It is heartbreaking, however, to see one-of-a-kind materials cropped, pasted down, or covered in decorative stickers—treatments that usually cannot be undone.

Best practices in scrapbooking means working only with copies when it comes to documents. With photographs, don't alter vintage prints; indeed, the same goes for recent prints unless you have a digital file or negative. If you are determined to include original items in a scrapbook, use photo corners to hold them in place rather than actually attaching them. Finally, to avoid the possibility of your photos sticking together, add a barrier sheet of acid-free paper between pages or place photographs in such a way that when you close your scrapbook, the surfaces of photographs don't touch.

Annotate Gently. When working around historical materials, archivists use pencil so that any marks—including accidental ones—can later be erased. If you feel you must add a note to an original document, do so lightly in pencil, usually on the back and preferably along an edge. Make sure there is a firm work surface beneath the document and take care not to press hard enough to leave indentions in the paper.

Label Photographs. Marking the backs of photographs with information such as date, occasion, location, and names of people pictured is very important to your family's history. If you have unlabeled photographs you can't identify, make copies to send around the family or community asking for help. Sooner rather than later is best, and ask the older generations first.

With older photographs, write information lightly on the back in pencil as described above. Modern photographs, however, are printed on RC (resin-coated) paper that is too slick for pencil. In this case, choose a soft-tip marker (not ballpoint) that is labeled as archival quality, lightfast, waterproof, fade proof, and nonbleeding. The ink will probably take a few minutes to dry, so don't stack the photos right away. Art or craft supply stores have such pens, but for a reliable product you might want to check reviews or see which brands are carried by archival supply companies.

Storing Paper-Based Documents and Photographs

We've already looked at keeping family materials safe while using them. The final step is to make sure you have proper storage so they can last as long as possible.

Create a Safe Climate. Unfinished attics, basements, and sheds are terrible storage areas for papers, photos, books, artifacts, or other items you wish to pass to future generations. Here are some important considerations:

- **Pests.** Storage areas without climate control can be a haven for pests that may feast on documents, chew up heirlooms to create nests, or leave behind staining droppings. The gelatin-based surface of some photographs may be particularly appealing to pests, as are old recipes or cookbooks flecked with food residue.
- **Chemical Acceleration.** An overly warm storage climate speeds up harmful chemical processes. Acids present in many types of paper turn it yellow and brittle over time, and this will speed up if papers are stowed in a hot attic. Similarly, inks may also have harmful chemical components causing them to fade or even decompose as the years go by. I have seen old documents that look like fine lace because each line and swoop of acidic pen ink has eaten away the paper under it.

ly over 25 million tons of paper, including box board but not including pulp. Of this amount the South accounts for a very high per cent, the speaker said.

Grades now produced in the South, he continued, include: news print, formerly a Canadian monopoly; kraft, formerly a Canadian and New England product; kraft board for hundreds of uses and bleached kraft for milk bottles, trays, and cups. The same mills also produce white writing paper.

As the result of this tremendous growth of the industry, Montag's after 65 years in business has seen fit to build a new plant in the heart of Atlanta to convert the many grades of paper into useful articles, the speaker said. The building covers about six acres of a 22-acre site

Acids weakened this paper, causing chips along the edges. It will tear very easily.

The glue used to affix this newspaper clipping quickly turned dark in a hot attic.

- *Mold and Mildew Blooms.* Warm air paired with moisture encourages the growth of damaging fungus. Even if halted, mold and mildew usually remain dormant, ready to take over when the climate conditions are right, such as during a temporary air-conditioning breakdown. Don't store family materials anywhere that warmth and moisture could become a problem. Isolate any heirlooms that could already have mold and mildew spores, usually identified by splotches of gray, black, or pink stains and sometimes (but not always) a musty smell.
- *Cycling.* Swings in temperature and humidity cause physical damage. Paper fibers expand when they become warm or humid, and then contract when they are cold or dry. Over time, the cycle of expanding and contracting weakens the fibers. Although each type of material has an ideal temperature and humidity level, a good "happy medium" for storing family materials is between 60° and 72°F with 40 to 55 percent relative humidity.

Choose Appropriate Containers. For long-term storage of family materials, use acid-free cardboard boxes and folders. These safely hold items together, keep dust at bay, and block light while allowing some healthy air circulation that helps prevent a microenvironment for fungus.

How do you find such boxes and folders? Unfortunately, this is a little tricky. The terms "acid free" and "archival" are currently unlegislated, so manufacturers can use them freely on product labels. The Library of Congress and other large archives have equipment for testing batches of new containers, but most archives and individuals don't have such resources.

A pH testing pen can help. After a small mark is made on paper or cardboard, the special ink turns yellow if acid is present. These pens have recently begun popping up in craft stores.[15] Since you would ideally need to gain permission to test containers before purchasing them, however, buying containers from a reputable source is probably the best course of action. For my family collection, I order from companies that I know many archives use.[16] Your local archives or library may be able to give you a recommendation.

Use Safe Storage Areas. Staff from the Georgia Archives helped after the Hurricane Katrina disaster, and it was heartbreaking to see how boxes on the floor soaked up oily floodwater when they would have been safe only a few inches higher. Keep in mind, however, that a disaster may take the form of an overflowing washing machine, broken window during a rainstorm, pipe drip, or ceiling leak. Think about possible hazards before choosing a storage area, and place storage boxes on shelves. If you must use floor space for storage, bricks placed under boxes can be a good stopgap measure that just might save the day. If you have to use a storage area with overhead pipes, a sheet of plastic draped over the boxes may similarly save your materials in case of a leak.

If you discover mold or current water damage in your family materials, isolate them and place them in a cool, dry climate right away so the problem doesn't spread or get worse. The next step would be to contact a professional archivist or paper conservator right away. If in-person help is not available, the National Archives and other reputable institutions have posted online emergency preparedness guides concerning archival materials.[17] I urge you not to toss family materials that seem ruined without first seeking help. Freeze-drying, chemical desiccants, and other methods may be able to save your materials or at least stabilize documents for making quality scans.

Make Backup Copies. If your home ever catches fire, you'll be very grateful that you made backup copies of important papers and photographs; even a small house fire can cause severe smoke and water damage. An excellent choice is to trade copies with family members who live far away, because region-wide disasters do happen.

Macon Good Will Tourists

In Account With

Harris House

McRae, Georgia

Luncheon September 8th, 1925

"SETTLED IN FULL"

We are delighted to have you good folks as our guests today.

Our only regret is that you cannot stay longer, so that we could know you better and you could get better acquainted with the best people in the best little city in the world.

Come Again.

Cordially,
McRAE BOARD OF TRADE

This paper was stacked with acidic papers. As the acid migrated, it turned the page old and brittle before its time. A small card of acid-free paper rested against part of it, shielding it and revealing "acid shadows."

Isolate Acidic or Soiled Papers. Yellowing is a sign that acid is breaking down the fibers in the paper. You'll see this quite often with newspaper clippings, which are common in most modern recipe collections, but it affects other types of paper too. Unfortunately, acids can migrate to other papers that touch them, leaving a yellow or brown shadow. Similarly, grease and other food residues on recipes can migrate if they touch other papers.

To protect papers from migration of acid or grime (including grease or food residue on heirloom recipes), make copies of yellowed or soiled papers to keep in your family files and then isolate the problem originals in a separate location. If you can't safely move a problem item, such as in a scrapbook, place blank sheets of acid-free paper in front of it and behind it so it does not touch other materials. Ideally, these barrier sheets should be changed every few years.

Backing Up Digital Materials

Most computer users would agree that it is important to update electronic devices and software periodically, to keep abreast of basic trends in technology, and to back up their work. As an archivist, however, perhaps I've heard more hard-luck stories of lost files than most. Let me share some helpful information to prevent a heart-sinking loss of your family's history.

Computer files are highly vulnerable, sometimes vanishing forever in a split second if equipment breaks down. The good news is that most backup systems are now high capacity and relatively inexpensive, so you can use more than one method, providing a second backup in case the first fails. At present, sharing and backing up electronic data is accomplished increasingly through online services rather than through personal storage devices. Technology changes so rapidly that any specifics printed here will almost immediately be out of date, so I'll just touch on some generalities.

Disks. For many years, disks of various types were the preferred way to share and back up electronic files. That has largely changed, yet some home computers can still write information to these disks, and data stored on them will be finding its way into archives for many years to come. Unfortunately, the forward march of technology means that the hardware and software needed to read disks is increasingly obsolete and consequently hard to find. In addition, longevity varies greatly. With compact disks, for instance, gold disks created on high-quality professional equipment might last a century or more, yet CDs created on a home computer may begin to lose data in a matter of months. One day you may pop a family history disk into your computer only to find it riddled with errors or even blank.

If disks are still your primary means of backup or you inherited information on some, seriously consider updating to other methods. In the meantime, make multiple copies in case of disk malfunction, and periodically create fresh copies to stave off data fade. Use a climate-controlled, low-light, dust-free area for storage, and place CD or DVD-type disks vertically in plastic "jewel cases." Because many markers and label adhesives contain harmful chemicals, write only on the hubs/centers of CDs or DVDs.

Electronic storage disks from the 1980s, 1990s, and early 2000s.

External Drives. In general, these devices are relatively stable and dependable. One of the drawbacks is that the uploading process may be confusing, so you might accidentally erase information by replacing files with outdated versions. If you avoid distractions when you back up files and label your electronic files clearly, however, this should not be a problem.

A far bigger drawback is that it may be tempting to rely on a single external drive for all your backup needs. Not long ago, one of my friends lost her home-based business files and almost every picture of her daughter when a thief zipped into her house on a sunny Sunday afternoon while she was at the grocery store. Despite an alarm system and a large dog, the thief took the computer and found the backup hard drive tucked away in another room. A house fire could likewise leave you with nothing. If you don't want to use an external drive in tandem with an online backup system, I recommend multiple external drives, frequently swapping out the most recently used external drive with another in a faraway location.

Online Sharing and Backups. An online backup can be as simple as e-mailing files to yourself so they are stored at least temporarily on a distant server. On a larger scale, linking electronic devices such as personal computers and smartphones means users have "anywhere access" to their files as well as a built-in backup service on a remote server. For those who don't wish to link various personal devices, an online backup service for just your computer is an option that still allows you to back up your work while traveling. An Internet search using terms such as "data backup" or "data repository" will turn up many backup service companies.

Before selecting any file sharing or data storage company, check to see where their computer system is located. You want one many miles from where you are living in case of a regional disaster—especially if you live in an earthquake, tornado, or hurricane zone. In addition, find out how often new data is backed up and how your information is kept secure. Check customer and magazine reviews to make sure the company's system works as promised.

Even if you have an online backup service, I recommend also backing up with an external hard drive. Most online services charge fees for efficiently restoring your files, and the process can take time—particularly if many customers are affected by problems at the same time, as in a regional disaster. An external hard drive may be the best way to get back on track quickly in case your computer fails. In addition, it is always good to have printouts of crucial files in case of multiple system failures, extensive computer viruses, or other unforeseen disasters. (In case of a zombie apocalypse, those beloved family recipes will be a true comfort if you can still access them—and adapt them for hearth cooking.)

Word Processing Files. Whenever you move up to a newer version of word processing software, do a "save as" and make an updated version with the new software to preserve your important files. It is also a good idea to save an extra copy of important word processing documents in Rich Text Format, a version that most word processing programs can read.

Print out copies of important word processing files. I once lost an electronic document of more than one hundred pages. Fortunately, I had printed it out. Not only did I still have the information, but I was able to scan each page and use OCR (optical character recognition) software to turn it into an electronic file again.

Other Digital Information. As with word processing documents, changes in technology over time will affect the usability of any image, sound, and video files you'd like to keep. Every couple of years, investigate what upgrades or software changes are needed to ensure your files are still usable. With digital photography files that you definitely want to keep, I recommend printing hard copies. For your most important photos, it is worth the extra expense to have a reputable photography lab create high-resolution prints. Check with your local camera shop to find a lab with quality equipment and well-trained staff.

You'll want to know that the staff frequently calibrate their equipment and check their inks/chemistry to make sure printed images are sharp and colors are true.

Family Artifacts

I have two aluminum cookie cutters that came from my great-grandmother. Making cookies with them a few times a year literally puts me in touch with family history, while the dough and gentle cleanup afterwards does them no harm. If you decide to use family kitchen heirlooms, do so with care and inspect them before and after use. Similarly, if you display family artifacts, make sure that exposure to light, air, and dust is causing them no harm. I have quite a few old cooking items on display in my kitchen, but I selected them carefully. Fluctuating humidity levels and airborne food particles make the kitchen a hazardous zone for heirlooms that are porous or vulnerable to rust, tarnishing, and mildew. When it comes to repairs or "face-lifts," be very hesitant to make any changes. Refinishing, repainting, or even a thorough cleaning can shorten the life or reduce the value of some items. A professional at a local museum may be able to give you advice or offer contact information for a reputable conservator. There are also guides available in print or online.[18]

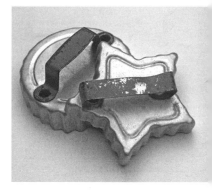

Aluminum cookie cutters that belonged to Dessie Jane Weekley Greene (1888–1958), the author's great-grandmother.

One of the most important steps you can take is to label or document family items. My mother had a cast-iron pan for molding small cornbread sticks. I remembered my mother using it only once and I hadn't used it myself, so I gave it to charity. I later learned that the pan belonged to my great-grandparents, and I felt terrible about letting it leave the family. Please learn from my mistake.

Taking time to label family artifacts can prevent accidental giveaways, but it also helps prevent subsequent generations from losing track of which pieces came from Aunt A and which from Aunt B. Similarly, if you are like me and enjoy antique shops, labeling family artifacts can keep them from being mixed up with purchases.

When labeling items, do not use permanent markers or adhesives. Grandpa Frey saved a nineteenth-century family hunting horn for me, but labeled it using masking tape that later turned stiff on the outside and gooey on the inside. Because of the softness of the horn, the professionals I showed it to thought it best to leave well enough alone. Now this family heirloom is forever wrapped in unsightly tape. Acid-free cardstock tags with soft cotton string ties

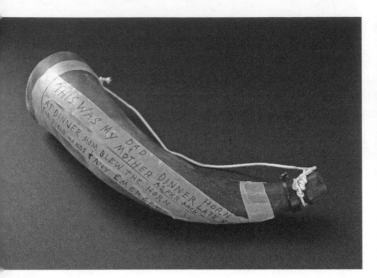

The label written by Robert A. Frey reads, "This was my Dad & Mother dinner horn as far back as late [18]80s. At dinner Mom blew the horn for field hands & any emergency."

This kitchen paddle used by the author's great-grandmother is now safely labeled.

are a much better labeling solution and can be purchased at most office supply or craft stores.

For items that can't safely be labeled, take pictures and label the photographs. This is actually a great step for all your family artifacts, because you can then create a single visual inventory. Make sure family members know where the photos are located, so if something happens to you, they can check this source before beginning to clean out your former living space. (A visual inventory is also helpful for wills and insurance purposes.)

If you do not have a clear idea about how your family kitchen artifact was used, a little research may make the item much more interesting to you and other family members. Your local library should have resources about daily life in various eras. Pricing guides for antique collectors are full of images that can be helpful, and you might also try asking a historian or a reputable antiques dealer to steer you in the right research direction.[19] And, of course, the Suggested Reading section at the end of this book should also be helpful.

Finally, if you don't think your family has many artifacts, it may be worth your time to ask around. Once I let it be known that I was taking photos of heirloom items for a family cookbook, I was truly surprised by the items brought out of china cabinets and closets—a rolling pin made by my great-grandfather, a carved wooden dough bowl from my great-great-grandfather's household, and chinaware that once traveled hundreds of miles by wagon train.

Robert A. Frey's kitchen knives speak to his blacksmithing skills. The top knife was used for dealing with bones and was handmade from a piece of pipe and a hacksaw blade. The middle knife was purchased, yet mended after the blade broke. The bottom "watermelon knife" is homemade and has been sharpened so many times that the blade is misshapen.

Sometimes artifacts wordlessly speak volumes. This orphaned grater was found at a junk shop. The labor-intensive repair, replacing a broken handle with folded sheet aluminum bolted into place, hints at its previous owner's thrift, skills, and resources.

Chapter Three

Adjusting Recipes

A good recipe is one that first encourages the reader to cook, and then delivers what it promises. A well-written recipe takes you by the hand and says, don't worry, it'll all be okay, this is what you're looking for, this is what happens when you chop or slice or apply heat, and if it goes wrong, this is how to fix it. And when you've finished, this is what it should look and taste like, this is what to eat it with. But above all, take joy in what you do.—Elisabeth Luard's commentary in Ostmann and Baker's *Recipe Writer's Handbook* (30)

One of the family recipes that came down to me is romantically titled "Daffodil Cake," yet a more descriptive name would be "Baked Yellow Paste." The finished dessert is dense and oddly flavored. Sadly, I know I'm not the only one to use a family recipe and find the results unpredictable, mediocre, or even unpleasant. A recipe is simply a list of ingredients and corresponding instructions, yet a sparse or confusing recipe makes cooking *anything but* simple.

When I was a relatively new cook, I always assumed it was my fault if a dish didn't turn out well. A cook's skill and care are certainly important, but recipe success also depends on the efforts of the person who wrote it down. Take a little time to read through the recipes you've identified as family heirlooms. For each one, ask yourself, "Will this recipe allow an average cook to successfully replicate the dish?"

If you are primarily interested in family recipes exactly as they were written, that is perfectly acceptable. Much can be learned from recipes "as is," and the reality is that just because a recipe was passed down from family doesn't mean it is a tasty or useful recipe worth cooking with. Please feel free to preserve recipes just as you collected them and move on to chapter 5.

Many who love family cooking, however, hope their recipes will consistently re-create the flavors that trigger memories or offer an authentic taste of the past. Others wish to transform humdrum or outdated family recipes into ones that suit today's demands and tastes even while paying homage to the cooks who came before them. To serve these needs, the information in this chapter is designed to help cooks adjust heirloom recipes in two ways. The first is to *clarify* the recipe through more effective language or additional information. If that isn't enough, you may also wish to *modify* the recipe, adapting ingredients or procedures so that the resulting dish is closer to the dish you remember and/ or more pleasing to the palate. And what if you are starting without a written recipe for a certain family dish? In that case, you'll need both clarification and modification know-how to create an effective one.

Let me pause here to add that how best to go about clarifying and modifying recipes may depend on the recipe's age and historical significance. Tinkering to lighten up your signature lasagna recipe or adding hints about seasoning Mom's potato salad may be relatively simple, but adjusting a bare-bones recipe to authentically recreate an ancestor's hearth cornmeal pudding is a complex task. This chapter offers some hints for handling older recipes, and chapter 6 as well as the Suggested Reading list will also be helpful. In particular, food historian Kay K. Moss's *Seeking the Historical Cook* offers background knowledge and cooking help but also explores what it means to faithfully interpret a historical recipe.

Recipe Versions

Whenever you feel an heirloom recipe needs adjusting—clarifying, modifying, or both—the first step is to preserve the recipe "as is." After you've made a copy to work with, the original should go into your genealogy files, preserving it as a historical document in its own right. Other cooks may wish for the chance to work with the original recipe someday, and it will also be there as a reference should you need to backtrack with your adjustments. As for the copy you'll work with, a printed scan or photocopy is fine to take with you into the kitchen. I prefer to type up each heirloom recipe before I begin to work with it, so a simple "save as" on my computer allows me to create my own version that I can print. However you create your version, add a notes section with your name, the date, and information about the recipe's history.

Once you're working on your own version of a given heirloom recipe, you're in for a treat. Creating a well-written recipe doesn't just involve the fun of cooking. It is a satisfying puzzle as well—unlocking culinary know-how but also effectively describing the process while keeping the directions efficient. The best way I can think of to move deeper into a discussion of adjusting recipes is to look at an actual recipe that has been both clarified and modified. Our family's recipe for teacakes, passed down through my paternal grandfather, is actually an orphaned recipe (discussed in depth in chapter 6). I've been using it so long, however, that it functions as my own. The original recipe turned out decent cookies, but the more I worked with it, the more knowledge I gathered and the better the cookies tasted. This is the original recipe, as dictated to me by Grandpa Frey:[1]

Teacakes

1 cup sugar

1 cup shortening

1 or 2 eggs

⅓ teaspoon soda

⅔ teaspoon baking powder

4 tablespoons water

4 to 5 cups flour

Mix first ingredients with hands. Drop into a nest made of flour. Mix. Roll on floured surface and cut into circles with a glass. Bake (400 degrees until crisp).

>> Did you just read through the recipe and think, that's not a teacake! Actually, "teacake" is a name used for various types of individual baked goods—some with yeast and some without, some soft and some crunchy. Particularly when looking at older recipes, terms and recipe titles evolve and change. This is just one of the challenges that lovers of old recipes face.

To be useful and consistent, my family's teacakes recipe went through many revisions—both clarifications and modifications—until it reached this point:

Ellen Moseley Teacakes

(Adjusted by Valerie J. Frey, November 2012)

This is a pale cookie that works well with cookie cutters, holding its shape with little puffing or distortion. The mild flavor pairs nicely with icing.

Scant 4 cups (475 grams) unsifted all-purpose flour, plus extra for handling dough

⅓ teaspoon (barely rounded ¼ teaspoon or 2.33 g) baking soda

⅔ teaspoon (gently rounded ½ teaspoon or 3.33 g) baking powder

1 cup (195 grams) shortening

1 cup (200 grams) granulated sugar

2 large eggs

1 teaspoon vanilla extract

1 teaspoon extract or bakery emulsion (orange, almond, or as desired)

2 to 3 tablespoons cool water

1. Preheat oven to 350°F.
2. In a medium-sized bowl, blend flour with soda and baking powder to create dry mixture, then set aside.
3. In a large mixing bowl, cream shortening and sugar with electric mixer until fluffy. Add eggs and flavorings, mixing just until well blended.
4. Gradually blend large spoonfuls of dry mixture into the creamed mixture, adding water a little at a time whenever dough seems crumbly. Dough will be very thick but not sticky and does not need to be chilled.
5. Roll dough out on a well-floured surface and cut with cookie cutters.
6. Place cutouts on ungreased cookie sheet and bake at 350°F, usually about 8 minutes for thin cookies (⅛ inch) and 12 for thick ones (¼ inch).
7. Let cookies rest on baking sheet for 5 minutes to firm up, but move to cooling racks before cold to prevent sticking. Store in an airtight container.

Makes about four dozen 2-inch cookies.

Comparing the two recipes, there are quite a few differences. First, I clarified the recipe. In general, the older the recipe, the more likely it is that the writer will assume the cook is experienced enough to fill in the missing details. I expanded the teacakes directions so any cook can better picture the process. Although I purchased a vintage ⅓ teaspoon measure for my own kitchen, I added additional measuring hints to the recipe to help cooks without one. (Such spoons are also available online or in some gourmet kitchen stores.)

Next, I modified the recipe to change the finished dish. Reading about food history is a favorite hobby, so at some point I would love to interpret this recipe as strictly as a food historian—complete with a wood-burning oven. In the meantime, it is a contemporary family favorite that shows up on our table at holidays. Thus I added extract for more flavor. Quite frankly, my family weren't fans of this recipe until I did. I also discovered that slightly less flour made for a more tender and moist cookie. However, I stopped short of reducing the flour enough to make the dough sticky and require chilling; when I did so, the resulting cookies no longer had their familiar taste and texture. I introduced using a mixer for shorter work time and a more even texture, and then reduced the oven temperature so that the cookies don't brown too quickly. The original recipe aims for "crisp," but my family prefers soft. The recipe is longer, yet even the newest cooks in my family need little help to follow it to success.

Because I preserved the original recipe just as Grandpa Frey dictated it to me, future generations can give it a go. The recipe is somewhat vague, so their results may or may not taste like mine. If my son, nieces, or nephews want to replicate the cutout cookies they remember from my kitchen every Christmas, however, they stand a good chance of being able to do so because my adjusted version of the recipe is thorough.

Kathleen Flinn, author of *The Kitchen Counter Cooking School*, reports that quite often original recipes created by food writers are later simplified by publishers.[2] Editing not only maximizes valuable page space but also makes a recipe look appealingly simple to the cookbook or magazine buyer. She points out, however, that just because a recipe is shorter doesn't mean it is easier to use or produces an optimal dish. Similarly, in order for an heirloom recipe to have a chance at being cherished and remaining in the family repertoire, it needs to be written well and contain enough information to ensure a positive cooking experience. Seasoned cooks can skip over familiar instructions or apply their creativity, but cooks needing guidance or seeking the authentic will be grateful for the help.

A good way to effectively write or rewrite a recipe is to imagine a novice cook as an audience. Perhaps it is inevitable for one who lost a mother early, but I think about what each recipe should explain to those getting used to cooking solo. I consider favorite cooking tips I'd like my son (and other descendants) to know, should I not be there in person to share cooking knowledge. In addition, there may be tips that positively transform a cook's experience with a recipe. For instance, cutting up gumdrops for an old bar cookie recipe meant that candy pieces tenaciously stuck to the knife, to my fingers, and to each other. I was about to forever swear off baking with gumdrops when I figured out the tricks of chilling the candy before handling, cutting it with buttered kitchen

Margaret Frey, Ellen Moseley's great-great-great-granddaughter, preparing to decorate teacakes in 2005.

For this book I enlisted the help of several home cooks as recipe testers. To my amusement, I soon learned that in order to be sure they would test a recipe *as it is written*, I had to make that request in bold, all-capital letters—and calling them on the phone to reiterate didn't hurt—because altering the recipe to suit personal preferences is a huge temptation. In fact, one of my testers wrote back, "It almost killed me not to change it." In order to refine your written recipes, however, you truly need someone to test them to the letter.

shears, and immediately dredging the cut bits with flour, so I added these tips to the recipe.

Jot down notes while actually making the dish, so that you will be more aware of each step. Try to be exact. Taking time to choose the right words to describe an ingredient size or a procedure can make all the difference later to someone standing at the stove trying to replicate the dish. Once you feel you have a well-written recipe, choose a tester from your circle of family or friends. Select someone who is not a highly experienced cook and have him or her use your updated recipe *exactly as it is written*. The feedback will help you further tweak the recipe. The best-case scenario is if you are actually in the kitchen with the test cook so you can observe the process. You want the other person to do the actual cooking, but you can make notes about problem spots and questions. It also gives you a chance to taste the finished dish to see if it turns out as you expect.

Tips for Clarifying Recipes

Let's first look at clarifying the language. If your recipe is fairly clear or for a dish that is easy to make, it may be in good shape already. If not, here are some tips:

Pay Attention to Order. By the mid-1800s, home economists and cookbook authors like Eliza Acton and Isabella Beeton as well as Fannie Farmer in later years campaigned for more efficient recipes. Their reforms moved recipes past the simple paragraph format, encouraging a list of ingredients at the beginning. The ingredient list should be in chronological order according to when the items will be used in the recipe. This helps the cook to have all the ingredients ready before starting, as well as to quickly review the list to make sure they have all been included once the preparation is done. In addition, I am a big fan of numbering the steps in the instructions portion of a recipe, as I find it creates good flow, helps me get back on track faster if I get interrupted while cooking, and makes it easier to discuss the recipe.

Measure Accurately. I can't overstate how important this step is. Many of us have been cooking so long that we measure ingredients automatically, usually the way we saw it done by others as we were learning to cook. I've

Detail from *Hood's Combined Cook Books*, produced by C. I. Hood & Co. of Lowell, Mass., ca. 1900.

Measuring utensils from the early to mid-twentieth century.

watched enough home cooks to know that measuring methods vary a good deal, particularly among those with enough experience to "wing it." When you're in the kitchen whipping up supper, measuring methods don't matter as long as you get good results. Writing recipes, however, is sharing knowledge. So that other cooks using your heirloom recipes will have success, the reality is that you can't do without the common ground of standardized measuring practices.

If you're serious about adjusting heirloom recipes but you also want to have more consistent results with all your recipes, an accurate kitchen scale is your best friend. Although measuring by weight is embraced by cooks around the world, most American cooks tend to stick with volume measuring utensils such as nonmetric cups and teaspoons. Since published American recipes are almost always by volume, I never considered any other way until I started working with very old recipes. When I learned the benefits of weighing ingredients, I found it was well worth the effort to expand my kitchen skills this way.

Why bother with weights? Professional bakers have long been aware that volume measurements for powdery ingredients like flour and confectioner's sugar can vary widely depending on how the handling fluffs or compacts them. The same holds true with many other ingredients from leafy greens to soft bread crumbs to cooked rice. Similarly, with ingredients like a cup of strawberries, do you leave them whole to measure them or do you chop them? How small the pieces are makes a significant difference in how much empty space versus berry there is in that cup. Measuring by weight takes out the guesswork.

If you've never cooked with a scale, know that it also makes cooking and cleanup easier. By using the "zero" or "tare" button on a digital scale, you can erase the weight of a container placed on it. Add an ingredient up to the correct weight and then hit the tare button again. As long as you go slowly (so you don't accidentally add too much), the next ingredient can go right in and will be measured without the weight of the container and previous ingredients. My scale isn't sensitive enough to handle small amounts of seasonings or leavenings, so I use measuring spoons for those, but my recipe zips along quickly. I find it blissful to add ingredients like honey or shortening directly from their containers; no more scraping or washing gooey measuring cups!

If a recipe you're working with calls for ingredients in volume measurements, take a moment to write in the equivalent weight measurements before you begin cooking. Looking up average weights of basic ingredients on the Internet is a quick way to start, although you'll want to test the recipe using weight measurements to be sure.[3] (I created a cheat sheet of weights for basic ingredients that I keep with my scale, but I also find it easy to remember the weights of ingredients I cook with often.) If you suspect the measurements written in your heirloom recipe may not be accurate, you can measure each ingredient the way you think the original cook did and then weigh it. Once your recipes have precise weight measurements added, potentially anyone can cook more quickly, easily, and accurately with them. (To help cooks who may not have scales, I add weight measurements in parentheses rather than replacing the standard volume measurements on recipes when I clarify them.)

If you're still not quite convinced about kitchen scales, it may help to know that prices have dropped greatly in recent years and, as we'll see in the next chapter, a scale is very handy for cooking visits. An additional benefit is that a scale usually makes it easier to work with recipes from other countries, expanding your cooking repertoire.

What if you just can't imagine measuring any differently than you've done for years? If you are going to stick strictly to cups and teaspoons, then, even if it seems a little humbling, it's worth your time to do a quick review about the way to measure various basic ingredients. Five minutes with a basic cookbook's general information section or online tutorial can save you from creating a long string of inaccurate recipes. Or you can add notes to the recipe about the way you measure your ingredients, so future cooks can measure your way too.

Avoid Abbreviations. If you've ever squinted at a recipe trying to decide if you're looking at an uppercase "T" for tablespoon or a lowercase "t" for teaspoon, you know why it is better to fully spell out each word. Even if your recipes are neatly printed via computer, using a full term makes it more likely a reader can decipher unfamiliar terminology. For instance, my mother always wrote "oleo" in recipes. This was short for "oleomargarine," an outdated term, and won't be deciphered by many of today's cooks if they don't see the full word.

Cookbooklet from Jelke's Good Luck oleomargarine, early 1920s.

Cookbooklet from Lawrenceburg Roller Mills Company, 1906.

Explain Brand Names. As with abbreviations, using just a brand name in a recipe may confuse cooks in years to come. If you inherited a recipe calling for a cup of Town Talk, King Midas, or Occident, would you know the recipe is asking for all-purpose flour? If the recipe should be faithful to a specific brand, add a note such as "1 cup all-purpose flour, White Lily preferred." Or give future cooks a clear picture of the recipe by calling for "1 cup White Lily (all-purpose flour from soft winter wheat with low protein and gluten content)."

Explain Package Capacities. Many recipes call for a can of this or a box of that. In such cases it is important to add a clarifying note about how much of the ingredient is actually needed. A cousin shared an obviously old but undated recipe for Vanilla Wafer Cake. How many wafers should be used? The recipe called for "a 25 cent package." Inflation jokes aside, I had to track down comparable recipes before I could make an educated guess.[4] If you stipulate a "large can" of tomato sauce, thinking of the 12-ounce size over the 6-ounce one, a future cook may shop in a store with more choices and interpret "large" as the industrial-size 18-ounce can. In addition, the amount of food in mass-produced containers can vary from brand to brand or may change over time. My father-in-law discovered that the ratio of custard to crumbs in his signature banana pudding recipe suddenly was off. It turned out that his usual brand of vanilla wafers had quietly subtracted two ounces of cookies from their standard box as a money-saving step during an economic downturn. Calling for "1 (12-ounce) box" or "1 (#2-size) can (2½ cups)" or "1 bunch spinach (1 pound including stems)" clarifies a recipe.

Compare Recipes. With tricky or complex dishes, search online and through cookbooks for recipes similar to the one you are adjusting. Compare ingredients, methods, word choices, and descriptions to glean ideas on how to clarify the recipe at hand. Depending on the recipe you're working with, it may be particularly helpful to compare it with others from a similar region and/or time period. Details for finding these can be found in chapter 6.

Consult Handbooks. Many food writers and journalists depend on *The Recipe Writer's Handbook* or similar authorities.[5] A handbook is a very helpful ready reference for home cooks as well. It explores recipe formats and styles while offering guidelines on preferred spellings, proper handling of specific ingredients, and measuring methods. It also serves as a quick reference on metric conversions, standard pan sizes, and commercial package capacities.

Recipe Clarification Checklist. Following are some questions that may be helpful to you whether you're mulling over clarifications for your own recipe or asking another cook for additional information. Please don't let the long list daunt you. Chances are your written recipe will already answer the majority of these questions. The checklist, however, may help you be more thorough or detect a weak spot in a complicated recipe. And you'll want to come back to this list for interviews or cooking visits (chapter 5).

Ingredients

1. What amounts or sizes are needed?
2. How do you properly measure each ingredient?
3. Are there preferred or specific types for each ingredient (e.g., cut of meat, variety of apple, type of oil, percentage of fat for dairy products)?
4. For ingredients that come in versions, which should be used (e.g., regular versus sugar free or low sodium, flavored versus plain)
5. If the ingredients are unusual items, where do you obtain them?
6. What is your selection process for each ingredient (determining ripeness, freshness, appropriate flavor, etc.)?
7. How do you store the ingredients so they maintain their quality?
8. How ready (ripe, steeped, cured) do the ingredients need to be before you begin cooking?
9. Is it essential that the ingredients be fresh? Which ones can be preserved and how (frozen, canned, dried, bottled)?

Seasonings

1. What seasonings do you use and how much do you add?
2. Do you prepare your seasonings in any way (toasting, grinding, soaking)?
3. If your seasonings vary depending on the quality or amount of other ingredients, how do you make decisions about flavoring this dish?
4. For herbs, are they dried or fresh?
5. At what point(s) in the cooking process do you add seasonings?
6. Are there other ways you build flavor into the recipe (searing meat, caramelizing onions, toasting nuts, slow cooking)?
7. Do any of your ingredients already contain hidden flavoring or come in versions that vary in flavor strength (salted versus unsalted butter, butter-flavored shortening versus regular, sharp versus mild cheese)?
8. Among the various types of salt (flavor and grain size), which do you use?

Equipment

1. What specific utensils do you use and why?
2. What specific cookware or bakeware do you use and why? (Size, material, thickness/weight, and color/finish of pans can all affect cooking time as well as the outcome of a dish. For instance, a copper mixing bowl helps to stabilize egg whites whipped in it; conversely, a hot aluminum pan may react negatively with acidic foods to leave an unpleasant aftertaste. Preferred cookware might be as simple as a glass lid on a pan that helps a cook know the moment a dish is done.)
3. How do you prepare the cookware for use (greasing/buttering, flouring, lining with waxed paper, seasoning cast iron)?
4. What appliances do you use, and how accurate are the settings on them?

Preparation Methods

1. Do any of the ingredients need special handling (tenderizing, marinating, scoring/pricking, sifting, beating, whipping) before they are added?
2. For cut ingredients, what size and shape should the pieces be?
3. What parts of ingredients are excluded (peelings, juices, seeds, fat, bones)? Are any of the excluded parts used later in the recipe?
4. For mixtures of ingredients, what is the desired color, texture, and consistency for each step?
5. Do any of the ingredients or mixtures need resting time (soaking, draining, rising, settling, cooling, chilling, gelling/setting up), and how do you tell when they are ready for the next step?
6. If mixtures are divided, what size should the portions be (diameter of cookies, amount of filling per item or layer, quantity of dough in each mold)?
7. How long should each step take?
8. Which steps of this recipe should be done slowly and which ones quickly?

Cooking Methods

1. What methods are used to cook this dish?
2. Is preheating necessary for the cooking surface or pans? What are the indicators that the heat level is ready for cooking?
3. Is the temperature consistent throughout the cooking process? If not, how and when should it vary? (In particular, keep in mind that old recipes developed for wood-burning stoves relied on residual heat that

slowly tapered off, while modern thermostat ovens fluctuate slightly over the cooking time.)

4. Are there any methods you use (adding fat, reducing temperature, covering with foil) to prevent heat problems such as sticking or overbrowning?
5. Are there any methods you use to prevent this dish from drying out or breaking down?
6. Is this dish cooked open, covered, or a combination? How is it covered?
7. Are there any parts of the dish that get skimmed off or discarded during or after the cooking process?
8. What are the indications (color, size, smell, taste, texture, sound) that this dish is properly cooked or ready for the next step?
9. How long should this dish remain in its cooking pan?
10. How should it be cooled or stored until serving?

Final Product

1. How should it look (color, texture, size, shape)?
2. How should it smell?
3. What is the ideal taste and texture for this dish?

Serving

1. What is the serving size, and how many servings does it yield?
2. How soon after cooking should it be served?
3. At what temperature should it be served?
4. How should it be garnished?
5. What should it be served with?
6. Is there a traditional way of presenting the finished dish at the table?

Storage

1. How do I safely and effectively store leftovers of this dish?
2. Are there any tricks to storing, reheating, or serving this dish so it remains appealing?
3. Are there any traditional or appealing uses for leftovers?

General Questions

1. Do you have any additional tips or tricks for making this dish?
2. Does the weather (humidity, barometric pressure, indoor temperature) affect this recipe?
3. If this is a particularly tricky recipe, what are the most common pitfalls?

History

1. How does this dish reflect personal or family history?
2. Who were some of the people who developed, cooked, or loved this dish?
3. At what memorable events was this dish served?
4. Can you share some anecdotes or stories about this dish?

Tips for Modifying Recipes

As you select recipes to include in the family collection, you may decide to go beyond merely clarifying the recipe and actually modify it so the finished dish is at its best. There are many reasons for doing this. If the recipe is your own, you want it to favorably represent your cooking and perhaps become a family favorite for generations to come. If the recipe came from another cook, you may feel the written recipe doesn't result in the dish you remember or needs updating to earn a spot in the current family repertoire.

Whatever your reasons, working with a recipe to alter a dish's taste, texture, or appearance takes time and attention. To begin, specifically identify how you feel it needs to be changed. After cooking with the recipe exactly as it is written, look carefully at the resulting dish. Smell it and taste it, filling in the blank: "This dish needs _____." If your response is "more flavor," you'll begin working with seasonings and cooking methods that build up taste and aroma. If you think the dish tastes like Grandma's yet is missing crunch, you'll zero in on the ingredients and cooking methods that can impart texture. Of course, if you identify many ways the recipe needs modifying, the process will take more time and effort.

The great news is that many recipes are quick and easy to modify, particularly if you're an experienced cook. In fact, if you have success, you may not even need the rest of this chapter. From here on out, chapter 3 is designed primarily for dealing with complicated family recipes.

Unfortunately, there are no guaranteed steps to success with tricky recipes. Yet as I stated in the introduction, with tenacity and thoughtfulness even an average cook like myself can almost always come through with a more satisfying dish and an effective recipe.[6] It goes without saying that the more cooking skills and sensibilities you've developed, the smoother and quicker the process will be. Reading cookbooks, comparing recipes, and consulting other cooks, however, will take you a long way. Keep in mind that you don't have to be

⏵⏵ Here is a comfort when it comes to older family recipes. I once compared twelve months of the nineteenth-century magazine *Southern Farm and Home* with a single current issue of *Southern Living.*[*] In a year, the older periodical carried 124 recipes calling for a total of 160 ingredients, while the single issue of the modern source contained 56 recipes calling for 199 ingredients. As is usually the case, the older recipes depended on a smaller base of ingredients repeated more often. In addition, those ingredients were almost completely local, whereas the modern magazine called for quite a few imported or commercially processed ingredients. This concept is a comfort when working with older recipes. If you're worried about becoming an expert on an older recipe, take heart that many of them are more basic than today's recipes.

* I examined *Southern Farm and Home* from November 1869 through October 1870 (vol. 1, nos. 1–12) and *Southern Living* for June 2008 (vol. 43, no. 6). My gratitude goes to archivist Laura Botts for telling me about the collection of this old periodical held by Mercer University in the Tarver Library Special Collections.

an expert chef; you just need to turn yourself into an expert on one recipe at a time. (For additional information, please see appendix 1.)

My research revealed four basic tips that help with modifying any recipe:

1. *Become a "Kitchen Scientist."* When modifying a tricky recipe, you want to take an observant, methodical approach. Save the task for when you have plenty of time and can shut out distractions. Work thoughtfully, being mindful of all aspects of the process from your first cooking preparations to the finished dish. What aspects of this dish do you want to change or enhance? For each aspect, brainstorm a list of variables that could affect your outcome and test them one at a time. A cooking log, even just in the form of scribbled notes on the side of your recipe, will be a huge help, especially if time will pass before you use the recipe again.

2. *Know Each Ingredient.* Sometimes it is easy to forget that every ingredient in a recipe should have some effect, altering the flavor, aroma, texture, or appearance of the dish. A little research online, in cookbooks, or in cooking guides will help you compare recipes and learn more about each ingredient. If necessary, creating a quick table or chart can help you

keep track of ingredient amounts, cooking times, and other details from recipe to recipe. When it comes to recipe websites, don't forget to scan through the user reviews and comments attached to recipes similar to the one you're working with. This is where cooks swap information about ingredients and altering recipes.

Modifying a recipe will be much easier once you understand how variables such as freshness or storage temperature affect your ingredients or the varied ways an ingredient can be cooked. Those few minutes of reading may very well result in an insight about whether you need to add more or less, try a different variety/brand, or substitute a different ingredient altogether. For example, I wasn't getting the texture I wanted from my grandmother's caramel corn recipe. From user comments on a similar recipe posted to a cooking website, I learned that beet sugar doesn't always perform the same way as cane sugar in high heat. Once I switched to pure cane sugar, the recipe worked fine.

3. *Take One Step at a Time.* It is tempting to save time, effort, and ingredients by making several changes to a recipe at once. With a tricky recipe, I don't recommend it. Even if you get lucky and have good results, you or other cooks may later have trouble consistently reproducing those results. In a broader sense, you won't understand the cause-and-effect relationship of each change and thus won't build your cooking knowledge.

4. *Use Instructional Sources.* While most cookbooks are primarily collections of recipes, others will teach you the techniques and even the underlying food science so you can truly understand ingredients and processes. A few of the cookbook authors who explore the hows and whys of cooking are Rose Levy Beranbaum, Alton Brown, Shirley O. Corriher, Regan Daley, and Harold McGee. In addition, there are many cooking periodicals, television programs, and online sources that provide similar instruction. *American's Test Kitchen, Cook's Country, Cook's Illustrated,* and *Cooking Light*—sources with supporting websites—are favorites that often explain the process of testing and altering recipes. Last, but certainly not least, in the United States we are lucky to have the Cooperative Extension System. Offices across the nation are staffed by experts who may be able to help you find answers about various topics including cooking and food preservation.[7]

Avoiding Recipe-Modifying Pitfalls

Still not getting the results you want from changes you've made to a recipe? If you have family recipes that are particularly challenging to modify because of their complexity or age, here are some additional tips:

Be Wary of Newfangled. Although it is wonderful that current cooks have more options than ever before, when attempting to replicate older family recipes, old-fashioned ingredients and methods may work best. Think about what options were around when the recipe was created. In other words, instant oats may not give the right structure to an old oatmeal bread recipe. Microwaved potatoes may not provide quite the same texture for your great-grandmother's boiled potato salad. Keep in mind that some ingredients now come in versions that may not be interchangeable. For example, today's nonfat or low-fat versions of sour cream don't taste exactly the same as regular sour cream, nor do they always perform the same way as an ingredient.

Pay Attention to Cooking Time. Talking with various cooks who prefer to do things "the old-fashioned way," as well as my experiences working with older recipes, has made me more aware that the speed of cooking directly affects the chemical and physical changes taking place in the ingredients.[8] Especially if you are adjusting an older recipe, give heed to recommended cooking methods and times. In fact, you might wish to avoid the microwave and the "speed bake" button on your oven altogether.

Make Healthy Changes to Recipes in Stages. Nowadays health concerns are one of the foremost reasons to modify a recipe. Interviewee Paula Eubanks regretted that many family recipes from her childhood contained processed ingredients.[9] For her mother's recipe for a meat dish called Fricadillie that called for condensed mushroom soup, she developed her own fresh mushroom sauce that is free from additives and preservatives as well as lower in sodium. In the family cookbook, Paula included the original version of the dish and then added a companion recipe jokingly titled "Paula-the-Food-Snob's Alternative Sauce for Fricadillie." Paula reported that since she modified only the sauce, the updated Fricadillie closely resembles the original dish.

Interviewee Willene O'Neal, when asked about modifying family recipes, related that she cut down on amounts of sugar and butter with good results. "But that was a gradual thing. You know, I cut back on one of the ingredients at a time." A slow but steady approach also is helpful with substitutions. Replace

A 1927 advertisement for Airy Fairy cake flour. The flour was sometimes packaged in colored cloth bags decorated with dancing fairies. These flour sacks found their way into a generation of kitchen towels, aprons, quilts, and baby clothes.

The N. K. Fairbank Company of Chicago introduced this shortening product in the 1800s. This image came from their cookbook, *Home Helps*, written by Mary Lincoln and published in 1910.

whole milk in a recipe with 2 percent, and then the next few times you cook, move down to 1 percent and skim. Each time you make your favorite coffee cake, swap out a bit more of the fat with pureed fruit. Trial and error will usually help you find a balance that works.

Research "Lost" Ingredients. If a recipe calls for a brand-name product now gone and the dish doesn't seem the same without it, try searching for the history of the product to learn more about it. This research process can be a bit like genealogy, with information found by following company product lines much as a genealogist researches bloodlines. Food company mergers are "marriages," but there are also "divorces," with companies selling off product lines that may continue with a new name. Although there are numerous "births" of new products, many do not survive. Names of now-dead products seem as quaint as those on old tombstones—Airy Fairy flour and Hip-O-Lite marshmallow cream, to name a couple. Old advertisements, recipes, or articles may explain the product in your recipe more fully. By looking at old advertising cookbooks, one learns that now-extinct Cottolene brand shortening contained cottonseed oil but also beef tallow.[10] A Cottolene recipe that fails to work well with today's all-vegetable shortening may possibly be improved by using a blend of Cottolene's two distinct ingredients.

Research is helpful with brand-name products, but it may also be useful to understand the general history of an ingredient. Perhaps you assume that a family recipe calling for "cooking oil" means olive oil, one of today's most popular choices. In the 1960s through 1980s, however, my mother and her friends would probably have reached for corn oil instead. Cooking oils vary in taste and performance, so it is worth a little research to narrow down the possibilities. For a delicate cake recipe, mild oil flavor will be important, while for a frying recipe, the smoke point of the oil may be crucial. Reading through similar recipes from the time period may help you figure out a type of ingredient.

And what if additional research doesn't give you any useful clues? If you simply don't know which alternate brand to use as an ingredient for an older recipe, try picking a brand that you think would have been available at the time the recipe was written.

Remember That Ingredients May Change. If you could go back in time and experience an apple, a chicken breast, and an egg from your great-grandmother's kitchen, you might be surprised at how they differ from those you'll find in today's grocery store. To a greater degree than ever before, today's commercial produce is developed and grown to visually impress consumers and maximize profits. Similarly, chickens and other animals raised for meat are now often bred to be larger and yet leaner. Much of food science seeks to create foods that require less resources to grow/raise, ship well, have a long storage life, and appeal to the eye.

If you're having trouble with an old recipe, keep in mind that it could be the modern ingredients and do a little research. Books like David Buchanan's *Taste, Memory: Forgotten Foods, Lost Flavors, and Why They Matter* and Rowan Jacobsen's *American Terroir* are enlightening on this subject.[11] In general, you may need to slightly reduce the amount of a modern ingredient to adjust for larger sizes or find ways to make up for flavor that was agriculturally lost in pursuit of other attributes. Minimally processed ingredients may also be the key. If you're willing to go the extra mile, the manager of your local health food store, farmers' market vendors, or the Internet may be able to help you track down free-range chickens, stone-ground grains, produce from heirloom seeds, and the like.

Chicken eggs vary greatly in size. *Photo by the author; eggs courtesy of the University of Georgia Poultry Research Center.*

Ingredients can and do change over time. For instance, if you have an old recipe that calls for a pint of oysters, you may very well decide to use around seventeen medium-sized shellfish in the dish. But in his book *Tidecraft* (page 188), William C. Fleetwood Jr. quotes Sonny Williams, an oysterman who was more than ninety years old in the 1940s. The retired harvester said that in the "old days" before overfishing, a pint cup could be filled with only *four* Carolina oysters!

Going back to my recipe for the regrettable Daffodil Cake, changes in ingredient sizes turned out to be the main culprit. My finished cake was suffering from too much egg yolk. When eggs were largely from the home coop, sizes varied widely. In fact, many old cake recipes were designed to take this into account, instructing the cook to pay attention to the proportion of ingredients rather than exact size—a recipe might call for "the weight of 5 eggs in flour."[12] In her work *A Thousand Years Over a Hot Stove*, author Laura Schenone recommends using three eggs for an 1881 recipe that called for five.[13] Anne Carter Zimmer, editor of *The Robert E. Lee Family Cooking and Housekeeping Book*, recommends using medium-sized eggs with nineteenth-century recipes.[14]

Be Aware Processing May Have Changed. Reading commentary in published manuscript cookbooks can forever change the way you think about old recipes and their ingredients. In the aforementioned Lee family cookbook, Anne Carter Zimmer points out that, long ago, milk may not have been skimmed or separated before it was poured into a recipe, so she suggests adding a little half-and-half to impart richness.[15] In addition, modern pasteurized and homogenized milk usually curdles differently than raw. And nowadays American milk usually comes from Holstein cows prized for impressive volume production rather than breeds known for the rich butterfat content of their milk. With flour, Zimmer's research told her that her ancestors' product would not have been as fine, so she suggests adding a tablespoon of whole wheat flour per cup of all-purpose in old recipes.[16] Cookbook commentary from culinary historian Karen Hess has also been very helpful in my journey to learn more about old recipes.[17] If your goal is an authentic dish, look at each ingredient and think about how it might have been processed when the recipe was penned. Do some research about how each ingredient has changed over time.

Be Aware That Food Names May Have Changed. When we use the word "catsup" or "ketchup," we mean a tomato-based condiment with a fairly standard taste and consistency. In days gone by, however, a sauce by this name could be made with a variety of fruits, vegetables, and spices. Sometimes it was even made with seafood. Thus whoever wrote an old recipe for catsup or called for it as an ingredient may have intended a very different color, flavor, and texture than you might assume. Similarly, in days gone by, pies used to be savory as often as sweet, and "pudding" resembled steamed cake. If you are using an older recipe that just doesn't seem to make sense, check a food dictionary or do a Web search to see if one or more ingredients—or even the dish as a whole—may mean something different than you assumed.

Don't Forget That the Secret May Be "In the Air." The hidden yet essential ingredients in many dishes are air and moisture. If a dish turns out too dense, dry, or crumbly, take a look at mixing techniques, oven size, and heat source, since all of these can affect the tiny air bubbles and residual liquids in your finished dish. Older recipes may have been developed before electric mixers and state-of-the-art large ovens.[18]

- Cooks of distant yesteryear may not have had electric mixers or even gear-driven egg beaters. If your batter doesn't seem right, it may be the amount of air in it. Try mixing for a shorter time, at a lower speed, or simply by hand.
- Be aware that convection or fan-assisted ovens may dry out dishes. Some ovens aren't labeled as convection but have a "quick cook" or "speed bake" button that activates this feature. If you're not sure about your oven, check for a fan.
- In today's climate-controlled kitchens we may disregard the outdoor weather, but the humidity level and barometric pressure on the day you're cooking can affect some recipes. This is especially true for candy, whipped mixtures, or foods with delicate or crisp textures.
- If your kitchen's altitude above sea level is significantly different than the kitchen where a recipe was developed, this can also affect your results. Many cookbooks and websites can tell you specifics on how to adjust for altitude.

Recheck Your Ingredients. Sometimes companies reformulate their products, or manufacturing batches vary more than you'd expect. Interviewee Jean Dirksen described problems making longtime-favorite baked goods after her usual brand of shortening changed to a trans-fat-free version, even though a company representative on the phone assured her she wouldn't be able to tell the difference. Similarly, by testing ingredients one at a time, cookbook author Doris Koplin discovered that it was a popular brand of flour causing her bread loaves to collapse, and changing brands was enough to fix the problem without other alterations to the recipe.[19] Make sure you understand the effect of each ingredient. Additional brand-specific research may also be helpful. Don't be afraid to experiment or switch brands.

Question Measurements. Earlier in the chapter we discussed how important it is to use proper measurements when clarifying a recipe. By the same token, if you're having trouble with a recipe recorded by someone else, don't assume that they measured properly. In fact, they may have just guessed at amounts. When I asked interviewee Norma McCoy how much oil she put in a recipe, she responded, "About *that* much." She pretended to pour oil from a bottle for about two seconds. "Well, I guess it would be about three tablespoons. I don't measure. I just do it."[20] Some cooks with finely developed cooking sensibilities may know the right amount only when they add it or see it in the mixing bowl. Regardless, when they share a recipe they may not be as articulate as Norma about their cooking process, jotting down an amount without thinking to mention it is only an estimate. If you're working with a recipe from a cook still living, this is when a cooking visit can be very helpful, and there are many helpful hints ahead in chapter 5.

One of the family recipes I worked on the longest was for my mother's Chess Tarts, mini pecan pies that she made each Thanksgiving.[21] Every time I made them, the filling was right and the crust tasted fine, but they just weren't quite the same as Mom's. Finally focusing closely on the task twenty years after her death, I remembered that she always used her measuring cup like a scoop. Despite being worried that the extra flour would just make the crust issue worse, I tried it anyway. That turned out to be the trick. Perhaps it isn't the exact texture or taste the cookbook authors had in mind, but now my crust is just as it was during my childhood. (It was a lovely breakthrough. My brother promptly dubbed my tarts "mini time machines.") So I can consistently "get it right" in the future, I used my electronic cooking scale to weigh the flour after it was measured her way and then added gram measurements to a transcribed version of the recipe. I also added a few notes about how she measured, so future cooks without a scale can choose which way to handle the flour.

If you are working with a recipe from a cook no longer living, measurements may be one of the keys to unlocking its secrets. Recipe evolution and the rise in popularity of printed cookbooks happened across many years—modest growth after the Civil War and then rapid after World War II. The farther you delve back into your family history, the more likely it is that you'll find cooks who worked from memory and estimated ingredient amounts. If they measured, it may have been their own system using whatever kitchen utensils were at hand. Perhaps their favorite coffee cup became a standard cup to them, their regular spoons a teaspoon with any other larger spoon (including a serving spoon!)

by default becoming a tablespoon. If you have many ineffective recipes from Great-Aunt Maude, see if you can compare them and come up with an idea about her "measuring scheme." In other words, knowing how much flour was "one cup" in her cake recipe may help you figure out her cookie recipe too.

And what if the recipes use a measurement standard that doesn't sound familiar at all—a teacupful or a gill? If an Internet search doesn't help you, please turn to chapter 6.

Compare Recipes and Flavor Profiles. This tip is probably starting to sound quite familiar, but comparison really is one of the best ways to understand a recipe. In a wider context, thinking about food on the basis of cultural origin may also be helpful. Cookbook author Tamara Patridge talked about the process of trying to re-create the flavor in a dish using "genre" or flavor profile/principle as a guide. "If you're doing a standard Asian dish, it is likely one of ten flavors."[22] Cookbooks that specialize in the type or nationality of the dish you're working with may be quite helpful. For instance, Greek or Italian cookbooks can help you understand ingredients and traditional flavors of Mediterranean dishes.

Get a Handle on Flavorings. If you need to work with herbs, spices, or extracts that aren't familiar to you, getting to know them on their own will be helpful. This allows you to develop what many chefs call "taste memory," a sensory understanding important to cooking and adjusting recipes. (See appendix 3.) Mix some of the flavoring with several tablespoons of unsalted butter or a mild, soft cheese. After letting the mixture sit for a few hours, taste it at room temperature either on its own or atop a plain cracker.

Even the most sophisticated, knowledgeable, and talented cooks gather recipes from others. They may modify or transform a recipe— or never follow it precisely—but the recipe provides a blueprint for their imaginative interpretations.
—Janet Theophano, *Eat My Words: Reading Women's Lives Through the Cookbooks They Wrote* (51)

Adjusting Recipes from Other Cooks

In this chapter so far, we've discussed adjusting recipes as though it happens in a vacuum, as if it were a process mainly affecting our work and the cooks we'll share with someday. In reality, there may be other family members' input, involvement that can lead to unwanted twists and turns. For instance, interviewee Anna Robinson found learning to reproduce her Italian grandmother's tomato sauce was a journey rather than a quick trip. "It wasn't written down anywhere. I had to talk on the phone to my aunt several times and to Nona. And Nona was just like, 'What do you mean, you want a recipe? Oh, I guess you throw some tomatoes in there.' And I said, 'Yeah, but it's not

> ❯❯ We recall things
> our mother did, how
> she cooked, what she
> cooked. And then you
> tinker, you play with the
> memory of how your
> mother did it.
> —Novelist Terry Kay,
> quoted in John T. Edge's
> *A Gracious Plenty* (44)

just tomatoes.' Bless her heart. She tried to talk me through it. It took a lot of sauce."[23]

If writing down or adjusting a family recipe begins to resemble a negotiation process, chapter 5 will be helpful. In the meantime, we should also look at the important issue of cook ego. Chapter 2 discussed giving fair credit for others' recipes and being sympathetic to other cooks' needs for recipe secrecy or exclusivity. In a similar vein, adjusting a recipe could hurt the feelings of the cook who shared it with you.

Some cooks are easygoing, viewing recipes as mere suggestions for any cook interested in giving them a go. May your family reunion be jammed with these generous souls! There are some cooks, however, who perceive their recipe as a perfected and complete work of art. If you adjust their recipe, you might as well tell them that their masterpiece wasn't good enough. Susan Puckett, food writer and former food editor of the *Atlanta Journal and Constitution*, discussed this problem with printing family recipes submitted to the paper.[24] She admitted, "It's been a huge challenge and a learning process because you don't want to offend a family. I'll include a recipe as it was written when I can. I'll note, 'Written in her own words' or something like that, and then I'll show the adaptations of it."

Similar to Puckett's, my advice is to preserve the original recipe in your family history files just as you received it, moving on carefully and diplomatically from there. If the recipe is used just in your kitchen, the original cook may never be the wiser. As for how to include an adjusted recipe in a family cookbook, you have the choice of including an updated version of the recipe alongside the original, including only the original but with suggested adjustments in the form of personal notes, or offering solely your adjusted version. Whichever way you choose, do make it clear that the recipe has been adjusted, explaining who, what, where, when, and why, as applicable. Personally, I try my best in such situations not to imply the original recipe was lacking, but rather suggest that I adapted it for my particular needs and situation.

When sharing adjusted recipes with family, the key to peace may lie in being forthright. If someone has shared a recipe with you and you are going to pass along an adjusted version of it to others, let the original cook know in advance. If the idea is not well received, at least you can handle the problem before it becomes a family-wide issue. Certainly don't let such concerns put you off working with family recipes, but know that glitches are possible.

The Recipe Adjustment Ladder

In light of recent topics, does working to adjust your own recipes sound easiest? Indeed, the task is usually at the bottom of a rising ladder of family recipe complexity. It is often a step more challenging to work with recipes from other cooks, with additional "toughness rungs" depending on whether there is a written recipe, how helpful the cook wants to be, and how well a cook can articulate what he or she knows. (There are suggestions and solutions for these issues in chapter 5.) While we just discussed the potential problems of handling other cooks' egos, having no cook to turn to for clarification or advice can be its own dilemma. Near the top of the challenge ladder is trying to reproduce the dish of a cook now gone, particularly if the recipe is sketchy. And a hug should go to the family recipe enthusiast who finds himself wobbling high on the top rung, reproducing a dish from a deceased cook who left no written recipe at all. Lest you despair, please know that higher on the ladder is also where a lot of improvisation and creativity can flow. If nothing else, it can be quite the experience to try out the mindset of another cook!

Before we move on from this chapter about adjusting recipes, let's look deeper into the process of working with sketchy or unwritten recipes without help from the original cook. In this case, your success may depend on how long the cook has been gone and how many other experienced cooks are left who knew their cooking. Although there are many challenges and you have to rely on ephemeral memories to verify that the finished dish tastes authentic, if your expectations are reasonable, then you'll probably be able to come up with a pleasing dish.

The Last Vestige of a Dish

When working with a late cook's sketchy or nonexistent recipe, the ideal situation is that you have some of the dish at hand. Thanks to canning and freezing, this is possible; two interviewees spoke of having Mother's preserved cooking left after she died.[25] Even if you don't have any of the dish you'd like to re-create, perhaps you'll come across a dish that closely resembles it. Interviewee Anna Robinson accidentally created pasta sauce that tasted exactly like her late grandmother's pizza sauce. Although she wasn't sure what she had done differently, she promptly froze the batch so she would be able to work with it later.

Anna had the right idea. If you have some of the original dish or something that tastes just like it, your first step is to preserve it until you can give it your full attention. Second, divide the dish into multiple taste samples—even if it means sawing up frozen pound cake or unmolding frozen casserole and breaking it into pieces with a kitchen mallet. Using tips from earlier in this chapter, work with the sketchy recipe to get it as close as you can to the dish you remember. (If you don't have a written recipe, find a recipe that sounds similar enough that you can use it as a surrogate and a starting point. More about this in a moment.) When you think you've created a winning batch that matches the appearance, taste, and texture of the original dish, you'll then prepare one of the preserved samples for comparison. Invite the most experienced cooks you know as well as family members familiar with the original dish to come for taste tests and give feedback. The more samples you have, the more chances you have to get the recipe right.

Re-creating a Remembered Dish

Whether you have some of the original dish at hand or not, re-creating a family dish without the cook's advice can be tricky. To meet this challenge, I asked various master cooks about steps for figuring out a recipe on your own. Professional chef Doris Koplin was particularly helpful. "First, try to determine what is in the dish. Sometimes that's difficult, if there's a sauce involved."[26] She noted that foods involving seasoned purees like sauces and soups may be the hardest to dissect because there are many possible ingredients and visual cues are largely hidden. To illustrate, she recalled attending a cooking class at a notable restaurant. Dinner was served to the students, and the woman sitting next to Doris thought the restaurant's signature soup was made with squash, while Doris herself thought it was sweet potato. It turned out that they were both right. An efficient kitchen does not waste food, so the soup contained many leftover vegetables, yet the dominant flavors were always the same— tomato paste and dill. Doris's soup story offers hope. To re-create a dish to your satisfaction, it may not have to be exactly the same as the original cook's but rather adhere to the dominant textures and flavors.

As with recipe modification, creating a written recipe from the memory of a dish involves methodical attention to detail. Think back on the original

Think you don't need to record the original version of a favorite recipe if it came from the package label of a food you use often? Think again. You never know when a company will stop publishing a recipe or alter it. The favorite cake in my parents' home was German's Sweet Chocolate Cake and my brother still asks for it on his birthday. My mother's recipe box contains the recipe clipped from the German's brand chocolate produced by General Foods with a note that it was from December of 1966. Several decades and company mergers later, the product is available as Baker's German's Sweet Chocolate Baking Bar sold by Kraft Foods Group, Inc. The recipe is no longer on the product label, and the website promotes German's Chocolate Cake made with a mix. A little searching leads to the "original recipe," but it calls for 2 cups all-purpose flour rather than 2½ cups cake flour. It does make a difference in texture, so I'm glad we have the recipe Mom used.

dish in terms of various sensory aspects—color, texture, serving temperature, smell, dominant tastes, and aftertastes. Going on what you know about the cook, including his or her living environment and cultural background, list logical ingredients and cooking methods that can give the dish each attribute. Once you build this "recipe scaffolding," a basic understanding of how the dish was probably made, then sift through recipes online or in cookbooks. You'll look for similar dishes, comparing and contrasting recipes until you can select one that seems close enough to use as a surrogate or base recipe. Using the methods described earlier in the chapter, you'll keep working on the recipe until you are satisfied.

If you are stuck on one aspect of a dish, do a little research. For example, if your sketchy or surrogate recipe results in a soup that is thinner than the original cook's version, a Web search for "soup thickener" will come up with suggestions such as flour/roux, cornstarch, arrowroot, potatoes, or pureeing some of the solids. Food substitution lists, available in many basic cookbooks as well as on the Internet, are intended for use when you are out of an ingredient, yet they can help give clues about ways to develop or modify recipes.[27] Obviously, the more experience you have as a cook, the better your knowledge base of potential ingredients and cooking methods will be. Don't be afraid to go to other cooks for ideas.

Family and friends who knew the now-gone cook can be a huge help. They may remember specifics about the dish in question and perhaps watched your cook in the kitchen. You may even wish to widen your search for help by taking advantage of the community where your cook lived. Cooks' know-how is often based in their culture, so community members of a similar age, socioeconomic group, and/or religion may make dishes that are strikingly comparable. Especially if your cook lived in a small or tight-knit community, try knocking on the doors of former neighbors or visit your cook's place of worship.

The Pitfalls of Re-creating a Dish

When you are trying to zero in on a specific taste another cook perfected, you are trying to duplicate something to which that person's taste buds were well attuned. And, like the tomato paste and dill soup mentioned above, your cook may have reached that taste in a number of ways. If you are trying to reproduce a dish from a cook with a particularly sophisticated sense of taste and many cooking sensibilities, this is going to be especially true. The list below of some of the common pitfalls and considerations may help you navigate the task.

Personal Tastes Change. We simply may not recognize when a food tastes just as it did when we were younger. Adults often learn to bypass bland, sweet childhood foods in favor of a more sophisticated palate. Preferences for amounts of salt or spice may change over time. If you think you made a dish just right, yet it doesn't taste as good as you remember, you may just have outgrown it![28]

Unexpected Ingredients. Someone trying to duplicate my Orange Almond Chicken without a recipe would probably try adding flavor with orange juice or zest, but the result would be too faint. What actually happened is that once when I was digging in the freezer for some chicken breasts, I came across a half-used container of orange juice concentrate and decided to pair the two. A cook trying to re-create that chicken would do well to brainstorm a list of as many orange products as possible and perhaps would discover the answer. On the other hand, sometimes an unexpected ingredient is altogether hidden. The secret to my dad's wonderful skillet popcorn was actually my mom's fried chicken; he used her leftover oil that was infused with traces of browned flour, salt, pepper, and chicken juices. If you are struggling to pinpoint a flavor, ask people who spent time in the kitchen with your cook if they know of any unusual ingredients or if they can describe the way the ingredients were handled.

Quality of Ingredients. Are your ingredients as fresh as the original cook's would have been? Some ingredients such as baking powder fail to work properly if they aren't relatively new. Also, storage greatly affects quality and freshness of some ingredients. For example, uncovered butter and other fats quickly pick up the flavors of foods around them. Baking soda is also known for this ability, yet many people store the box with the cardboard flap partially open. Spices shouldn't be stored too near kitchen heat sources or their flavors fade. The cook you're trying to imitate, however, could have practiced poor storage habits—perhaps a part of the recipe puzzle!

Terroir. Food writer Rowan Jacobsen and others have examined the phenomenon of terroir.[29] This French term (pronounced *tare-wahr*) means "the land" or, by extension, "taste of place" and is used to describe how weather, altitude, soil composition or drainage, and other conditions affect the food raised in a specific place. Georgia's sweet Vidalia onions taste different from similar onions grown in other parts of the state. The oysters of Louisiana taste different from those of the Chesapeake Bay because of the water where they are found. If a family dish doesn't taste like you think it should, perhaps you are missing the elusive taste of the farm or region where the dish used to be cooked! If you can return to the location where your recipes originated, farmers' markets or "u-pick" farms may be the missing piece for your recipe. If you have friends or relatives there, social media can help with locating food sources. When I moved back to my hometown, a social media "shout out" helped me locate wild persimmon trees, and each autumn local friends help me determine when the forest muscadines are finally ripe.

This selection from *Favorite Recipes Save Time and Money*, published around 1919 by the Lydia E. Pinkham Medicine Co. of Lynn, Mass., might have been given the heading "How to *use up* apples." Harvesttime often brought a temporary overabundance of ingredients, which gave many chances to practice recipes.

Recipes from Cooks Outside of Living Memory

We've talked about working with your own recipes as well as recipes from others—both living cooks and those now gone. But what about recipes from cooks *long* gone? For more information about developing cooking skills and knowledge for significantly older recipes, please see chapter 6.

Sweet Failure and Recipe Evolution

I wish I could say that adjusting recipes is quick and easy. With complex family dishes, however, it will likely take trial and error as well as research, new skills, and creativity—but it is worth it. Whipping up a batch that "isn't quite it" can be disappointing, yet there is definite exhilaration once you know you've got it. I know for myself, once I have a recipe "just right," it becomes a part of my repertoire, and I love knowing that dishes dear from my childhood or otherwise connected to family history are now becoming dear to my son.

I would be remiss, however, if I didn't admit that sometimes heirloom recipes never do match your memories. Family cookbook author Glenda Major reached this point with her mother's Sweet Bread.[30] There was no recipe, so Glenda coaxed her mother into writing one. Glenda stated, "Hers always worked, but mine doesn't quite taste like I remember. But I don't have the childhood memories in mine that she had in hers. Maybe my grandchildren will put some childhood memories into it when I make it for them."[31]

Glenda's "imperfect" Sweet Bread was an important lesson about heirloom recipes for me. I have no idea how Mrs. Ralston's original version tasted, nor do I know how Glenda's tastes. But I know that for me the recipe consistently turns out a gingerbread-like bar cookie with a pleasingly moist texture somewhere between cake and brownie. In our house, it quickly became an autumn favorite for company, an appealing dessert that makes the house smell welcoming. When I make it, I think of fondly of Glenda and some of the stories she told about her mother. What's not to love? I sympathize with Glenda, because that is how I felt about my mother's Chess Tarts before I figured out the flour amount. Still, authentic or not, Major's grandchildren are surely adding their own memories to this wonderful dish connected to family history. Likewise, if you feel you've done all you can with an heirloom recipe, yet it doesn't seem authentic, there's no failure if it creates a dish you enjoy. Simply add your notes about working with the recipe and how you feel it is different from the dish you remember.

In my interview with her about re-creating dishes from cooks of the past, food writer Susan Puckett said, "Honestly, there's not a magic formula to it. Even having a highly trained chef is by no means a guarantee that whatever they come up with is even going to resemble the original dish. If you've got a sketchy recipe, there's only so much you can do." That sounds a little bleak, but then Susan added, "Recipes evolve. I guess the goal should not necessarily be duplicating or trying to get this exact flavor, but rather something close to it or to find some part of that recipe that's going to allow you to connect with it. . . . I think 'inspiration' is the optimal word. Often with these dishes, it wasn't that they were the most wonderful tasting in the world. Instead it reminded you of warm memories from somewhere or somebody."

Mama Ralston's Sweet Bread

Recipe shared with Glenda Major's kind permission

The author's son, almost-two-year-old Eli, helping make Mama Ralston's Sweet Bread in 2010.

Sift about 4 or 5 cups self-rising flour in a big bowl. Make a hole in the flour and add 1½ cups sugar, 2 eggs, 1 cup molasses, 1 teaspoon baking soda, ½ cup buttermilk, 1 heaping teaspoon ginger, ½ teaspoon cinnamon, and ½ cup shortening. (Hang in here with me now!) Mix with fingers (clean hands, of course) as you would for biscuit dough. (That's how Mama made biscuit dough—with her hands.) Batter should be rather stiff, if not, add more flour. Work on floured board as you would cookie dough. Divide in half and pat into a greased and floured pan that has one-inch sides. Mother called these "biscuit pans." I have also seen her bake the bread in an iron skillet. Bake at 350 until knife comes out clean when tested.

I have made this many times, but somehow mine never tastes like Mama's. It is always good though, and I like making it this way because that's how I remember Mama making it.

My Mother was Mary Elizabeth (nee Postell) Ralston born at Suches, Georgia, in 1900. By the time she was 11 years old, both of her parents were dead. She spent several years in an orphanage in North Carolina, and four years at a boarding school. (I think it might have been called a "finishing school.") She taught school in Robbinsville, North Carolina, for a short time before marrying my dad. They had eight children and we grew up near Blue Ridge, Georgia. Mother passed away in 1979.

In fact, giving yourself permission to take a new direction with a recipe may be a relief. Susan noted, "Sometimes we end up dismissing recipes because they are too bland or they are not made well. But you can take the idea and use it for something that makes more sense today or something that is more to your liking now but still is grounded in its history."

Studio portrait of hula master Ione and family eating poi, ca. 1885.
Photo from Bishop Museum Archives, Honolulu, Hawaiʻi, E.C. Hawaiian,
Domestic Life, Foods, Poi, folder 2.

Chapter Four

Working with Regional or World Recipes

Recipes are strange things. The power of great food resides in the fact that, like music, its meaning is beyond words.—Robert Girardi, "Spaghetti," in Mark Winegardner's *We Are What We Ate: 24 Memories of Food* (102)

During my years working at the Georgia Archives, I became friends with Birgit Debeerst, a Belgian recently married to an American army officer with deep southern roots. She soon introduced me to the Beer Pancakes and "Mouse Poop" of her childhood.[1] (Fear not. The latter is actually tiny beads of chocolate enjoyed sprinkled across buttered bread.) In return, I took Birgit with me on a family visit to rural Arkansas in hopes it would expand her understanding of the region where her husband was born and raised. She had culinary adventures at the local tomato festival, and my cousins taught us the ways of homemade biscuits and sawmill gravy.[2] When she got home, the meals she cooked for her husband began taking southern twists. Birgit and I learned more about each other's countries and food traditions. At the same time, we both found that explaining the "hows and whys" brought clarity about aspects of our own history and culture. What was ordinary became a source of pride, we both learned new kitchen tricks, and Birgit meshed more deeply with her new family through food.

If your family connections involve "exotic" recipes and foodways either through heritage or through marriage, embrace them. Recipes can be a window

Biscuits and gravy made by Norma Reaves McCoy and Birgit Debeerst.

into the lives of relatives and ancestors. In a similar vein, you may be living far from your homeland and have trouble finding the right ingredients for beloved family recipes or want to instill a love for old favorites with new family. This brief chapter explores some of the challenges cooks experience when working with recipes foreign to the location of their kitchen. (And, as the stories in the introduction to this book indicate, "foreign" may simply mean another region or subculture within the United States. When I lived near San Francisco for several years, you wouldn't believe the trouble I had finding a bag of decent grits!)

Translating Recipes

The most basic of hurdles in dealing with world recipes may be language. If a recipe's language is somewhat familiar to you, a little help can come in the form of foreign language dictionaries (print or online), free online translators, and foreign cookbooks. The latter can be particularly helpful for comparing recipes, understanding basic vocabulary, and learning about unfamiliar ingredients.

Finding a native speaker to help translate recipes is another avenue, and one you'll need if you have little experience with the language in question. The Internet or your local library's reference desk can put you in touch with individuals, companies, and organizations that specialize in translating a particular language. If budget is an issue, colleges and universities often have international students who will be willing to work with you for reasonable fees or in exchange for practicing their English. Contact your local school to find out where you may publicly post requests.

Working with Foreign Recipes

Even if you are bilingual or have recipe translations, you may still find difficulties in using recipes from other countries. In addition to Birgit, I interviewed Leslie Browning Pourreau, a foreign language teacher who married a Frenchman and now works with family recipes from both sides of the Atlantic. She and Birgit echoed each other on some basic challenges and also solutions. After compiling their observations into a single document, I shared this with ten consultants, experienced home cooks who could add valuable advice concerning recipes from various parts of the world. The resulting information may prove helpful in your kitchen as well.

Adjusting Tastes. Leslie noted of her marriage, "A lot of it was merging our cultures more than anything else when it came to the culinary." As an example, she found that her husband was used to considering corn as merely something to feed animals, "So with corn on the cob and things like that, he had to change his way of thinking. Now he loves it." Similarly, Birgit grew up without peanut butter and still struggles with the flavor even if her husband and American-born daughter love it. Other cooks I consulted for this chapter mentioned that ingredients that are common in some countries may yet have strong taboos associated with them in other parts of the world. Meat from horses, dogs, or snakes is a good example. Insects is another. Adding a foreign recipe to your regular cooking repertoire may require repetition and patience.

Home cook Hadley Haekyong Koo (birth name Yun) came from a South Korean background, but her parents raised their family in Europe. She pointed out that an amalgamation of foods can help families learn to love flavors and ingredients. "My mom wanted to incorporate as many Korean dishes and tastes as possible while my brother and I grew up and loved German/European food. We were therefore served dishes such as Wiener Schnitzel with rice (always sticky), kimchi, and red cabbage." She also mentioned a couple of other blended meals—rice omelets with fresh German bread, and ramyun (Korean instant noodles) with a slice of American cheese on top.

Leah Koo, who is learning to enjoy dishes from many countries but also amalgams of various regional ingredients. *Photo courtesy of Hadley Yun Koo.*

Converting Measurements. In the last chapter we touched on the fact that volume measurements are favored in American home cooking. Most modern recipes around the world, however, call for ingredients primarily by weight. In addition, foreign recipes usually rely on metric measures. Therefore, for your kitchen ventures it may be helpful to have a scale and measuring cups and spoons marked with both American and metric measurements, as well as oven, meat, or candy/fry thermometers with both Celsius and Fahrenheit increments.

Leslie pointed out that some recipes have proportional relationships between ingredients that may fall apart if you use them in a country with different processing techniques or measurement methods. "The tough thing for me is that here a cup of flour equals a cup of sugar in terms of volume. But if you go to do a dessert recipe from France, the flour and sugar have different densities. Therefore, you have to remember that a cup of sugar weighs more than a cup of flour. You have to go ingredient by ingredient."

Home cook Andrew Kim, who has South Korean ancestry but grew up in Hong Kong, pointed out that you may need to research measurement methods before launching into unfamiliar recipes. A "catty" is a familiar nonmetric measurement used in the marketplace in parts of Asia, but one that most Americans don't know. Home cook Suruchi Gadkari Krieglstein, who uses recipes from her ancestral homeland, India, warned that even with straightforward measurements you should do some investigating if something seems off with a dish. She told of an Indian friend who followed a family recipe that called for five onions—only to later learn that American baseball-sized onions are already as large as about five from that region of India!

Learning Vocabulary. Sometimes a foreign recipe contains ingredients or cooking terms that are completely new to you. If you are bilingual, try finding a popular foreign cookbook (in the same language as your recipe) that has been translated into English. By comparing the two cookbook versions, you may gain clarity on ingredients or techniques. Community or regional cookbooks from the same area as your recipe may also be helpful. Mexico native Julissa Ilizaliturri-Keenan finds that the Internet—specifically home video sites like YouTube—helps her with local expressions or words too specific to be found in most language dictionaries, such as varieties of fruits, indigenous herbs, or types of local fish. Home cook Mahnee Shawananoak Titus pointed out that even within the same language there can be challenges. After her move to England, figuring out that shopping for an eggplant entailed asking for an "aubergine" and that a "courgette" was the same vegetable she knew as a zucchini was just the beginning of a long list of differently named ingredients.

Bobbie Nordwall and her granddaughter plucking ducks on the Paiute/Shoshone Stillwater Reservation, Fallon, Nevada. *Photo courtesy of Mahnee Shawananoak Titus.*

Leslie pointed out that with a country like France, their language is going to have a greater number of cooking terms and more a specific vocabulary than English. A few sentences may be necessary to describe something French cuisine long ago coined a word to describe. "Otherwise you just need to learn the basic terms—mix, stir, cook, sift. It's not terribly difficult," she encourages.

Finding Ingredients. The right ingredients are usually crucial to a recipe, so many cooks hesitate to use a recipe if it calls for something not found in their usual supermarket. Leslie admitted that items common in France may be hard to come by or very expensive in the United States. "A lot of the ingredients are very specific to France in terms of fresh produce and the kind of things that are available."

One of Leslie's biggest ingredient challenges has been reproducing the family's prized Black Forest Cake, otherwise known as Schwarzwälder Kirschtorte. Her mother-in-law, Helga, is from the Black Forest or Schwarzwald area in southwest Germany but has dual German/French citizenship. On several visits, the two worked to transcribe the recipe into English and adjust it so it can be made in an American kitchen. Leslie stated, "A challenge I find is that there are some ingredients that are very European, very specific. If you don't use them, the end product doesn't taste bad, but it doesn't taste as authentic." Two of these important ingredients are *sucre vanillé*, vanilla-infused powdered sugar, and *Bitter-Mandel Aroma*, a bitter almond extract packaged in small vials.[3] Leslie also reported that flours are sometimes processed and used differently in Europe, which may affect some recipes. For the Black Forest Cake, Helga uses Maizena brand flour, an item that can be hard to find in the United States. Maizena is actually corn flour, akin to very finely ground cornmeal yet different from more highly processed cornstarch. Leslie stated that the difference is more in the cake's texture than in the taste and suggests using American cake flour, very fine bleached wheat flour, instead.

In this day and age, obtaining nonperishable ingredients is usually as close as your Internet connection. A huge variety of preserved or otherwise shelf-stable ingredients are available to home cooks across the globe through the World Wide Web. For extra shipping costs, some perishable items are available as well. A little sleuthing may be necessary to figure out quality sources and brand names.

Ingredient home delivery, however, is not always an option. Shipping costs, wait times, and the sheer amount of ingredients needed may make online purchases unreasonable. Other ingredients may be too fragile or perishable. Birgit and several of the consultants for this chapter reported that finding specific ingredients locally is a challenge, but that availability has improved greatly in recent years thanks to America's ever-more-global trends in shopping, cooking, and eating out.

Since she lived near a city, Birgit eventually had good luck finding Belgian products or ones comparable to them, but she had to explore specialty markets first—farmers' markets, foreign grocery stores, even upscale kitchen shops. She noted that many cities have enclaves rich in foreign markets and ethnic restaurants, and that sometimes a market that focuses on one cultural group will still have a large variety of foreign foods from other regions of the globe. She sometimes finds European ingredients at Middle Eastern, Asian, and Latin American markets. She found additional sources by getting to know other European immigrants and asking about their cooking and shopping experiences. Through a Web search, she located a local social group for Belgian expatriates and descendants, the Belgian Club of Atlanta. Many members shared hints for finding ingredients from the motherland.

Several consultants mentioned that a manager at a grocery store may be able to place a special order for unusual ingredients they don't usually stock. Likewise, a manager at an ethnic restaurant might serve as a middleman, helping you obtain unusual ingredients even for items not reflected on their menu. In general, businesses that are locally owned are more likely to say yes to

Belgian Beer Pancakes

Recipe kindly shared by Birgit Debeerst

◈◈ This recipe was passed from my grandmother, Maria Camerlynck, to my mom, Lutgarde Marescau, and then to me. My mom must have been nine or so when she first ate these pancakes.

1 liter (4 cups + 3 tablespoons) 2% or whole milk	1 355-ml (12-ounce) bottle of dark or Belgian beer
6 large eggs	
75 grams (⅓ cup) of sugar	1 tablespoon of vanilla extract*
550 grams (4 cups + 6 tablespoons) all-purpose flour	125 grams (about 9 tablespoons) butter**

Mix the milk, eggs, sugar, beer, and vanilla extract together. You add little by little the flour (make sure you sift it while adding to avoid big chunks of flour). While you do that, you melt the butter in a T-fal [nonstick] frying pan. (Make sure it does not cook [brown]!) You add the melted butter to your mixture (wipe out the pan a little with some kitchen paper), and you are ready to start cooking! I always use a "Made in France" T-fal pan. Otherwise you might end up with a sticky disappointment.

* In the original recipe, my mother added one pack of vanilla flour instead of vanilla extract. Since I have not found vanilla flour on the American market, I just add vanilla extract. It works just as well. Use more depending whether you want your pancakes more bitter or sweeter. It also depends on the kind of beer you use. The more bitter the beer, the more vanilla extract you might want to add.

** I often use less, about 90 grams (6 tablespoons) or so, because I prefer my pancakes not as fatty.

Author's note: To my American way of thinking, these are crepes; the thin batter spreads out to the sides of the pan to create one large pancake and the finished food is rolled up before eating. The beer imparts a faint but pleasing toasted grain flavor. With help from my Belgian friends Birgit and Isabel, I learned the following techniques. With my 12.5-inch pan, I use ¾ cup of batter. With my 8-inch pan, I use ¼ cup of batter. I cook them on medium-high. Once the pancake is no longer wet, I loosen the edges and flip it over to brown slightly on the other side. We eat them warm with jelly, chocolate hazelnut spread, banana slices, or berries inside. Isabel's family sometimes adds sprinkles of brown sugar. A dusting of powdered sugar also goes nicely on the outside after rolling.

this type of special request. If they can't get the ingredients for you, they may at least be able to point you in the right direction or advise on substitutes.

Another trick to try is visiting a nearby town with a sizable university or military base. These towns tend to have larger populations of people from other countries or who have lived overseas. Knowing there is a steady market for international ingredients makes it worthwhile for local stores to carry them.

Unfortunately, some perishable ingredients for foreign recipes may simply not exist here in the United States. Mexican cook Julissa misses various wild greens and exotic fruits that grow in her native region, and she has to substitute similar types of produce as she is able. She wistfully reported that American zucchini taste bitter compared with the ones she grew up with, so she tends to steer clear of this vegetable unless she is visiting home. One solution for produce problems is to see if it is legal to obtain seeds and grow your own. A backyard greenhouse or indoor grow lights may be needed to ensure the right climate, but it may be well worth the effort.

Some ingredients are available but handled differently in the United States. Julissa and Leslie both noted that in America animals are butchered differently, so it is hard to find the cuts of meat they need for foreign recipes. This was particularly frustrating to Julissa, who grew up with service-focused butcher shops and fresh fish markets. Now that she lives in the United States, she skips regular grocery stories when it comes to these items and has tracked down

Rabbi inspecting wine in a kosher shop in New York City, 1942. *Photograph by Marjory Collins, courtesy of Library of Congress.*

Six-braided Challah, baked by Emily Wiese and Aviv Hod using Sarit Warshawsky's recipe, on a traditional platter. *Photograph by Aviv Hod, June 2009.*

shops or markets with staff that will work with her. She uses the Internet to find pictures of cuts of meat or specific fish that she can carry with her, showing butchers or market workers what she needs. If you are from another region or country, trips back to your homeland (or pleas to kin still living there) may help you create a collection of photographs of needed ingredients that you can show to store clerks. Saving package labels for tough-to-find ingredients can also help serve this purpose.

Yet another ingredient challenge is that some foreign foods are outlawed in the United States. Probably the best example is cheese. Many artisanal raw-milk cheeses from Europe cannot legally be brought into this country, yet our homogenized and pasteurized versions don't develop the same flavors and may not work as well in recipes. If you're told it is impossible to get a particular ingredient here in the United States, try a little sleuthing to find out why, and whether substitutes might be available. For instance, in recent years some small-batch raw-milk artisanal cheese producers have popped up in the United States and may be able to provide what you need for a recipe.

Working with foreign recipes may be a challenge but is often rewarding. Recipes from other lands can be memorable and exciting, teaching us about a culture outside our usual experience. They are a wonderful way to keep in touch with your family's roots and promote a shared family identity. Last but not least, the knowledge you build while adjusting a foreign recipe may give you some unusual kitchen tricks and provide knowledge about uncommon ingredients that may make you a better cook.

Black Forest Cake

Recipe kindly shared by Leslie Browning Pourreau and Helga Dierenbach Pourreau

▸▸ My mother-in-law, Helga Dierenbach Pourreau, shared this recipe with me in French. It is an authentic German recipe handed down through her family from her maternal grandmother.

CAKE
(Prepare one day in advance or very early in the day)

⅓ cup flour
⅓ cup Maizena or cake flour
2 tablespoons cocoa
2 teaspoons baking powder
4 tablespoons cold water
4 large eggs, separated
A pinch of salt
1 (8 gram) packet *sucre vanillé* (vanilla sugar)
1 level teaspoon cinnamon
1 small pinch ground cloves (enough to fill the tip of a paring knife)
2 drops of *amandes amères* (bitter almond flavoring)

CHERRY GLAZE
2 cans pitted cherries, packed in water
⅓ cup Maizena or cake flour

FROSTING/TOPPING
1¼ pints heavy whipping cream, beaten until stiff
Raspberry jam
Grated dark chocolate
Kirschwasser (cherry liqueur)

Prepare the Batter. Preheat the oven to 340°F. Grease the bottom and sides of a 9-inch springform pan with butter and overlay the butter with parchment paper precut to fit the sides and bottom of the pan with a slight overlap; set aside.

In a medium bowl, mix the flour, the Maizena or cake flour, the cocoa, and the baking powder. Pass once through a flour sifter. Set the mixture aside.

In a large bowl, mix together the water, egg whites, and salt. Beat with an electric mixer until very stiff. Next, add sugar, cinnamon, and cloves and continue mixing until well mixed. Add egg yolks and then almond flavor. Gradually reduce the speed of the mixer to low. Add dry ingredients and continue mixing with the machine until dry ingredients are just incorporated. Pour batter into prepared pan. Bake approximately 30 minutes or until a toothpick inserted into the cake comes out clean. Allow the cake to remain in pan until completely cooled or until the next day. Cut the cake (about 3.5 cm thick) two times horizontally to yield three very thin cake layers.

Cherry Glaze. Open the canned cherries and set aside 1 cup plus 2 tablespoons of the water from the cherries; discard any excess water. Mix the Maizena/cake flour with the reserved water and cook the mixture over low heat, stirring often and until the mixture just starts to thicken.

Assembling Cake. Set aside 8–12 cherries to use at the end of the cake assembly. Put one cake layer on a plate and sprinkle it evenly with drops of kirschwasser, then put half of the remaining cherries on the cake layer. Put a thin layer of cherry glaze over the cherries. Allow this layer to cool and set for several minutes (refrigerate if possible). When the layer has cooled, prepare the whipping cream. Spread one layer of whipping cream on the cake layer with the cherries and glaze. Next, put another layer on the cake, sprinkle it evenly with drops of kirschwasser, then top it with a thin layer of raspberry jam. Put the third cake layer in place and sprinkle it evenly with drops of kirschwasser. Take ¾ of the remaining cream and use it to frost the top and sides of the cake. Next, sprinkle the top and sides of the cake with grated dark chocolate. Use the rest of the cream to decorate the top of the cake by dropping the cream around the perimeter in small dollops, one dollop for each of the 8–12 reserved cherries. Take the 8–12 reserved cherries and place one cherry in the center of each cream dollop. Refrigerate the cake until ready to serve. This cake is best when eaten within forty-eight hours of being completed.

Author's Note. This cake is not as sweet or tall as the Americanized version but has wonderful, sophisticated flavor. Our family asks for the whipped cream sweetened, so I add 4 tablespoons of confectioner's sugar and a teaspoon of vanilla extract to it. We also like to use the leftover cherries by adding them chopped to fruit salad.

Gillie McDonald's full table, including purple hull peas, fried chicken, deviled eggs, macaroni and cheese, coleslaw, mashed potatoes, skillet gravy, and chicken and dumplings. Dessert was three-layer Red Velvet Cake and fried fruit pies.

Chapter Five

Interviews and Cooking Visits

Like all good cooks our mother seemed to be guided by a sort of instinct for her recipes were extremely vague. On being asked by a friend how she made her plum cake which had something of a reputation she answered: 'I hardly know. When eggs are plenty I use four, but when they are scarce, three will do. Then I take as much butter as I can afford, a bowl of sugar, some milk, flour enough to make it of the right consistency, a bowl of raisins and stir them well together adding spices, salt and wine or brandy to my taste.' It is perhaps needless to say that very few persons ever attempted to follow this rule and those who did were not entirely successful.—Laura Russell, *Laura Russell Remembers: An Old Plymouth Manuscript* (16)

If you collect family recipes for very long, chances are you're going to run into some interesting challenges. Interviewee Dusty Gres told me about learning to make Divinity from her aunt.[1] After Dusty's recipe request, Aunt Mabel cheerfully brought out a cookbook and began to make the candy from what she said was her preferred recipe. Yet Dusty began to notice a pattern. Aunt Mabel altered almost every ingredient—less sugar and salt but an extra egg white as well as double vanilla and pecans. "Luckily I wrote down what she did as opposed to what she said. But to her death, if you asked her for her recipe for Divinity, she would pull out that cookbook, open it, and have you copy it down."

Even when somebody is happy to share a family recipe with you, cooking a successful and recognizable dish from it may not be as straightforward as you'd hope. Chapter 3 offers many insights into adjusting recipes, but often an

Aunt Mabel's Pecan Divinity

Recipe kindly shared by Dusty Gres

(The amount called for in the original cookbook recipe follows in parentheses so you can see how Mabel altered this dish.)

2½ cups sugar (2 cups)
½ cup light corn syrup
½ cup water
1 pinch of salt (¼ teaspoon)

3 egg whites (2 egg whites)
1 tsp vanilla extract (½ teaspoon)
1 cup chopped pecans (½ cup)

Make sure that it is not a day with high humidity—even with air conditioning. (Mabel said: "The divinity *knows*.") Line a cookie sheet with waxed paper. Beat the egg whites (brought to room temperature) until stiff. In a heavy saucepan, over medium heat, stir the sugar, corn syrup, water, and salt. (The recipe said put the salt in with the egg whites. Mabel said: "Egg whites are too delicate for salt.") Cook until it starts to boil. Reduce heat and cook until mixture is in the "soft ball" stage. (The recipe said 250 degrees on a candy thermometer.) Turn the mixer on. Beat the egg whites just for a couple of seconds. (The recipe did not say that. Mabel said: "Everyone knows to do that!") With the mixer on high, slowly and steadily pour the hot mixture into the egg whites. Add the flavoring and continue to beat until the mixture begins to hold its shape. (This can take 5 minutes or more and the mixture will stop being shiny). Fold in the pecans. Working very fast, spoon the mixture onto waxed paper. (It helps to use two spoons, one to spoon out the candy mix, the other to push the mixture off the spoon.) Twirl the spoon so the drops have a bit of a point. If the remaining mixture becomes too hard to continue spooning, you can add a little bit of hot water to it, but it is important to spoon fast before the candy hardens. (Mabel said if you can't spoon fast enough, just pour it into a waxed paper lined pan and when it cools, cut it into squares.) Make sure the candy is very cool before you take it off the waxed paper and store it. Store in an airtight container—but not in the refrigerator.

❯❯ Mabel A. Wilkinson was born in Bonifay, Florida, in 1926 and died in Glennville, Georgia, in 2007. A eulogy on March 1 in the *Glennville Sentinel* called her "a loving wife, mother, and grandmother" but also "a ball of energy, a good homemaker, an excellent seamstress, an accomplished artist, a maker of wonderful quilts, and a top notch cook and pastry chef."

Author's note: If you're used to the grainy sort of divinity that you buy in a log shape at the truck stop, you're in for a treat. Mabel's is smooth and marshmallowy. I use my stand mixer with the whip attachment and use parchment paper rather than waxed paper. As for the temperature, "soft ball" begins at 234°F but most divinity recipes instruct cooks to heat to "hard ball," which begins at 250°F. Mabel's Divinity works well if I go to 250°F. I'll admit that this recipe always tests my faith. I'm always afraid I haven't beaten it long enough at the end and that the candy is never going to set up. In the end, all is pillowy bliss.

important part of the solution is to go back to the source and discuss the recipe. Better yet, watching the original family cook make the dish may reveal crucial knowledge.

At first, it seems that the interview part of the project should just come naturally. We've been asking questions and wading into discussions with family our whole lives! What you want, however, is not just talk, but information that is complete and effective enough to give you and future cooks recipe success. This chapter contains quite a few tips that will help you get better results when you interview family. And please don't let the term "interview" put you off. If it sounds too stiff and formal, then call it a "recipe discussion" or even just a "visit." Whatever you call it, this chapter will help you avoid common pitfalls.

Creating an Interview Plan

If you don't have a specific recipe or cook already in mind, determining whom to interview is the first step. Perhaps with the help of other family members, make a list of people to interview for their recipes and stories:

- What family dishes would you miss the most if you never tasted them again?
- Are there recipes that particularly represent your family's culture, religion, or regional background?
- Are there any recipes in your family that seem unusual or unique?
- What are the oldest recipes and food traditions in your family? Who may know the most about these?
- Who are the best cooks in your family?
- Are there delicate considerations of timing? Which cooks, given their advanced age or poor health, may not be around a lot longer?

Considering Technology

Sitting down with a family member, pad of paper and pen in hand, is a perfectly acceptable way to capture recipes and stories. Some old-school journalists wouldn't have it any other way, stating that recording devices prevent the development of good listening skills. For myself, I found that a recording relieves me of taking too many notes. I can concentrate on what I'm hearing now rather than still jotting down something important that was said a moment ago. I also love being able to accurately capture quotations, those shining sentences that sum up an interviewee's personality or viewpoint.

Recording devices are helpful for collecting information, but they can also be wonderful simply for the sound recordings they create. A few years back, my brother's young daughter Margaret looked at a picture of Grandpa Frey and asked what he was like. I have forty-five hours of my grandparents' stories that I captured on audiotape during the 1990s and that I later digitized. My laptop computer was nearby, so I played one of Grandpa's stories for her. She listened intently, concentrating far longer than I expected for her age. When Grandpa wrapped up his childhood tale about wrecking his bicycle, she giggled. Then she experimentally repeated some of his words, pronouncing them in his southern drawl as best she could before saying wistfully, "He sounds so nice!" The great-grandfather she couldn't remember meeting as a baby became a vivid person and shared a story with her.

If you are trying to decide whether or not to record interviews, here are some questions to help you:

- Are you comfortable using technology or will it be a distraction?
- How important is it to you to be able to hear family members' voices in years to come?
- Are there some family kitchen techniques that can only truly be captured by video?
- Does your budget limit you to technology you already own or can borrow?
- Will you want to transcribe (type up) recordings so as to include parts of the interview with a recipe or in a family cookbook?

Even if you decide not to record interviews with audio or video, considering using technology you may already have at home to help you collect information:

Camera. Ask yourself what images would help you explain or tell the story of each recipe you're working with. Also, think about documenting the best cooks in the family and their kitchens as well as family events that involve food.

A camera is not just a way to create images for a photo album. Photos capture information. If an interviewee offers to share written recipes, I usually take pictures of the recipes rather than take up valuable interview time writing them down. With today's digital cameras, you can immediately make sure a recipe image is legible. In addition, I often take reference pictures of each

Antique dough cutters, photographed with alphabet labels. Sometimes during an interview a large number of ingredients, kitchen tools, or artifacts can be confusing, especially if you aren't sure what they are all called. Group the items, place letters or numbers on pieces of paper next to each one, and snap a reference photo. You can then ask details about each item by letter or number.

step of a recipe during a kitchen visit. Later I can look back at the photos to remind myself about size and brand of ingredients, the dimensions of diced ingredients, the texture of batter, and so on.

When taking reference photos, scale is sometimes important. Having a ruler to place in the shot is the best way to show accurate sizes. If you don't have one, putting a penny or even your hand in the shot may help.

Scanner. I'm thankful that prices on scanners have plummeted in recent years, because my scanner is one of the best genealogy tools I have. I can reproduce family materials in a way that can be backed up electronically for safekeeping. So that I don't have to worry about damaging precious originals, I make high-resolution copies of photographs, recipes, and documents to pass around at a reunion, carry into the kitchen, or frame for my walls. I can also easily share copies.

When I'm traveling for research, I often carry my laptop computer and scanner along. (I wrap my scanner with towels for padding and place it—along with a couple of extension cords—in a plastic storage tub. Bungee cords on the outside secure the lid.) Asking for copies of family materials is easier and more fruitful while on location; people don't have to let treasures out of their sight, and I don't have to be responsible for the safe return of delicate items.

Getting Started with an Interview

Set a specific time and place with your interviewees. Let them know in advance what the project is for and if you plan to record them. It also helps if you let them know what topics and time periods you are most interested to hear about so they can be mulling. If you want to see family items such as photographs, recipes, and documents, let them know this in advance so they have time to find the items in question.

Picking a Place. One of the most important details is to pick a meeting space that is quiet and free of distractions. I let my interviewees pick the place because it helps them to be comfortable, but I do try to steer away from restaurants. It is difficult to concentrate (and later hear a recording) when the server interrupts, the interviewee is eating, and lots of other diners create background noise. If a public place is necessary, coffee shops are usually quieter, especially after the morning rush. Public library meeting rooms and hotel lobbies are other public spots out of the weather that often have a quiet corner.

An interview in the home tends to work best. Not only is your interviewee comfortable there and can control the noise level, but sometimes there are items the person can spontaneously pull out to show you—recipes, photographs, old kitchen utensils, and the like. On the other hand, you can't control who else will be there. The worst-case scenario is the extra person who constantly interrupts, taking the discussion off topic or pestering your interviewee. You can ask the interviewee in advance for some alone time, which is probably a good idea if you don't know the person or the others in the household very well. I will add, however, that I have conducted interviews where the person's spouse or adult child helpfully glides into the discussion now and then to jog the person's memory or clarify meaning.

Prepare a Small Gift. Bear with me a moment for sounding like Emily Post, but here is a helpful tidbit that could help you as much as it helps me. Especially if I don't know the person well, starting off a visit with a small token of my thanks puts my interviewee at ease and promotes a spirit of sharing. What to bring?

A favorite recipe is usually well received. Food gifts also work well if I know the interviewee doesn't have dietary restrictions. Sometimes I bake a favorite family treat (and include the recipe) or bring a popular local/seasonal ingredient like pecans or a small bag of peaches. For a family interviewee, often the ideal gift is genealogy related—a copy of an old photograph or newspaper article.

Background Research and Preparation. It doesn't have to be elaborate, but homework on your part can go a long way toward getting great interview results. Will you be collecting recipes and stories from the time of the Great Depression or the civil rights struggles of the 1960s? Even a general encyclopedia article will help you review key people, events, and places, allowing you to better understand the interview content and formulate follow-up questions. If you're interviewing an extended family member or someone who knows a great deal about long-ago generations, homework may also involve your family tree. Before an interview, look over family charts to refresh your memory. Finally, if there are particular dishes you want to ask about, reading recipes for similar dishes will be helpful. Then you'll have background knowledge about ingredients and methods.

Items to Bring to an Interview

- *Recipes.* If you already have a copy of a recipe and are simply seeking more information, be sure to bring it with you as a reference. (I learned to never assume other people will quickly be able to find their copies!) Slowly reading the recipe aloud, asking the interviewee to stop you with suggestions and comments, can get great results. Looking the recipe over beforehand and using the clarification list from chapter 3 can be very helpful.
- *Family Papers.* A family tree or pedigree chart can be a boon for clarifying details or prompting memories.
- *Writing Materials.* Paper and pencil are useful for making notes. You'll also be ready if your interviewee wants to draw a map to a former home place or sketch the shape of an old cooking tool.
- *Images.* Bringing copies of old family photographs can be helpful, offering a new topic of discussion if the interview falls into a lull. You may also learn more information about the people, places, and events pictured.
- *Interview Questions.* Some interviewees are like racehorses at the gate, raring to get started. Others have to be coaxed. Writing out some clear, short questions in advance will help with either situation. You can look the questions over at the tail end of a speedy interview to see if you've covered

the topics you need, or you can ask the questions one by one in slower interviews. Create open-ended questions—those that ask your interviewee to describe and elaborate rather than just respond with yes or no. Your questions may focus on the recipe you're working with, but here are some basic questions to give you additional ideas related to family foodways:

- How did you learn to cook?
- Who taught you some of your most important kitchen lessons? Tell me about them.
- What are your oldest recipes and where did they come from?
- What are some of our family's unique food traditions?
- How was cooking in your home (either growing up or when you were raising your family) like or different than other families in your neighborhood?
- What do you remember about holidays and special events?
- What are some of your earliest food memories?
- What are some of your best food memories?
- What are some of your funniest or most unpleasant food memories?
- Who are/were the best cooks in the family? Tell me about them.
- What changes in cooking or kitchen trends have you noticed over time?

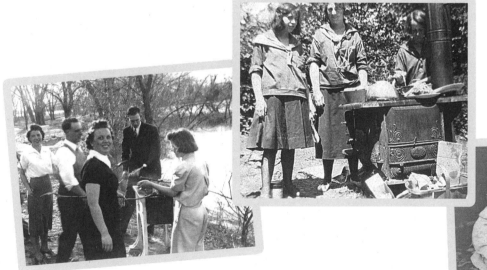

Additional Interview Tips

Bring an Extra Ear. On one visit to my grandparents, I brought a friend with me simply to share the long road trip. When the stories started flying the first evening, however, I realized my grandparents told more complete versions of their familiar tales. Because they had a new audience, they made an effort to explain family relationships and give background details. Over the next few years, I made sure to bring several more friends for visits, coaching them to ask questions while the audio recorder was running. I explained to my guests that if they didn't understand some of the details of my grandparents' stories, future generations might not either.

Set Up Technology Beforehand. If you are using recording technology in an interview, you'll want to have all the pieces ready before you begin. I've taught workshops on oral histories, and you'd be surprised how many people forget this detail. (Humbly, I have to admit that years ago I once had to pause an interview to fly to the nearest convenience store for overpriced batteries!) Even if you're sure your equipment works, test it after setting up, as sometimes buttons or wire connections get bumped during transport. Make sure you have extra batteries, plenty of data storage, and backup power cords close at hand.

Collect Basic Information. The start of an interview is a great time to make sure you have background facts. If you don't know each other well, ask for the interviewee's full name with any name changes (maiden name, names from other marriages), date of birth, and birthplace. Verify spellings. For extended family, you may also wish to clarify how the two of you are related. If you are using a recording device, this information becomes a permanent part of the interview, so you'll also want to state your name, the date, where the interview is taking place, and the full names/relationships of anyone else attending the interview who may contribute information.

Interview Pitfalls

Act Only as a Guide. Asking one short, clear question at a time is key to a successful interview. It is also important to remember an interview is not a discussion, so steel yourself for pauses and lulls while you wait for answers. Your job is to simply give a nudge in the right direction when necessary, allowing the information or story to flow.

I find a two-part process works best. First I serve as a guide for the question-and-answer portion, allowing my interviewee to do most of the talking. When I feel I've gotten what I need and the person seems content with what's been shared, I announce that I am at the end of my written questions and offer my thanks. Then, if I think there is potential for a quality discussion, I'll ask if we can chat while I leave my recorder running. By easing into a casual discussion, sometimes I get particularly rich information. At the same time, I know I captured the other person's viewpoint in the original portion of the interview, before I "muddied the waters" with my own ideas and perspectives.

Embrace Serendipity. It is easy to go into an interview thinking you know exactly what you need and what you'll find, but be prepared to follow someone else's lead and be charmed. Your interviewee may be an expert in something you don't know about or witnessed interesting history in the making. Save your prepared questions for later if you strike rich new topics.

Be Objective. Trust and rapport are important to the interview process, so your role is the nonjudgmental listener and recorder. Especially when learning about the past, keep in mind that society as a whole but also local communities are works in progress, changing and hopefully evolving. The same is true of the person you're interviewing. One of the first times I taped Grandpa Frey, he told a childhood story about kicking his older sister in the shin with his big farm boots. I blurted out, "Grandpa, that was mean!" His jovial mood deflated and the stories ground to a halt while he began to speak about how important it is to respect others. An interviewer reacting to politics, religion, and cultural differences during an interview can be even more damaging.

Fill in Information Gaps. During the interview, jot down additional questions to ask at the end. Think about details that need to be clarified. What are the full names of the people mentioned, and what are the relationships between them? Where are the specific locations for places discussed? Are there any proper nouns that need spellings verified?

Follow Up. This tip is worth mentioning because it can greatly affect how successful you are at a larger-scale family recipe project. For many of the same reasons that I bring a small gift to an interview, I send a thank-you note afterwards. People of older generations may expect one and be hurt if it does not follow. The important thing is the kind gesture, but I also find my gratitude fosters goodwill should I need additional information. It is common to need follow-up calls or even a second visit, especially after creating a transcription or testing a recipe.

The Cooking Visit

When it comes to recipes, interviews are great but cooking visits are usually even better. This eyewitness experience can be highly effective for gleaning tips as well as troubleshooting. One of Grandpa Frey's best dishes was skillet-fried potatoes, and I watched him make them many times. Still, after his death I sadly had to admit that mine didn't taste as good. I confessed my potato failures to my cousin Joe Robert McClellan, a great cook who worked with Grandpa in the kitchen on many occasions. He shook his head and grinned. The process was so simple he could do it in his sleep! But when the two of us cooked side by side, I remembered Grandpa used *red* potatoes and realized I'd assumed canola oil would be fine when in fact peanut oil works best. And with hot oil right there, Cousin Joe was able to show me techniques for shifting foods in the frying pan so they cook equally.

Joe Robert McClellan's skillet-fried potatoes, 2005.

Grandpa Frey making skillet-fried potatoes, 1995.

Basic Cooking Visit Etiquette

Once again, etiquette may not seem important, yet the following real-experience tips can truly make a cooking visit more enjoyable and effective. It wasn't until after I'd done several cooking visits that I realized how much time and effort they can take. I learned to arrange for a long enough visit that no one would feel rushed. In that same vein, if the cooking session may last until time for the next meal my visit means both cook and kitchen will be occupied, so I offer to bring in food for everyone in the house. It is important, however, to ask first. I've been on cooking visits where it was a source of pride and joy to the cook to serve up a great meal for the guest.[2]

So that my host cook senses my appreciation and has fewer preparations to do before my visit, I offer in advance to pay for or bring ingredients for the

Red Velvet Cake shared by Gillie McDonald, who also insisted on sharing a table full of homemade southern classics.

Despite a busy morning teaching the author to make biscuits, Bonnie Crowley still served up a noontime dinner worthy of a holiday meal.

recipe(s) we'll be working with. I ask about preferred sizes and brands, so the supplies will actually be useful. Finally, my two cents is that a thank-you note or a small gift is especially important after a cooking visit, as someone has not only spent time to help me with my project but has most likely gone to great effort and used some personal resources to do so.

What to Bring to a Cooking Visit

Prepare like a scientist; brainstorm all the variables in a recipe and how you can measure them. If you have a copy of the written recipe in advance, it is quite helpful. If not, take a look at similar recipes before your visit.

A Helper. If your interviewee doesn't mind you bringing a friend along, an assistant may be your best asset. An extra pair of hands and eyes—preferably those of an experienced cook—can help you take notes and ask questions. Your helper may think to ask things you won't. Immediately after the visit, the two of you can compare thoughts.

Measuring Utensils. I find that the more experienced the cooks you are visiting, the more developed their cooking sensibilities are and the more they may take their skills and know-how for granted. No matter how well-meaning they are, it will most likely be up to you to ask questions and record specific details. I also discovered the hard way that those wonderful old-fashioned cooks often don't even *own* measuring utensils. Grandpa Frey's one measuring cup wasn't to be found in the kitchen. It sat on the edge of the table where he paid bills, filled to the brim with dusty pennies.

Working with Cooks Who Don't Measure

Some cooks with finely developed cooking sensibilities may not be able to give exact measurements for a recipe. They know the right amount when they see it in their hand or in their familiar mixing bowl but are no longer sure when the ingredient is placed in a measuring cup. This is when a cooking visit can be very helpful. Here are a few tricks:

- *Start with Full Ingredient Quantities.* For instance, have your cook use milk from a full quart. After the cooking is done, measure the

remaining milk and a quick subtraction will tell you know how much
was used.

- *Use a Scale.* When measuring ingredients before and after someone has cooked with them, it is worth noting that most commercial ingredients these days are packed by weight rather than volume and many products settle. For these reasons, as well as the reasons outlined in chapter 3, the easiest and most reliable way to determine ingredient amounts is with a good-quality kitchen scale. All ingredients can remain in their familiar containers. Simply weigh all the ingredients before the cooking begins and again after it is finished to learn how much was used out of each container. If your scale is not sensitive enough to weigh seasonings, leavenings, and other small quantities, an inexpensive "pocket," "micro," or "pharmacy" scale may do the job.

- *Use the Empty Pot or Foil Trick.* Sometimes a cook has developed a sensibility for small amounts of an ingredient based on how long the salt shaker is upended, the number of shakes a spice jar is given, or the seconds it takes to drizzle some oil. Ask your cook to shake or pour into an empty bowl, collecting the ingredient for measuring purposes before it gets added to the main cooking pot.

    If an empty bowl seems to break your cook's stride too much, briefly cover the actual cooking pot or mixing bowl with a sheet of foil to catch what they add. Making a depression in the foil covering, curving its surface into a valley shape, keeps the ingredient from spilling out. If you have a sensitive kitchen scale, you can weigh the foil before and after each seasoning is added. If not, after your cook tosses in each seasoning, carefully remove the foil and curve it into a funnel shape so you can pour the ingredient into a measuring spoon. Many cooks add seasonings periodically as a dish progresses, so don't forget to pull out the foil each time.

Cooking Visit Packing List

What you bring along depends, of course, on your preferences and needs. So does the way you bring it. I carry everything in a large plastic storage tub with a lid. This safely corrals items, seals out the rain during transport, and keeps curious kids or pets from pawing through my supplies.

- Camera and/or video camera, perhaps with a tripod, along with extra memory cards, necessary cords, and backup batteries
- Audio recording device with necessary cords and backup batteries
- Measuring cups and spoons
- Kitchen scale (many have long-life batteries, but you might wish to carry extras)
- Aluminum foil (a wide roll is more versatile than a narrow one)
- Oven thermometer (you may be surprised how much ovens vary)
- Other thermometers, such as meat, candy, or refrigerator, depending on the recipe(s) you'll work with
- Ruler and tape measure, to accurately record the circumference of pans, thickness of rolled-out dough, and the like, as well as to provide a visual scale in photos
- A watch with a second hand, or the stopwatch feature of your cell phone, to measure not only cooking times but also the time for processes such as mixing
- If photographs of the visit will be important to you, portable backgrounds make it easier to take uncluttered images of ingredients, finished dishes, or kitchen artifacts. It is good to have backdrops in white, gray, and black to help with contrast. One option is large sheets of matte-textured foam board or poster board, although they can be tricky to safely transport. Plain, wrinkle-resistant tablecloths or lengths of fabric are also good. While cloth can be difficult to smooth out, it can cover more surface area and can be draped.

Interview Transcription Techniques

How do you transform a bit of recorded dialogue into a usable recipe? Here is one example from an interview with Bonnie Crowley of Athens, Georgia, who taught me about cakes from scratch.[3]

Crowley: My grandmother told me this—one, two, three, four. One cup of butter, one cup of milk, two cups of sugar, three cups of flour, and four eggs.

Frey: What percent milk do you use?

Crowley: Whole milk. It's better. I'm supposed to be eating this skim milk, but skim milk ain't nothing but ol' blue jar. Ain't nothing to it.

Frey: What size eggs do you use?

Crowley: Large.

Frey: You didn't say baking powder or soda, so I'm guessing the flour is self-rising. Is that right?

Crowley: Uh huh.

Frey: And how much cake does that make?

Crowley: Three layers.

Frey: Eight-inch pans?

Crowley: Nine.

Frey: What do you bake it at?

Crowley: Three-fifty. Until it browns. Sometimes I make it into Pineapple Pourover Cake. I do my 1-2-3-4 and cut it in half. I make just a loaf one, you know. When it got done, I took it out. You have to do it before it gets cold. You know, while it's hot. I make me a sauce to put over it. I take pineapple juice and powdered sugar. Mix it up real good. And your pineapple too. Put your pineapple in too. Stir it up real good and beat it up real good. Spread it over your cake. Take a knife and let it go down the sides of it and everything. I stick little holes in my cake. I'll tell you, I take it out of the stove and they can eat half of it.

The above dialogue doesn't include many cooking techniques, yet most butter cakes require similar procedures that helped me build a workable recipe. If your own kitchen knowledge doesn't go far enough to fill in important details for your recipe, refer to cookbooks or compare similar recipes for ideas.

For Mrs. Crowley's pineapple sauce, I needed a follow-up call to verify some details. She assured me that the sauce was hard to get wrong, but that cans of pineapple vary in amount of juice, so cooks should just experiment with the sauce until they are pleased. I also sent the written recipe back to Mrs. Crowley and adjusted it according to her further suggestions. (Note: Most written recipes list ingredients in the order of use. In this transcribed recipe, they are in the order of amount, so as to suit the memorable title.)

Mrs. Bonnie Crowley's 1-2-3-4 Cake

1 cup butter
1 cup whole milk
2 cups granulated sugar
3 cups self-rising flour
4 large eggs

1. Preheat oven to 350°F. Prepare three 9-inch cake pans by greasing and flouring.
2. Cream butter and sugar together until light and fluffy.
3. Add eggs and then milk, mixing between additions.
4. Add the flour a little at a time, mixing well.
5. Immediately pour batter into pans and bake for 25 to 30 minutes or until cake is golden brown and a toothpick inserted in the center comes out clean. Allow to cool slightly before loosening the edges with a butter knife and inverting the cakes onto wire racks.

PINEAPPLE POUROVER CAKE

1. Halve the ingredients in the 1-2-3-4 Cake recipe and bake in a greased and floured loaf pan (9 by 5 by 3 inches) for about 50 to 60 minutes.
2. While cake is baking, make the pineapple sauce (see below).
3. When the cake is golden brown and a toothpick inserted in the center comes out clean, remove from oven but do not remove from pan.
4. While cake is still very hot, poke holes in it with a knife and drizzle with pineapple sauce, making sure to cover the edges. Start by pouring about three-fourths of the sauce over the loaf cake, adding the rest only if you like the cake so moist it is pudding-like.

Pineapple Sauce. Mix one small (8-ounce) can of crushed pineapple with one cup of powdered sugar. You may need to add more powdered sugar, but do so gradually. You want a sauce that is thicker than the pineapple juice so it makes a visible glaze when cool, yet thin enough to drizzle and soak in easily.

When creating a working recipe after your interview or cooking visit, you'll want to make sure to add notes on aspects such as temperatures, ingredient brands, and sizes of ingredients and pans. When you describe ingredients or finished dishes in your notes, think about comparisons that others can relate to well. Is the mixture as thick as mayonnaise or thin like soy sauce? Writing "beat until stiff" is rather vague; "beat until stiff peaks form but egg whites are still glossy" is more informative. The list of recipe clarification points in chapter 3 may help. And for another example of a cooking visit turned into a recipe, please see appendix 2.

Negotiating with Cooks

You know you are talking to a generous soul when you compliment a dish and the creator responds with, "Well, all you do is take a cup of . . ." During my late teenage years, I asked Cousin Evelyn Morgan Bowen for her white cake recipe, which I later learned the family humorously calls Fat Mama Cake. Her response was to have me over for a cooking session that inspired a lifelong quest for more family recipes. I have since learned that I had a lucky start.

As discussed in other chapters, it is sad but true that egos and family politics can come into play when collecting recipes and family materials. Uncle A gets his feelings hurt that you didn't approach him first. Aunt B won't participate until she gets wind that Aunt C has agreed to be interviewed too—or until she decides that Aunt D is surely giving you inferior recipes that must not represent the family. Uncle E hoards all the photographs. Sigh but remind yourself you're doing this for future pleasant hours around the table as well as to benefit generations to come. A few potential roadblocks are listed below with some tips that may help you.

Dueling Cooks. Like feuding gunslingers, sometimes family cooks get a little carried away with competition, either seeking the title of "best cook" or laying claim to having the superior recipe for X. In such a climate, choosing cooks to interview or versions of a recipe to include in a family cookbook can be daunting.

Should you find yourself in such a situation, take a look at *Julia and Jacques Cooking at Home.* This volume by master chefs Julia Child and Jacques Pépin illustrates a wonderful way to celebrate the differences between cooks. The book gives recipes—his, hers, and theirs—with general commentary in the center panel. Beyond the thoughtful layout, the text frequently compares the cooks and addresses opposing viewpoints in a positive way. The book may give you inspiration. And perhaps if you show it to your dueling cooks, they might find it inspires tolerance as well.

"Determined" Cooks. One of my interviewees sadly stated, "Dad collected all these recipes and he wanted to put a cookbook together. So I worked with him on the cookbook and I put lots of history in it, but he didn't want it in there. I had put lots of old pictures, but he didn't want the pictures in there either. You can trace back families and you can trace back friends and you can revisit events if you know the people. It's just fascinating. But I had to take all that out." She was understandably frustrated that he was determined to have the

cookbook completely his own way. In another example, I knew a master cook who turned down her beloved niece's request for recipes for a family cookbook.

It's difficult to know a person's motivation for refusing to fully work with you, but what looks like whim on the surface may come from a deep desire to leave a singular personal legacy, a need to promote a particular view of the past, or a desire for quality control over a family collection. My experience is that if you already tried reasoning with that person, and after some mull time the answer hasn't changed, you may just need to revise your project—at least for the time being.

Secretive Cooks. The Peach Cobbler Story (see sidebar on the following page) was only the beginning. After all the research for this book, I could probably write an additional volume titled *Recipe: Impossible* filled with tales of mysteriously lost recipes, snooping cooks, and spurned gourmets. Barring unethical spy methods, there's no way to get a recipe from someone who doesn't wish to share. Promising to give full credit may not be enough, because some cooks want nothing less than to hold special knowledge and garner praise for a dish only they can create. Appealing to common sense and the cook's desire for legacy sometimes works. Here are some arguments that may help you plead your case.

- Cooks have an entire repertoire as well as preferences, skills, and insights to call their own, so sharing a single recipe or even a handful of recipes is not going to divulge all secrets.
- Professional cooks often share recipes and ideas. Le Cordon Bleu–trained chef and cookbook author Doris Koplin is a member of Les Dames d'Escoffier, an international group of leaders from the food world including chefs, food writers, and others. Mentoring, advocacy, and charity are among the group's goals. "You could call any one of them and ask, 'How do you do so and so?' It's a wonderful opportunity for networking and sharing. That's what we do. That's what we're about."[4]
- In a selfish way, a cook refusing to share a recipe makes a certain amount a sense—but only for a few years. People will talk longingly of Nana's special dish after she is gone. But in time, most likely in the span of a single generation, the legend of her expertise will fade from family memory. A well-written recipe means that the cook's great-great-grandchildren and beyond may make the special dish, admiring the expertise of their forebear.
- Ask if the person would be willing to give the special recipe as a gift. I coveted a family member's chocolate cake recipe for years but didn't push

Bertha Schulze Ashley holding her mother's well-loved *Home Helps* cookbook by Mary J. Lincoln. Although Bertha lived her whole life in a small town in Tennessee, her family had strong German-Swiss roots that included interesting foodways from sauerkraut to rabbit. Nearly a hundred years old, Bertha recalled cooking with a wood-burning stove, a chant to help the butter churn faster, and stories about keeping leftovers on the windowsill before the family had an icebox.

My favorite story about recipe secrecy came from a trip to the furniture store, of all places. While I was purchasing a sofa, I chatted with the salesman about this book project. Before long, a story unfolded about his mother's prized yet secret peach cobbler recipe. When he realized she was getting older and beginning to cook less, he begged. "C'mon, Mom. Tell me. I'm your baby boy." Finally, she consented. She wouldn't write a recipe down, but she would make it with him. Soon they were in the middle of making the cobbler and she said, "Son, I need you to get me more flour from the top shelf of the pantry." He found a step stool and looked carefully but didn't find any flour. When he stepped back into the kitchen, he discovered his mother feverishly adding her secret spices while she thought his back was turned.

when a couple of requests seemed to fall on deaf ears. Then one birthday she presented me with a beautifully wrapped gift that turned out to be the cake recipe printed on a thick sheet of fancy paper.[5] The delivery and the fact that it was given in lieu of a purchased gift showed how much she valued it and made me all the more grateful.

- If all else fails, ask such cooks to write a detailed recipe, seal it in an envelope, and leave it with their last will and testament. The recipe is all their own until after they are gone.

The truth is that sharing special recipes is a great way to establish a legacy for a family member. Family cookbook author Tamara Patridge said, "My Grandmama Harlow made the best pound cake. And I thought, 'Hmmm. Maybe this is a recipe I could kinda keep close.' Then I thought, 'No, I'll share it. I'll just put her name there so people will know.' Now people will say to me, 'For the picnic, are you going to bring Mama Harlow's?' They didn't know her name before but they do now."[6]

This idea, the written legacy of a cook lasting longer than the living reputation, may come in handy with a second secrecy issue—the cook who shares a recipe but makes sure it is incomplete or inaccurate so that no one else can follow it to success. If you suspect you've been given such a recipe, a general discussion of cooking legacies and a nonaccusatory request for any additional tips to make sure the recipe has a long, successful life may yield more information from the cook.

And perhaps a spirit of competition can actually work in your favor. Interviewee Anna Robinson talked about the fact that in her mother's family, rivalry actually stimulates sharing recipes: "Who can come up with the best recipe? Who can remember a recipe the best from when we were kids, and can you make it like Grandpa did? We're not competitive to the point where we don't share recipes, because—it's actually kind of narcissistic—we all want everybody else to make our recipes!"

Egos aside, there are two other challenges you may face when working with family cooks:

Shy Cooks. While some cooks may be unwilling to give recipes because they value them so highly, you may find cooks who feel they have nothing special that warrants sharing. In this case, asking for a specific recipe that you can praise may be more effective than making a generic request for recipes.

Another type of shy cook prefers to cook alone and may turn down a request for a cooking visit. Interviewee Martha Eubanks said of her mother-in-law, Dot Eubanks: "She was able to carry on a conversation and laugh and talk to everybody, never get flustered, and turn out a perfect meal." I'm in awe because I don't have that talent, and perhaps your potential interviewee doesn't either. If seeing the cooking process is particularly important, ask if the cook is willing to work with another family member who can fill in for you—someone the cook is comfortable and familiar working around—or would even try cooking alone but with a video camera set up on a tripod.

Inarticulate Cooks. Cooking well and writing well are separate skills. A brilliant cook may be embarrassed by her lack of writing ability, which may result in a refusal to share recipes. Some cooks would far prefer to talk through a recipe, so an interview or cooking visit may overcome the problem.

Interview Guides

If you plan to conduct many interviews—and you may, because they are addicting—this chapter is a good start, but I recommend further reading. By the time I discovered interview and oral history guides, I had already collected dozens of hours of stories from my grandparents and others in their community. While I treasure every recorded minute, reading a guide would have helped me improve as an interviewer much more quickly. Please see the Suggested Reading list.

⟫ My mother's family in the Pacific Northwest used to go clamming and then cook up what they caught. Unfortunately, by the time I got interested in family foodways, those days were gone. Years later, on vacation in Martha's Vineyard in June 2002, I jumped on the chance to learn an East Coast style of clamming. The Green family invited me to join in a New England foraging and cooking session. I pulled out my laptop computer and point-and-shoot camera to capture the action both for nostalgia's sake and for the next time I want to make start-to-finish Clam Sauce on my own. They kindly gave me permission to share the experience and recipes here.

Three generations clamming on a Pacific beach in Oregon: Sharon Cowles Frey with son Eric and mother Marjorie Greene Cowles, fall 1967.

From my journal:

Carl [father], Danielle [daughter], and I went over to a saltwater inlet called Sengekontacket Pond with a clam rake as well as a clam basket set inside an inner tube. The latter had a rope that was tied to someone's waist. Instead of trudging back to the bucket to deposit your finds, you could pull it over every time you had a clam to drop inside. You could also find your bucket no matter how deep the water got, although we stayed around knee deep.

   The water was cold, but not awful. In a few minutes we were used to it. It was also rather clear. The bottom was sandy, but had lots of seaweed, rocks, muddy patches, shells, and tiny spider crabs too. The dark grey areas of mud seemed to be where all the clams were located. I wore shoes into the water at first but later discovered I loved finding clams using my toes. You kinda do a wiggle dance to get your toes deep enough to feel their smooth shells. Using the rake is more productive, but also more difficult on your arm, shoulder, and back muscles. The long and thin tines of the rake are pressed into the bottom, then a basket area built into the rake beneath them holds the clams you scoop up. Systematically, you press the rake in then drag it toward you. When you hit a clam, you can feel it. The difference between a rock and a clam, however, is the sound. When the tines hit a clam, it rings with a quiet, hollow sound. You have to press the rake in a little deeper so the tines don't roll over the clam, then you twist it sideways to scoop it up.

Also in my journal, on June 17, 2002, I wrote down the following procedures and recipes. After that night's meal, I read the recipes back to the Greens to be sure I had my facts straight.

Steaming Open Clams

In a large pot, put about two inches of water in the bottom. Using a stiff brush, scrub well 25 midsized live quahog ("co-hog") clams, rinse, and place them in the pot. It is probably best to put the largest clams at the bottom where they will cook faster. Turn heat on high and bring to a boil. Wait about 15 to 20 minutes. When clams open easily, falling completely open, they are done. Smaller clams will get done first and can be lifted out with a spoon. Don't eat clams that don't open up during this process. Save and strain the water/juice left in the pot for use in cooking. (Mother Bebee uses cheesecloth or clean panty hose for straining.) Our clams yielded about 7 cups of juice. Carl froze the extra in Mason jars to use in clam chowder later.

Red Clam Sauce for Pasta

(Recipe captured as Danielle and Bebee "wing it.")

Remove twenty-five steamed quahog clams from their shells and chop. (Bebee uses a meat cleaver.) In a skillet over low heat, sauté three cloves of crushed garlic in about two tablespoons of olive oil. Add a 14½-ounce can of diced tomatoes. Add about ¼ cup white wine, 1 tablespoon dried parsley, 2 teaspoons crushed dry basil leaves, and black pepper to taste. (Fresh tomatoes and herbs would be best.) You don't need to add salt because the clams and their juice will be salty. Let the sauce cook down for about five minutes, then add about 1 cup of strained clam juice. Add chopped clams, then add another can of diced tomatoes if desired. Cook down for a few more minutes, then ladle over cooked pasta.

The Greene family clamming and cooking on Martha's Vineyard, Massachusetts, summer 2002.

Chapter Six

Orphaned Recipes and Conducting Research

Slowly, as information accumulated, I began to see the entries in this shabby little notebook as so many windows, through which to glimpse, sometimes only dimly and ambiguously, other lives and times, answering fragments of that bigger question that can never be fully answered: What was it really like?—Anne Carter Zimmer (great-granddaughter of Robert E. Lee), *The Robert E. Lee Family Cooking and Housekeeping Book* (70)

There is an old saying, "When an old person dies, a library is burned." This metaphor for loss of experience and knowledge rings true when it comes to a family's cooks. Even if they leave behind written recipes to share some of their know-how, the passage of time erodes recipe context. It becomes harder to find a source to authenticate an "orphaned" recipe, to find someone with sharp, firsthand experience with the dish or the cook who created it. A family begins to forget how old recipes fitted into past foodways. Eventually, with complex recipes or ones with unusual ingredients, later cooks may no longer have the everyday skills and resources required to use them. This natural decay of knowledge is regrettable, but this book can help prevent it from happening.

More good news is that a little research can often breathe useful life back into an old recipe. Learning a trick or two about outdated cooking methods can allow you to bring yesterday's dish to today's table, but don't stop there. You can also learn to use a recipe as a historical document. By looking with the eye of an archivist, historian, genealogist, or linguist, you can sometimes tell more about a recipe's origins and creator by the very ingredients or cooking methods it calls for or by the way it was written.

This chapter explores orphaned recipes, helping you on the research path for learning more about old ways of cooking, genealogical searches related to family foodways, and possibly uncovering recipes you didn't know existed. I promise to share some of my best archivist tips.

The Teacakes Recipe as a Document

To better grasp how to look in depth at an heirloom recipe, let's return to the Moseley Teacakes recipe as an example. (It appears in chapter 3.) Since I know the identity of the cook my grandfather credited with the recipe, I first turned to family papers and basic genealogy sources. The Teacakes are a present-day family favorite, yet they originated with a woman born in 1830 when Andrew Jackson was president and Arkansas was largely wild territory. Ellen Harbus/ Harbers was actually born in Bristol, England, and emigrated to Charleston at the age of nine. She married a Mr. Black, but was soon left a widow. In 1848 she married Mason A. Moseley, and they moved to Arkansas around 1851. She had nine children and died at the age of sixty-nine, a day after her husband.

Cemetery records informed me that Ellen Moseley lived to see the turn of the century, but since she died in the summer of 1900, the Teacakes are most likely a nineteenth-century recipe. To determine how typical these cookies may have been and possibly find relevant baking cues, I looked for similar recipes from the period and the region. Unfortunately, there are not many older recipes available from rural south-central Arkansas. In addition, because of Ellen's background, I explored older cookbooks from England and South Carolina, but have yet to turn up any recipes I feel are a very close match. As I continue to do family research, comparable recipes for teacakes are something I'll look for. You never know what collections will be donated to archives or what historical cookbooks will be published.

After so long a time, the Teacakes recipe is definitely orphaned, a creation living on past its creator and even firsthand knowledge. Census records reveal that Grandma Moseley lived long enough to possibly bake her Teacakes for six of her grandchildren, yet even the youngest of these died of old age decades ago. There's no one left to ask, "Do the Teacakes I made with this recipe taste like hers did?"

Mason A. and Ellen H. B. Moseley, the author's great-great-grandparents.

The graves of Mason A. and Ellen H. B. Moseley in the Moseley/Mosley cemetery east of New Edinburg, Arkansas.

Taste aside, authenticating the Teacakes recipe itself is a puzzle. Is the recipe really hers? My connection to the recipe is gone; Grandpa Frey died in 2000. Since he was born eleven years after the death of his Grandmother Moseley, at the very least I know he didn't get the recipe directly from her or record it while watching her in the kitchen. His mother, Ellen's daughter, didn't leave any written recipes that I know about. Then where did it come from? The original slip of paper with the recipe on it can't be examined for handwriting, age of paper, or other clues. It disappeared from my grandparents' house sometime after Grandpa dictated it to me in 1990.[1] Thank goodness I wrote it down!

I then turned to family members for help. The John and Hepsey Frey family won a cup at the state fair in 1925 for the "Largest and Fittest Family in Arkansas" and once held huge annual family reunions.[2] Now the fifteen children are all dead, as are many of the thirty-six grandchildren. The descending cousins are largely scattered. It is stunning for such a large family, but there aren't many people I could find to ask, and none knew anything about the recipe. (Trust me, I do wish now that I had asked more questions when Grandpa Frey was alive! He was the last one living of all his siblings.)

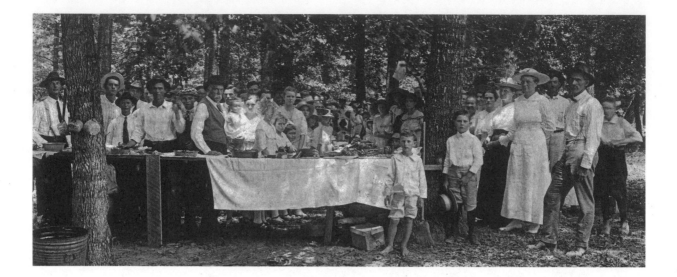

Frey family reunion, Cleveland County, Arkansas, date unknown.

The recipe's structure and components are the next clues, and reading old cookbooks helps with placing a recipe in a historical context. Secondary sources about food history are helpful as well. (Please see the list of cookbooks later in this chapter as well as the Suggested Reading section.) One clue is that the Teacakes recipe is written in the modern ingredients-first-and-instructions-second format. Most recipes in cookbooks or periodicals during Ellen Moseley's day would have been in paragraph form, yet this was changing during the last years of Ellen's life.[3]

Similarly, the amounts of the ingredients hold clues. The fact that the measurements are given by volume suggests the Teacakes recipe is from the latter half of the nineteenth century. Culinary historian Karen Hess noted that prior to Mrs. A. L. Webster's 1844 cookbook *The Improved Housewife*, most ingredients were usually called for by weight rather than volume.[4] Despite the fact that not many rural cooks of the time owned measuring utensils, the Teacakes ingredients are called for in standard measurements. Still, such utensils were available and becoming more popular in Ellen's day. And even if cooks did not have "official" measuring utensils, they generally tried to estimate them when writing down or using recipes. That the leavenings are called for in thirds of teaspoons rather than quarters or halves is another clue that this recipe is older and that measurements may have been estimated. Although ingredients are sometimes called for in thirds of cups, my research experience is that thirds of teaspoons were not common in older American cookbooks and are downright rare after the mid-twentieth century. Finally, the amount of egg in the recipe is given as "1 or 2," which points to this being an older recipe developed in a time when many households raised chickens for their eggs. As discussed in chapter 3, the size of home-raised eggs may vary considerably.

Was each ingredient in the Teacakes recipe available in the late 1800s? Yes, although "shortening" as an ingredient is curious. To my modern way of thinking, this means a thick vegetable product found at the grocery store, and I can't imagine an ancestor in the rural, agricultural South not using lard. But according to food dictionaries, lard is indeed a "shortening." Fat substitutes such as margarine and rendered mixtures were available in Ellen's day, although in her rural area she might not have had access to them.[5] Another ingredient-based indicator of the time period is that if the recipe came from earlier in the nineteenth century, it might have dictated that the sugar be pulverized. In early America sugar was sold in a hard cone or "loaf." Also, baking powder didn't come into common use in rural America until the late 1800s (see appendix 2).

One true anachronism in the recipe, however, is the cooking temperature. Judging by her birth year and her travels, Ellen most likely experienced a good deal of hearth cooking in her early life. Her socioeconomic status (indicated by property holdings in census records and also hinted at by her substantial tombstone) probably meant she had the means to follow social trends and embrace woodstove cookery. With knowledge gleaned from family stories and from looking up when natural gas and electricity came to be used in rural Arkansas, it would have been most unusual for Ellen to stick with hearth cooking, but also unlikely for her to move past a wood-burning stove to something more modern. With all but perhaps the most expensive and state-of-the-art oven models, wood-burning cooks of Ellen's day would have relied on cooking sensibilities rather than a thermometer. Experienced cooks knew by sliding a hand quickly in and out of the oven whether it was hot enough. (For delicate baking projects, they might place a piece of white paper, some wool, or a pan containing a handful of flour in the oven. How long it took before the material became toasty brown helped them know if the oven was ready.) Many older recipes assume the cook will know how to bake a dish once it is ready for this step. If baking instructions were included on older recipes, oven temperature was usually described in terms of a cool/slow, moderate, or hot/

fast oven. (I find that these descriptive heat indicators in recipes increased in popularity during the late 1800s and not long after the turn of the twentieth century were often accompanied by numeric temperatures. They came to be used less and less in recipes after World War II. A conversion table of oven temperatures is provided later in the chapter.) A specific temperature written in the Teacakes recipe indicates that a cook sometime after the advent of modern cooking appliances added that detail. Unfortunately, there's no way to know who or when.

My great-great-grandmother's nonelectric kitchen would probably have seemed very basic to my modern eyes. The Teacakes instructions are indeed ideal for such a cooking space. They ask the cook to work by hand, and the "nest of flour" suggests this cooking task wasn't much different from what was required for the soft biscuits that were so popular in that region (see appendix

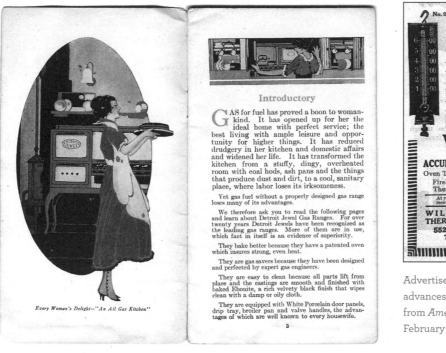

Advertisement promoting advances in cooking methods, from *American Cookery*, February 1917.

Opening spread from *Detroit Jewel Recipes*, produced by Detroit Stove Works, ca. 1916. Ellen Moseley likely witnessed the transition from hearth to wood-burning stoves. By the turn of the twentieth century, the transition to gas or electric stoves depended upon location and the family's socioeconomic level.

2). The rim of a drinking glass was used for shaping the dough rather than a task-specific cookie cutter. Although I don't know the size or thickness of Ellen's Teacakes, at least I know the shape.

As you can see, some questions about the Teacakes recipe can be reasonably answered while others probably will never be solved. Still, the knowledge and pleasure I've gotten from the recipe far outweigh the blank spaces in my understanding. Learning more about the recipe and, by connection, rural southern kitchens at the turn of the twentieth century taught me more about what life was like for my great-great-grandmother. Since I have no artifacts she owned and know few details about her life, without this recipe she would simply be a name on a family tree. Instead, my child smiles when he hears her name, associating her with warm cookies.

Challenges of Authenticating Existing Recipes

There will be more about research, historical documents, and old recipes in this chapter, but first let us look at some of the challenges you may find when trying to authenticate your own heirloom recipes.

Differing Versions. My paternal grandparents left behind three versions of banana pudding recipes. It wasn't a dish they made often, so I can't just cook all three and go by taste to pick a definitive version. I made sure to save all three versions in my genealogy files, but how would you handle this in a family cookbook? That is up to you. If there is room, including multiple versions of a recipe from the same cook or even different cooks is perfectly acceptable. Add as many notes about provenance as you can—when each recipe came into the family, who created or used it, and other relevant information.

If you are making a cookbook that is limited in size, it may be helpful to decide on a version-determining factor before such a situation arises. For example, automatically pick the oldest recipe or the one from the cook who isn't as heavily represented in the cookbook yet. You can add a note that additional versions from Cousin A and Cousin B are available in the family files.

Disputed Versions. Several interviewees reported that family members have difficulty agreeing on authentic versions of particular recipes or dishes. For some, like the Eubanks mentioned in chapter 2, this is a matter solved by group discussion. Sometimes, however, this problem harks back to chapter 5's discussion on recipe secrecy. In one clan, such disputes about recipe versions are the result of carefully guarded knowledge. With a laugh, an interviewee launched into a sinister voice to mimic the family mindset:

> No one else will make a moister stuffing better than the one I make! Because I've got the *best* recipe! And if I put it in that cookbook, not only will those other people—who just happen to be my blood relatives—have access to it, but they won't make it as well as I make it! 'Cause they're going to put green pepper in it! They think it should be that way because they have this recipe that came from Grandma, but that's the *wrong one*!

What do you do if this sounds like your family? A couple of aspirins may help with your tension headache. As for the family cookbook, perhaps offer to include as many versions of a recipe as you can coax out of family members.

Knowledge of the Cook's Preferences. If you found a recipe for peppermint cake credited to my father, I'd have a hard time believing it. I never knew my father to bake. Also, despite the fact that he married a peppermint farmer's daughter, he felt strongly that mint was a flavor reserved for gum and toothpaste— nothing you'd want to swallow. If you have a recipe that you're not sure belonged to the cook in question, see if you can find out more about cooking style and preferences. Keep in mind, however, that recipes can be in a cook's family files to please others, even if it isn't something they like to eat.

Knowledge of Food and Cooking History. For older recipes, it may help to look up some of the required ingredients or utensils to see when they became available in the area where your ancestor cook lived. A reference librarian (or this book's Suggested Reading section) can help you find suitable sources. One quick search method, the Food Timeline, is an independent online resource created by reference librarian Lynne Olver.[6] Unlike many online resources, the information is checked for accuracy. You can also consult period cookbooks to see how similar your recipe is to the ones recorded. If a recipe calls for a brand-name ingredient, do a background check to see when the company began marketing that product. Sometimes it is possible to trace recipes with brand-name ingredients back to advertising cookbooklets or product labels.

Language, Spelling, and Vocabulary Choices. Interviewee Robert Curry showed me his mother's recipe for oatmeal cookies. The recipe calls for "sweet milk" and also instructs the cook to cool the dough in the "ice box." Sweet milk is an older term used to distinguish milk from buttermilk. Refrigerators became popular soon after electricity arrived, although "icebox" still hangs on as slang for "refrigerator" in a few households.

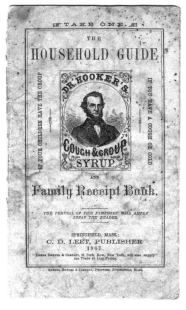

The Household Guide and Family Receipt Book, promoting Dr. Hooker's Cough & Croup Syrup, from C. D. Leet of Springfield, Mass., 1867. Clues to the age of old cookbooks and recipes can sometimes be found in how the words in them are spelled.

As with Curry's cookies, the very words of a recipe can give clues about time period. "Receipt/recipe," "cocoanut/coconut," and "cooky/cookie" are all examples of words that slowly changed in popular usage or spelling around the close of the nineteenth century.[7] It may be difficult to find a historical linguist to help pin down shifts in specific words, but reading older cookbooks or secondary sources by food historians can help you get a feel for various changes. Online searches for an outdated term may also help you to find digitized recipes for comparison that have publication dates.

Penmanship. I'm fairly certain that a lemon pie recipe I found among Grandma Frey's papers is from her mother, El Myra Reaves, because I've read enough family letters to recognize the handwriting.[8] A distinctive style of handwriting (or wording) can help authenticate recipes, so see if you can find additional documents with a cook's writing or signature on them for comparison. But even if the recipe is the only writing sample you have, handwriting styles in general change over time, so a reference book on various styles (see Suggested Reading) may at least help you narrow down a time period for the recipe writer.

Materials. The physical look and feel of the recipe can offer quite a few clues. A quill or fountain pen leaves distinctive patterns that cannot be achieved with a more modern ballpoint or felt-tip pen. Paper styles and manufacturing processes change over the years. Papers, inks, and pencil residues also degrade at least somewhat over time, giving clues about creation and age. Iron gall ink, for example, is a black ink created from plant tannins and iron salts that was popular from America's beginning and into the early twentieth century. Over time it fades to a distinctive brown. An archivist, conservator, historian, or other expert may be able to help you glean clues about a recipe's age from its physical appearance.

Lemon Pie recipe believed to have been written by the author's great-grandmother El Myra Trammell Reaves (1882–1950).

Lemon Pie (my receipt)

FILLING
¾ cup sugar
1½ cups boiling water
3 heaping Tablesp. starch
1 lemon (juice & inside)
1 Tablesp. butter
2 egg yolks

Mix corn starch & sugar add water & lemon juice. Beat egg yolks & mix with rest of ingredients & put in double boiler & cook until thick
When cool put in baked pie shell. Beat 2 egg whites until stiff. add 2 Tablesp. sugar & vanilla & spread on pie. return to oven to brown.

Recipe Hide-and-Seek

Sometimes we are handed a stack of orphaned recipes, but there are also times when they have to be sought out in a person's home after they move to an assisted-living facility or pass away. You may be lucky enough to find a card file or recipe notebook waiting in the kitchen, but be prepared for a treasure hunt for recipes scribbled on envelopes, napkins, and the like. As someone who has conducted professional on-site appraisals for estates, I can tell you that likely places to look for loose recipes include between the pages of printed cookbooks (which might also have manuscript recipes jotted down on the inside covers or blank spaces), at the bottom of kitchen drawers, inside kitchen cabinets (sometimes taped to the inside of the doors), junk drawers, interspersed with coupons or grocery lists, and with warranties or manuals from kitchen appliances. The best hunting is usually in the kitchen, pantry, or utility room, but also check desks, correspondence collections, diaries, and between the pages of vegetable gardening books or seed catalogs. Bulky cooking equipment such as canning supplies or ice cream churns might be stored in outbuildings and have recipes tucked away with them.

Deciphering Handwritten Recipes

Once you've collected some orphaned recipes, deciphering handwriting is often the next challenge. For a display at the Georgia Archives, the staff Exhibits Committee examined a handwritten recipe for pudding, yet because the letters were so looped and fancy, we had a hard time deciding if it was for "Cabbage Pudding" or "Cottage Pudding." Then we found the first word was a challenge as well: 1 pf. Poof? Puff? Comparing it with other recipes, we realized it must be "pt." for pint. What with damage, fading, or simply poor handwriting, accurately reading recipes can be a challenge, and you don't always have the benefit of a committee full of history professionals. Here are some steps that may help you decipher old recipes:

1. Slowly read the recipe aloud. (This may be particularly helpful if some of the words are misspelled or if your recipe comes from a time when spelling was less standardized.)
2. Transcribe the recipe to the best of your ability, working line by line. Your transcription should include the same number of words per line as the

original so that it is easy to compare the two side by side. (See Lemon Pie recipe example on page 141.)

3. On your transcription, mark any problem words. If a word seems incomprehensible, list as many of the individual letters as you can.

4. Brainstorm a list of possible spellings or word choices for each problem word.

Ask for Help. If you're still stumped, two heads can be better than one. Ask someone else to go through the four steps above. (A high-quality scan of the recipe will keep you from having to pass around the original.) Another person may interpret problem words differently, so don't share your transcription until your helper has tried solving it alone.

The most productive helper is probably going to be a family member or friend who knows the cook's handwriting well. (And hopefully the recipe can also be compared to other documents in the cook's handwriting.) A good second choice is to seek the help of someone who often works with old handwriting—a genealogist, archivist, historian, or rare manuscripts dealer. If you find a handwriting helper who also knows a lot about cooking, you may have hit the jackpot!

Researching Problem Words. If you've done the steps above by yourself and with help but still don't know all the words in the recipe, the next task is to do some research on the Internet, in your local library, or at an archives. Compare the recipe to other recipes that share the same name or have similar ingredients. Recipes from the same region and period stand the best chance of being a helpful match, so community cookbooks (compilations of recipes from a community or group, usually created for charity purposes) may be particularly useful. Food dictionaries or cooks' dictionaries as well as comprehensive cookbooks may be helpful.

Keep in mind that the problem word(s) may come from a culture or language unfamiliar to you. For instance, if the recipe comes from Louisiana, check Cajun cookbooks to see if perhaps the word is one specific to that area, such as "mirliton" (a member of the gourd family, more commonly called chayote) or "tasso" (a type of highly seasoned smoked pork). Foreign cookbooks might also be helpful, as the Cajuns descended from French-speaking Acadians, and Louisiana is also rich in Spanish and African influences. Check to see if your cook was a recent immigrant or lived in an area abounding in immigrant culture. If so, foreign language dictionaries may also be helpful.

Handwriting Guides. For more clues about handwritten recipes, check the Suggested Reading section of this book or your local library for reference guides to American handwriting, outdated abbreviations, and historical acronyms.[9]

Faded Recipes. Here are some archivist tricks to read faded lettering:

- Try looking at the writing under various light sources such as incandescent, fluorescent, and natural daylight. Try both strong and soft light, but also tilt the paper to see if it helps to have shadows fall into any indentations left by the writing instrument.
- A photocopy of the recipe may be more legible than the original. There are several reasons for this. Because the copy process involves light, indentations in the paper may give the letters a slight shadow, or traces of shiny graphite from a pencil may reflect. Also, a black-and-white photocopy machine turns colors to grayscale. Because of the wavelength of light involved with various colors, red-toned inks may photocopy darker than the original and thus be more legible. (As you move down the spectrum, this becomes less successful; pale blue ink may completely disappear in a photocopy.) Don't forget to adjust the light/dark and contrast settings on the copier to see if this helps.

This recipe was penciled on the back of a 1922 cookbooklet, and the handwriting faded with time and handling. Digital scanning and adjustment of the image allows the words to be read more successfully.

- Scanning is another trick to try. The scanner may pick up more than you can see with the naked eye, so try making a high-quality scan and adjusting the contrast. Some textures of paper, however, can get in the way of creating a legible scan. If you don't have good luck, also try creating a low-resolution scan.

Recipe Collections: Files and Scrapbooks

So now you've found some family recipes and perhaps tried to decipher and authenticate them. An important next step is to look at them as a group, especially if they came to you as a collection. In the course of my research, I spent an afternoon at the antebellum house of Robert and Susie Curry in Sparta, Georgia.[10] While rain flecked the windowpanes, we sifted through their old wooden file box. The couple shared tales and memories evoked by various recipes—generous cooks from Robert's hungry bachelor days, cocreations from their early marriage, and their children's favorite dishes. "There are cards here, Robert, that really run through our lives," Susie remarked.

Robert and Susie Curry of Sparta, Georgia, looking through their collection of recipes, 2008.

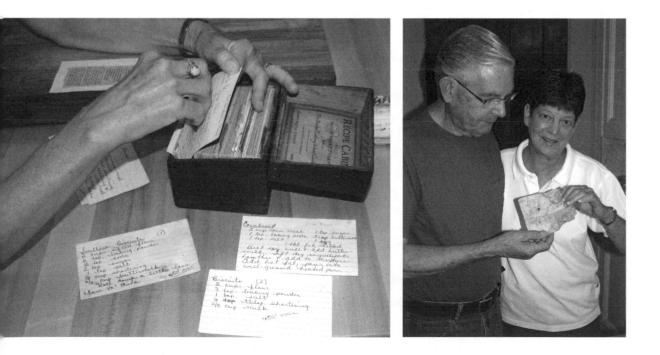

Ina Shipley's recipe book, spanning from ca. 1851 to 1956.

Recipe collections can indeed speak eloquently about the lives of cooks and their families. Perhaps the best way to showcase this idea is by looking at a recipe compilation separated from all information about its origins. Several years ago, I adopted the most battered, overstuffed recipe notebook I'd ever seen.[11] Sold by a Florida auction house that never replied to my queries about its provenance, the book is full of mysteries. While examining the volume first as an object and then for its contents, I found useful clues. Below are some of the basic questions I used to begin looking at the volume, which may help you examine your own family's recipe collection.

1. *What is the physical condition of the volume/container and contents?* The recipe notebook began as a school composition book. Repeated creases and soiling patterns suggest it began to fall apart from overuse. At some point, someone tried to sew the book back together. I also noticed that the book was in chronological layers—recipes written in pencil were covered with clippings attached by glue or straight pins.[12] Later, loose items were placed between full pages.

2. *Who created it?* The front cover has a name written across it, but the handwriting is florid and difficult to read. One recipe inside, however, is written on the back of a typed envelope, verifying the name as Ina Shipley. Some of the handwritten recipes inside are credited to "Mama" or "Aunt Mary" while other names give no clues to family

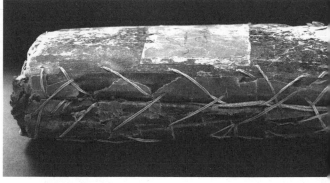

connections—Annie, Bill, Mrs. Durner. The handwriting on the pages themselves seems to be the same throughout.

3. *Where did it come from?* I first assumed the book was from Florida but found no clues to support the idea. The typed envelope with Shipley's name had a Baltimore address, so I turned to the U.S. Census records for Maryland. She is enumerated in the 1920 census as a married woman of thirty-eight (therefore born around 1882) with three children. Previously, according to the 1910 census, she lived in the household of her parents along with her two children and her husband, a carpenter for the railroad. Sometime between the two census records, the family moved down the street from Shipley's parents; almost every person on this street claimed railroad occupations for the census.

   A few of the recipes are marked as originating with Lansdowne School from "B&O Town," an area of Baltimore largely filled with Baltimore & Ohio Railroad workers. There are product labels for Baltimore products and clippings from Baltimore newspapers in the volume.

4. *What time period is it from?* The date "1954" is legible on the front cover. Inside I found notes, clippings, and recipes with dates ranging from 1900 to 1956. There is one loose handwritten recipe for Pork Pie marked 1851.

5. *What does the volume reveal about its place and time of creation?* Here is one example of an interesting historical item found in the recipe book. A handwritten entry on one of the first pages is for "1918 World War

Receipt. Salvation Army Donut Queen Reveals the Secret of Her Art."
Apparently a news article copied into the notebook, this entry continues:

> I guess I've made more donuts than any woman alive! I used to think two or
> three dozen was "a batch." Now I've seen Yankee soldiers eat donuts during
> and after a big battle and I know that "a batch" is not less than 500 donuts!
> There's a hole in a doughnut and I believe there is an unfillable hole in a
> doughboy![13]

A donut recipe follows the text. Shipley also recorded a list of food prices
from 1918: sugar 15 cents a pound, bread 16 cents a loaf, butter 75 cents
per pound, and milk 20 cents per quart.

But what about the owner? What can you glean about a cook or a family
from a recipe collection? What is included or not included can bring up some
interesting questions. An overabundance of dessert recipes makes me wonder
if Shipley had a sweet tooth or else had social commitments that required her
to frequently serve refreshments. The volume includes some non-recipe items—
poems, articles about flower gardening, clippings about beauty remedies, and
information on how to live frugally give indicators about Shipley's interests
and hobbies.

The juxtaposition of various aspects of a collection can also provide clues.
In the Shipley collection there are recipes for Easter candy, pork, and oysters.

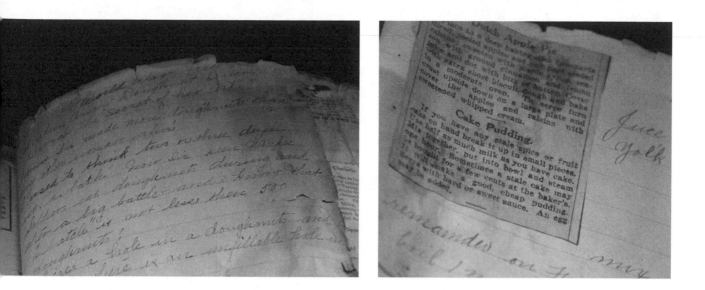

Does this indicate Shipley was neither an Orthodox Jew nor a Muslim? There are some Christian poems copied into the notebook, yet also a cookbooklet for hard beverages and a dandelion wine recipe. Does this mean Shipley was Christian but not a member of a fundamentalist denomination, as they usually eschew alcohol?

In a recipe collection, a change over time can also hint at changes in a cook's life or even society as a whole. The handwritten recipes near the front of the Shipley book are for dishes strictly from scratch. In later pages, brand-name ingredients appear in the recipes, and some are obviously clipped from food packages. Later recipes also call for processed ingredients such as a can of soup or a packet of flavored pudding mix. What does this perhaps say about how the cook's lifestyle changed over the years?

Ultimately, the family facts you learn from a recipe collection will be fewer in number than your hunches. It's wise to resist the temptation to draw conclusions. Still, a recipe collection can give you the flavor (pun intended) of the cook's life and raise interesting questions that additional family research might resolve. Good sources about how to glean information from manuscript recipe compilations include Janet Theophano's *Eat My Words: Reading Women's Lives through the Cookbooks They Wrote* and Diane Tye's *Baking as Biography: A Life Story in Recipes*.

When looking at your own family recipes, here are a few additional aspects to keep in mind:

- *Examine the Paper Itself.* Interviewee Martha Eubanks laughed about the appearance of her recipes. "Does it have spots on it? If it's clean, I probably meant to make it but never did." Quite often you can follow the trail of food specks through a recipe collection or cookbook to find favorites.

Pages from the recipe stash kindly shared by the author's cousin Evelyn Morgan Bowen. It is easy to see that these recipes from her grandmother Cora Mae Lash "Fat Mama" Frey (1901–1961) are still being used.

- *Don't Forget the Backs.* As with the envelope in Shipley's volume that gave her name and address, clippings and other additions to the recipe collection may yield useful information. Be sure to check both sides of recipes and clippings. Don't jump to conclusions, though, as your cook may have borrowed a stray scrap of paper to jot down that recipe. Wait and see how the clues add up.
- *Search for Writing Clues.* Recipe format, vocabulary, spelling, and handwriting style may tell you more about when the recipe was written. It may also give you clues about the education level of the recipe author or whether English was a second language.
- *Look at the Recipe Collection as an Artifact.* Types of papers and inks as well as the manner of pen marks can give additional information about the way the collection was compiled. For example, are the recipes written on scrap paper or fine stationery?
- *Examine the Recipes as a Whole.* Are the recipes geared for a beginning cook or an expert? Do the recipes often call for expensive or exotic ingredients, perhaps denoting a well-to-do or well-traveled household?

Recipe Collections: Printed Cookbooks

We've looked at handwritten and clipped recipes. But perhaps someone in your family left behind well-loved cookbooks. These volumes are a source of familiar recipes but can also tell about the previous owner's life—or at least more about what society was like during that lifetime. The British Library website asks some interesting questions about published cookbooks: "Who wrote these books? Who were they writing for? Who bought the books? Who actually read and used them?" Of their fourteenth- through eighteenth-century collection of cookbooks, the British Library Board states:

> The books should give a sense of the way food has for so long been used to define class—much of this food would only ever have been tasted by the wealthy few. The books also illustrate vividly how social, economic, technological and cultural factors fuel language use and development. And they suggest how tastes, fashions, and ideas of social status were shaped, developed and maintained.[14]

Rising literacy rates and plunging printing costs meant that more "ordinary people" used cookbooks by the late nineteenth century, so these questions and observations are useful for published cookbooks owned by recent generations of your family as well.

The content and tone of a cookbook can inform us about the communities where it was written and used. After I gave a lecture on preserving family recipes in Savannah, several women came forward with cookbooks owned by previous matriarchs. I was surprised to find that the heirlooms were the same two cookbooks—*The Twentieth-Century Cookbook* and *The Settlement Cookbook*.[15] I later learned these were indeed popular texts in Jewish communities at the dawn of the twentieth century.[16] Two of the women with the cookbooks, Bobbie Levy and Matiel Leffler, are friends and brought copies originally belonging to women who were also friends—Bobbie's grandmother and Matiel's mother-in-law. We looked over recipes for labor-intensive desserts to serve guests but also for Green Turtle Soup ("Cut the head off the turtle, let bleed overnight . . ."), for a few moments visiting a world somehow both more genteel and more frank about the realities of life.[17]

If nothing else, the illustrations in old cookbooks can be enlightening as well as amusing. For instance, it is interesting to see how women are portrayed.

Images from the 1910s–1930s. Right, from *Favorite Recipes Save Time and Money* (Lynn, Mass.: Lydia E. Pinkham Medicine Co., ca. 1919). Left, from *Ingleheart's Cake Secrets* (Evansville, Ind.: Ingleheart Brothers, 1928). Center, *A Handy Guide for Busy Cooks with 77 Ways of Using Crystal and Dial Brand Baking Soda* (Wyandotte, Mich.: Detroit Soda Products, ca. 1931).

(Unsurprisingly, few men are pictured unless they are professional chefs or at the barbecue grill.) In general, the rosy milkmaid-type cook of the late nineteenth century gave way to two images by the 1920s—the dainty flapper and the crisply dressed nurse-like home economist. By the 1930s the womanly ideal was the sensible and somewhat plain housewife of the Great Depression. In the post–World War II cookbooks my mother learned with, cooks appear in pearls and high heels, their idealized waists tiny and accentuated by crisp aprons.

On a more personal level, the cookbooks dear to a cook now gone can give you clues about that person's preferences and tastes—especially if you can tell which recipes were actually used. Sometimes the impact of a particular cookbook or cookbook author spreads across a family. My mother was quite loyal to *Betty Crocker's Picture Cook Book*.[18] (See chapter 1.) As I was learning to cook, I usually used Mom's copy or the 1980s updated version she gave me one Christmas. Now that I own my mother's cookbook, I passed the 1980s version on to my niece.

Several cooks interviewed for this book professed similar family loyalty to one or more cookbooks. Paying attention to such "cookbook dynasties" can give you a valuable reference to look for the recipes that may have formed the basis of favorite family dishes, as well as a source for understanding the underlying cooking knowledge for a family. Thanks to online sellers of used or rare books, it is often possible to track down additional copies of old cookbooks—even specific editions—to share with current generations.

Expand Your Circle of Interviewees

You've now looked through the materials a cook left behind, hoping to find traces of the person's kitchen legacy. Now what? Check back through the recipe collection once more, this time looking for personal names.

Even though your cook is now gone, see if you can make contact with coworkers, neighbors, or friends the person may have cooked for. They may be willing to share their memories. These contacts may also have swapped recipes with your cook. Keep in mind that sometimes cooks will not need a recipe to make a common dish and therefore will have kept no written record for themselves, but they may have taken the time to write a recipe down for a friend, a new bride, or a young relative setting up housekeeping for the first time.

Does it seem like a long shot to track down a cook's friends? More than two decades after my mother's death, a former neighbor gave me several of Mom's recipes, including two that my brother and I had lamented as lost forever. Excited by this turn of events, I tracked down a couple of her other friends. Along with lovely trips down memory lane and stories about Mom's cooking, I found still more recipes.[19]

I've known many researchers who are hesitant to contact nonfamily or a distant relative they have not met. If you're nodding your head, see if a family member can provide an introduction. If I have to make a "cold contact" myself, I usually try to do so in writing so I don't put somebody on the spot, following up with a call if I don't hear anything. I briefly outline my project and tell how I am connected to the cook or family I am researching. For context and to instill confidence about the legitimacy of my request, I include background information about the cook (full name, life dates, how the cook knew the person I am contacting, and so on). Sharing a copy of one of the cook's recipes I already have, a photo of the cook, or a similar gift helps establish a spirit of generosity.

Even if you are searching for recipes from a cook gone much longer, one trick that experienced genealogists use for finding additional information or locating a missing branch of a family is researching their ancestors' neighbors and friends. As America expanded, families sometimes found it safer and more comforting to migrate with neighbors and friends—or letters mailed back to the old community sometimes enticed others to follow. In remote or faraway places, friends and neighbors often served as a crucial support system and were the ones that shared life events, celebrations, and meals. If you can find evidence of such ties and relationships, additional research on those individuals or families could possibly lead to archived troves that include your family's recipes, letters, or stories.

Checking Community Sources

If you are new to family research, finding information at an archives or in the special collections area of a library is a rewarding process. Staff can point you to sources where you can verify facts and perhaps turn up a story or two. What you'll find varies by the size and scope of the archives but also by what local primary information sources still exist, such as letter collections, newspapers with firsthand accounts, and government documents. Available secondary sources such as local histories, cemetery indexes, and newspaper indexes also vary from archives to archives.

Your results will further depend on how active your ancestors were in society. Unfortunately, that means gender, race, religion, or ethnicity does come into play; yesteryear's discrimination still affects what today's researcher can uncover. But if this concern has been holding you back, know that there are many historical sources out there, including records created by special interest groups, minority social clubs, and places of worship. In recent decades, archivists have been proactive about finding and preserving such sources so that researchers can develop a more balanced understanding of the past.

Finding cookbooks and food-related materials in online catalogs or computer databases can be tricky, so don't be afraid to ask archives staff for help. The usual search terms are "cooking" and "cookery," but you may find additional items by conducting searches for "cook," "cookbook," "recipe," and the outdated term "receipt." You may be one of those lucky people who discover that an ancestor wrote a family history or contributed to a community cookbook. Or there may be other materials available. In my grandparents' county, for instance, the local newspaper ran a regular column for many years that highlighted a local cook each week and printed some of their favorite recipes.[20] From time to time, my relatives were featured in this column.

If you are just starting out in genealogy, your local library or bookstore will have resources on how to get started in family research. Once you verify and organize the information you already have, you can work your way backward chronologically to collect new information, researching one fact or examining one source at a time.

Although many researchers end up like the proverbial kid in a candy store, excited by all the possibilities around them, new researchers are sometimes unprepared or even upset by operating procedures at archives. Let me offer a few helpful tips. Before you go, verify research hours; many archives do not keep full business hours and may readjust schedules near holidays. Also check policies about what you can bring into the research areas with you. Because archives must protect one-of-a-kind materials from loss and damage, rules are far more restrictive than you'll find at public libraries. Most archives will not let you take in drinking water, pens, highlighters, pads of "sticky notes," purses, computer bags, backpacks, envelopes, binder notebooks, or outerwear (coats, heavy jackets, or hats). Sometimes archives require you to use their notepaper and pencils rather than your own. Computer devices, scanners, cameras, and phones may need to be examined before you enter the archives reading room, and there may be restrictions about their use. You will want to bring valid photo identification, paper, pencils, and a light sweater. (Archives are notoriously chilly, as a cool temperature helps preserve rare materials.) You may also need coins or small bills for photocopies and possibly for a locker deposit to secure your personal items. A small external hard drive (flash/jump/thumb drive) is often helpful for saving digitized information.

If you have already used archives for family research, it may be worth a return trip. You never know what materials have been discovered, donated, or processed by archives staff since your last visit.

And what if there is no archives in your area? An archives many miles away may collect items relevant to the whole state or region, so give them a try. On the other hand, sometimes local historical societies, public libraries, or worship centers keep troves of historical papers and books. Your state archives or local library may know about these sources. In rural areas, I've had luck finding information by asking at the nearest courthouse or library where I can find individuals or organizations that are interested in local history.

Community Cookbooks

Author and director of the Southern Foodways Alliance at the University of Mississippi John T. Edge wrote an illuminating essay in praise of community cookbooks for his book *A Gracious Plenty: Recipes and Recollections from the American South*. He points out that such books are "a voyeur's treat, a window into the everyday life and foods of a group of churchgoers, a clutch of quilters, or a league of ladies inclined towards service."[21] In a later book he writes, "We read community cookbooks as informal histories of people and place told through recipes."[22]

Grandma Frey left behind two such books, one from the Cleveland County Home Demonstration Club Council (1963) and one from the Cleveland County Extension Home Makers Club (1975).[23] Although my grandmother didn't contribute recipes, some of my cousins did, and I'm glad to have those recipes. These volumes are certainly a source of useful comparison recipes from my grandparents' time and region, helping me understand cooking practices and the types of foods eaten in that community. In addition, the photographs and sponsor advertisements give more clues about my grandparents' world. Similarly, I discovered that an elderly cousin, a former teacher, once helped edit a school cookbook that contains twenty-three of her recipes.[24] Since her mother was one of the great-aunts who excelled at cakes, I was gleeful to find baking recipes in the bunch—possible trickle-down cooking knowledge. If your family doesn't own community cookbooks, you may wish to check with neighbors or family friends in the area to see if they know of such sources. Archives, libraries, and historical societies are good places to look as well.

When searching for community cookbooks in a library or archives, be aware that they may also be described as charitable, compiled, fund-raising, local, or regional cookbooks. Places of worship, schools, social clubs, scouting groups, charities, and schools are the most common creators of these cookbooks, so it may be worth checking for archival collections (or making a few phone calls) to see if such groups in your family's area put together recipe collections or even just included recipes in newsletters. When you're ready to look beyond your local archives, you may find not only community cookbooks but also yesteryear's general cookbooks and even manuscript recipes in archives that specialize in American culinary collections—Harvard's Schlesinger Library, Michigan State University Library (Feeding America: The Historic American Cookbook Project), Michigan University (Longone Culinary Archive), the University of Minnesota Library (Kirschner Cookbook Collection), Virginia Tech (History of Food and Drink Collection), and the University of Wisconsin–Madison Library, to name a few. Some of the websites for these institutions provide a network of links to culinary collections and even allow access to scanned materials.

For developing your own collection, community cookbooks can be found for purchase in local used book sales, thrift stores, and antique stores as well as through used bookstores and online booksellers. Also, some community cookbook presses have online stores where you can search by state or keyword to purchase their publications.[25]

If you are looking for a general understanding of foodways in your family's region, statewide cookbooks may also be of interest to you. The bibliography of John Egerton's book *Southern Food* contains a list of some of the best cookbooks for each southern state.[26] Online searches for "cookbook" and the name of your state can help you find titles beyond the South, and Lynne Olver's online Food Timeline offers a list of traditional state foods and recipes. Some state fairs also publish cookbooks. Last but not least, organizations like American Food Roots,

Cookbook, Cleveland County (Arkansas) Home Demonstration Club Council, 1963.

the Slow Food Foundation's Ark of Taste, the Southern Foodways Alliance, and the United Nations Educational, Scientific, and Cultural Organization (UNESCO) Intangible Heritage Project, as well as the bibliography of this book, can help you discover regional or national specialties.[27]

Searching for Specific Lost Recipes

Perhaps the most compelling of research puzzles is the recipe that you know was once in written form but is now simply lost. Sometimes lost recipes can be re-created using your knowledge, recipe comparisons, help from family members, and guidance from other cooks. At other times, a recipe you think is lost forever turns up in another person's recipe collection. Cookbook author Glenda Major included the recipe for her sister's mock plum pudding in her family cookbook, not knowing that the sister thought the recipe was lost.[28] "It's been in my drawer all these years," Glenda said with a laugh. "She was delighted to have that recipe again." Asking around for recipes may have great results—with your own lost recipes or those from other cooks.

Recipe for Boiled Cookies, otherwise known as Mudballs. The recipe came into the family via the author's maternal grandmother, Marjorie Cowles. Nucoa was a brand of margarine; the author uses ¼ cup butter.

The author's grandmother Marjorie Eileen Greene Cowles Macpherson (1920–2003) in an undated photo.

The occasional recipe may become lost simply because the title isn't what you assume. I searched high and low for the stovetop cookie recipe that my brother and I loved growing up and called Mudballs. Eventually, the recipe turned up in my mother's recipe file after all, just under a different name. Shakespeare's Juliet says, "that which we call a rose by any other name would smell as sweet," yet "Boiled Cookies" makes me think of stinky cabbage while "Mudballs" is humorously descriptive of these cocoa and oatmeal mounds. I flipped past that card many times before I finally thought to read through the recipe.[29]

Some recipes become popular enough that they turn up in many collections. You may have luck finding a recipe almost identical to one you lost if you ask an experienced cook from the right age group or look in a community cookbook matching the region and time period. Some recipes can live a long time in the public record. For instance, my aunt told me that she remembered her grandmother making cookies called Cherry Winks.[30] It turned out that this was a well-known Pillsbury Bakeoff winner during my great-grandmother's lifetime, and the recipe is still available through that company's website and cookbooks. This cookie is now back in our family repertoire.

Because a single recipe may have various titles, an advanced online search that includes the most unusual or important ingredients may have better results. By searching for "recipe," "orange juice concentrate," and "coconut," one can find a favorite no-bake confection recipe that Grandma Frey used to make but that went missing long ago. I didn't know to search for "Ambrosia Balls" or "Orange Coconut Balls" because we always called them Orange Sunsets, but I sure was glad to have the recipe back in the family. If a general Web query isn't fruitful, some cooking websites allow users to conduct advanced searches for recipes that include specific ingredients while eliminating recipes that contain unwanted ingredients.[31]

There are a few sources where one can appeal to others for help with lost recipes. Some cooking magazines and food sections of newspapers invite readers to write in with lost recipe descriptions, publishing a small number to see if their readership can help. Some cooking websites, blogs, and recipe message boards have similar features. One site titled Ask Uncle Phaedrus, Finder of Lost Recipes is designed for such searches and has an extensive archive of past queries and answers.[32] Social media like Facebook or Twitter may be helpful as well, allowing you to ask many family members and friends at once about a recipe.

An example of a family food tradition you might *not* want to follow: the author's paternal grandfather, George Lyman Cowles (1916–2004), and his brother John (1907–1985) in 1937 on Balanced Rock near Castleford, Idaho. *Life* published a similar version of the photo in March 1956 and captioned it "Precarious Place for a Picnic."

Grandpa George Cowles and the author in 1987 on a hill above the area where his Rainier, Oregon, peppermint farm was located.

Here is an example of an anecdote that can be used in a family cookbook to include a person who didn't cook much. My maternal grandfather, George Lyman Cowles (1916–2004), was born in Castle Rock, Idaho, but lived most of his life in Rainier and Clatskanie, Oregon. He was a peppermint farmer for much of his adult life, and his daughter, my mother, loved this deeply familiar flavor so much that peppermint recipes abound in our family files. But there are other foodways as well. My brother, Eric Frey, wrote a eulogy for our Grandpa after his death titled "Impressions of George Cowles" that included details about his food preferences. It would make a humorous and memorable addition to a family cookbook:

George Cowles never passed an ice cream stand without stopping. It had to be soft-serve ice cream, though. If it were regular hand-dipped ice cream, he would load us all back into the wagon train and try the next one. He seemed to have all of northwestern Oregon mapped out in his head, connecting one ice cream stand with another. Definitely an excellent traveling companion for a couple of kids with a sweet tooth.

He would watch like a hawk as the guy served up his ice cream cone. He didn't want his cone to be massed up to the sky, to drip all over his hands and clothes. So once the cone was the way he liked it, he would call out to the server, "That's enough!" But sometimes the kid wouldn't pay attention, load the cone until ice cream was six inches above the rim, and then hand it to Grandpa. Grandpa would grunt in disgust, "Bah!" and take out his pocket knife. With one swift stroke, he would lop off the top four inches of his ice cream cone, letting it fall into the dirt with a sad plop.

The first time I witnessed this, I was aghast. "Holy cow! You wasted half of your ice cream!" "I told him to stop," he would reply.

When it happened in the future, I knew to stay at his side, so that when he sliced off the top of his ice cream, I could catch it bare-handed and eat it. Naturally, once Val saw what was going on, she had to get in on the action. So after an adult stepped in to stop the fight, we had to take turns eating Grandpa's cast-off ice cream.

Later on, I watched Grandpa scrape manure off his boots with a pocket knife. I asked, "Is that the same knife you cut the ice cream with?"

"Yep."

My brother's essay ended with the fact that camping trips with his daughter always include stopping for soft-serve ice cream. Even without a recipe, the great-grandfather she never met becomes more real to her through family foodways. (Grandpa's ice cream, by the way, *had* to be vanilla.)

Surrogate Recipes

Purists may balk at collecting recipes not strictly from family members. Sometimes, however, recipes are simply gone from the family's history, and thus an important cook may not be represented in a family cookbook. For instance, the only recipe I have from Great-Grandma Reaves is the aforementioned one for lemon pie that I'm pretty sure is in her handwriting. The recipes I'd truly love to have are the ones for treats her daughter and grandchildren bragged about—gingerbread, teacakes, and biscuits. (See appendix 1.) I tried to gather as much information about her specialties as I could (size, shape, flavor) and then found or developed recipes that are, in my mind, suitable stand-ins. These recipes help to keep her memory alive, now that she has been gone more than half a century.

Using surrogate recipes may be especially challenging if you haven't experienced the dish yourself. Great-Grandma Reaves remains in living memory thanks to her grandchildren. But since those grandchildren haven't experienced her cooking for many decades, the reports were conflicting. The oldest grandchild thought her cake-like gingerbread was cut into squares.[33] "It wasn't very thick. I don't recall for sure." The next grandchild also remembered the gingerbread as cake, but when asked how thick, he moved his hand to indicate about five inches. "May have not been but four, but I don't remember exactly. I just remember sinking my teeth in."[34] The information seemed conflicting, but then we realized the gingerbread may have been cooked in a loaf pan—therefore a slice cut by a generous grandmother could have been large in each direction. If you're stuck on an aspect of a dish, a little discussion and comparing sources may clarify the matter.

When using such surrogates in a family recipe collection, clearly mark them as being "in honor of," "dedicated to," or "inspired by" and note the actual origin of the recipe. If the idea of surrogate recipes appeals to you, start by pulling together a list of the foods the person liked or was known for and select quality recipes for each.

For a family cookbook, simply including a list of foods a person liked or a food-related story may be interesting to future generations.

Learning to Cook the Very Old-Fashioned Way

If you have significantly older recipes from your family or would like to reach back in time to learn about the daily life of distant ancestors through foodways, research and practice are required, yet this is a rewarding journey. Even if you've only used a modern oven and stovetop, learning to handle a wood-burning stove or open hearth is quite possible. In an interview about the topic, Colonial Williamsburg food specialist Dennis Cotner stressed a hands-on approach. "More than anything, to get a jump start, you have to develop your cooking skills first." Through reading old cookbooks such as Hannah Glasse's colonial-era volume and also practicing basic cooking skills, he slowly learned to be a successful hearth cook. "I bumped around a good bit before I learned how to develop those skills. They're not that hard. They're very basic. But it's really doing it continually that maintains that level. My advice has always been to get into the kitchen. Jump in and teach yourself."

Root House Museum kitchen, Marietta, Georgia. *Photo by the author; permission courtesy of Cobb Landmarks and Historical Society, Inc.*

If you have the desire to learn the basic skills of yesteryear's cooking, there are resources available. In time and with a little research, you'll come to understand various ingredients, utensils, and methods. Educational venues such as Georgia's Foxfire, North Carolina's John C. Campbell Folk School, and Virginia's Colonial Williamsburg periodically hold demonstrations or classes.[35] An Internet search, your state's tourism office, or the Association for Living History, Farm, and Agricultural Museums (ALHFAM) can help you find local house museums, living history sites, or similar venues that teach historical foodways.[36]

There are also various books available to help with learning historical cooking methods. Cotner and the others at Colonial Williamsburg use period cookbooks to glean information. Later in this chapter, you will find a list of early cookbooks that may be helpful. In the meantime, one of the best sources I've seen to explain older cooking terms and equivalents is Lily May and John Spaulding's *Civil War Recipes: Receipts from the Pages of Godey's Lady's Book*.[37] Many other historical cookbooks or food history websites contain similar notes. Modern "how-to" books listed in the Suggested Reading section may be beneficial as well.

Translating Old-Fashioned Measurements. Often one of the most difficult hurdles with very old recipes is measuring. I've seen recipes that call for "a teacup" of butter or ask you to form dough balls "the size of a hickory nut." Exactly how much is that? As for liquids, what is a hogshead or a pottle? In the 1847 *Carolina Housewife,* a recipe for Pumpkin Chips compares the correct size for the pumpkin slices to a dollar coin.[38] But what diameter and thickness was a dollar back in 1847? (An Internet search took me to a coin dealer's website that provided information on the last point.)

Recipe calling for "butter the size of a walnut," in an uncredited and undated ledger purchased from an estate sale in Indiana. The entire recipe is pictured; the recipe writer assumed readers would know what to do with those ingredients.

Guide to Older Food Measurements

❯❯ Please note that, in general, the older the recipe, the greater the likelihood that measures were "rough" or estimated. Also, I have come across contradictory sources, so the list below is not foolproof but rather a good starting place.

Blade of mace = scant ¼ teaspoon

Bushel = 8 gallons (dry measure)

Coffee cup = scant cup

Coffee spoon = ½ teaspoon

Dessert spoon = 1 to 2 teaspoons

Drachm/dram = ¾ teaspoon

Drop = about ⅟₆₀ teaspoon

Firkin = 9 to 10 gallons (liquid measure)

Fistful (usually flour or cornmeal) = ⅓ cup

Gill/Jill = ½ cup (liquid measure)

Glass = ¼ cup (liquid measure)

Goblet = scant cup

Half-pinch = amount lifted between thumb and first finger

Hogshead = large barrel, usually 63 gallons

Jack = ¼ cup (liquid measure)

Jigger = 1½ fluid ounces, about 3 tablespoons

Jill, *see* Gill

Kenning = 4 gallons (dry measure)

Kitchen spoon = 1 teaspoon

Lump of butter = 1 rounded tablespoon

Mouthful = ½ ounce (liquid measure)

Noggin = ½ cup

Nutmeg (whole) = 2 to 3 teaspoons ground spice (stronger than bottled)

Peck = 2 gallons (dry measure)

Pinch = amount lifted between thumb and first two fingers

Pint = 2 cups

Pottle = 2 quarts

Salt spoon = ⅛ to ¼ teaspoon

Saucer = 1 cup plus 1 tablespoon

Size of an egg (chicken assumed) = ¼ cup

Size of a goose egg = ¾ cup

Size of a guinea egg = ⅛ cup or 2 tablespoons

Size of a hazelnut = 1 teaspoon

Size of a hickory nut = 1 to 2 tablespoons

Size of a quail egg = 1½ teaspoons

Size of a turkey egg = ⅓ cup

Size of a walnut = 1 to 2 tablespoons

Soup spoon = 2 to 3 teaspoons, scant tablespoon

Spoonful = 1 tablespoon

Teacup = 4 to 6 fluid ounces, usually around ⅔ cup

Thimbleful = scant teaspoon

Tumbler = 1 cup

Wine glass = around ¼ cup (liquid measure)

Turkey, chicken, and quail eggs. Turkey eggs weigh an average of 70 grams. Chicken eggs, which vary by breed and other factors, range from 25 to 65 grams, with store-bought large eggs weighing around 60 grams. Quail eggs average 6 grams. *Photo by the author; eggs courtesy of the University of Georgia Poultry Research Center.*

Because of my interest in old recipes, I began making notes about unusual or outdated measurements whenever I came across them in archival collections or old cookbooks. See the "Guide to Older Food Measurements" and the "Guide to Oven Temperatures" sidebars.

As with so many other recipe quandaries, comparing your old recipe to others (from the time period and beyond) as well as seeking the advice of other cooks will be helpful. If a very old recipe seems to be particularly difficult to decipher, some of the organizations mentioned earlier in this chapter that are involved in preserving and teaching historical foodways may be able to help you.

Sources of Older Recipes. If you love history and love cooking but have never read through a cookbook from yesteryear, you're in for a treat. Most first-time readers are fascinated by ingredients and dishes that are no longer common. Certain flavorings (butternut or white walnut, rosewater, horehound) and ingredients (quince, suet, sweetbreads, currants) have largely fallen from favor, at least in America. Although cultural shifts can affect how much we appreciate older dishes as well as our ability to find the ingredients we need to make them, you may discover recipes that give you ideas few cooks are using anymore. In the household column of an old farming magazine, I found a recipe for spiced strawberries using mace.[39] Not only is this spice less popular

Recipe for Spiced Strawberries, from *Southern Farm and Home* magazine, April 1870.

A Few Cookbooks from America's Past

The books listed below in chronological order can help you find recipes to compare with ones in your family collection, learn about the kitchens of your American ancestors, and cook interesting dishes to celebrate history. Many of the best-selling cookbooks a century or more ago were published in the eastern portion of the United States or even in England, reflecting America's early days and growth patterns. Still, the list provides a manageable start, and a little sleuthing will turn up additional cookbooks representing various regions and traditions. The publication place is provided for each work below; complete citations can be found in the bibliography. One or more editions of each listed book—as well as many other notable historical cookbooks—have been reprinted or are available online through digitization efforts such as Google Books, Feeding America: The Historic American Cookbook Project (Michigan State University), the HathiTrust, Internet Archives, and Project Gutenberg.

1727 Eliza Smith, *The Compleat Housewife* (London)
The 1742 edition published in Virginia is often thought to be the first cookbook published in the United States.

1747 Hannah Glasse, *The Art of Cookery Made Plain and Easy* (London)

1796 Amelia Simmons, *American Cookery* (Connecticut)
This volume is usually noted as the first American cookbook, and it includes ingredients indigenous to North America.

1824 Mary Randolph, *The Virginia Housewife* (Virginia)

1827 Robert Roberts, *The House Servant's Directory; or, A Monitor for Private Families* (New York)
This manual and cookbook was written by an African American in Massachusetts.

1829 Lydia Maria Child, *The American Frugal Housewife* (Massachusetts)

1839 Lettice Bryan, *The Kentucky Housewife* (Ohio)

1845 Eliza Acton, *Modern Cookery for Private Families* (London)

1846 Catharine Beecher, *Miss Beecher's Domestic Receipt Book* (New York)

1847 Sarah Rutledge, *The Carolina Housewife* (Charleston)

1857 Eliza Leslie, *Miss Leslie's New Cookery Book* (Philadelphia)

1861 Isabella Beeton, *Mrs Beeton's Book of Household Management* (London)

1867 Annabella Hill, *Mrs. Hill's New Cook Book* (New York)
The author was from Georgia.

1877 Estelle Wilcox, *Buckeye Cookery* (Minnesota)
The author was from Ohio.

1881 Abby Fisher, *What Mrs. Fisher Knows about Old Southern Cooking* (San Francisco)
The author was an African American from Alabama.

1885 Lafcadio Hearn, *La Cuisine Creole* (Louisiana)

1896 Fannie Farmer, *The Boston Cooking-School Cook Book* (Massachusetts)

1901 Lizzy Kander, *The Settlement Cookbook* (Wisconsin)
The author, from an enclave of Bavarian immigrants, was Jewish.

1905 Times-Mirror, *Los Angeles Times Cook Book—No. 2.* (California)
This compilation contains "old time California, Spanish and Mexican dishes."

than it once was, but the idea of spicing fruit is nowadays more for apples, pears, or stone fruit than for berries. I had to significantly tone down the recipe's spice level for my modern palate, but I used it as inspiration for a simple dessert sauce that gets surprised reactions but also requests for more.

Some old recipes are decidedly unappealing for today's kitchen, but they can still be fascinating and enlightening reading material. I balk at using recipes calling for lard, but they abound in older cookbooks (especially in the South) and help me to realize how important the family hog was to my ancestors. My great-grandmother once made a cake using several ingredients purchased in bulk.[40] After it was baked, she realized she'd mixed up her kitchen barrels; there was a half teaspoon of sugar but well over a cup of salt in that cake. She tossed it into the hog trough with the rest of the kitchen scraps and baked another. The next time she went outside, the unfortunate pig was dead and had turned a shocking blue. As a child, I felt sorry for the pig yet thought the story had a cartoonish quality. Now I know from cookbooks of the region and period that almost every family meal depended on ham, lard, salt pork, and the like. My great-grandparents were largely subsistence farmers, so the loss of the hog was a family disaster that must have affected their resources for months.

Other recipes may be downright appalling, such as those for animals we nowadays primarily think of as roadkill. Late one night while curled up with an 1800s cookbook in bed, I found myself reading unsettling and somewhat graphic instructions on how to use a broom handle to break an opossum's neck. The information made me feel squeamish, yet when I look at genteel photos of my rural great-grandmothers in their Sunday-best dresses, I still know that they needed farm skills like expertly and humanely wringing the head off a live chicken. Recipes and foodways can be a fascinating window into a vanished world.

One of my favorite hometown treats was a cookie called Cinnamon Toast sold by a local café called Cookies & Co. in downtown Athens, Georgia. When the business closed in 2009 after almost thirty years, I was bereft. Those cookies were very thin, chewy, and buttery with gentle spice, and I never came across anything else just like them. (In fact, some recipes give tips on how to *avoid* thin cookies!) I began experimenting. There were lace cookie recipes out there, but even if the thinness was right, the texture was wrong. I searched the Web for articles on how to adjust cookies and then started to monkey with a favorite recipe for Best Big, Fat, Chewy Chocolate Chip Cookies posted to Allrecipes.com by user ElizabethBH. I hit upon a series of changes to transform it into a surrogate recipe. Enough years have gone by since I tasted the original that I know these cookies aren't exactly right—in fact, my cookie edges are too uneven—yet they satisfy similar cravings. This surrogate recipe allowed youth's reminiscences to become a family favorite that will gather even more memories.

Cinnamon Toast Salute Cookies

1 cup (226 grams) salted butter, European preferred

2 cups (250 grams) all-purpose flour

½ teaspoon baking soda

¼ teaspoon salt

1 tablespoon cinnamon, korintje preferred, plus extra for dusting

¼ teaspoon ground nutmeg

1 cup (245 grams) firmly packed light brown sugar

¼ cup (80 grams) light corn syrup

1 large egg plus 1 large egg yolk

1 tablespoon vanilla extract (yes, that much!)

1. Preheat oven to 350°F and grease cookie sheets.
2. Melt butter and set aside to cool slightly. (European butter has a higher percentage of butterfat, which adds to the flavor and texture.)
3. Blend flour, baking soda, salt, and spices in a small bowl with a whisk. Set aside. (Measure flour carefully. Too much flour affects the cookie texture.)
4. In a mixing bowl, blend sugar with corn syrup and then stir melted butter into it. Blend in eggs and vanilla. (I use an electric mixer on low speed, but arm power will work fine for this recipe.)
5. Add dry flour mixture a spoonful at a time to the creamed mixture until completely blended. Mixture will be quite soft.

6. Drop cookie dough 2 teaspoons at a time, at least 3 inches apart, onto cool, greased cookie sheets.

7. Bake for 7 to 10 minutes or until edges are just toasty brown. Do not overbake, as this will make the edges stiff and crumbly. It looks pretty if you lightly dust each warm cookie with a little extra cinnamon. A small mesh strainer works best for this task.

8. Cool slightly on baking sheet before transferring to cooling rack. You want the cookies firm enough to not wrinkle when the spatula goes under them, yet they will stick if they cool too much.

8. When completely cool, store cookies in an airtight container. If there are somehow cookies left after a day or two, my mother's cookie-reviving trick was to place a slice of apple or bread (not touching the cookies) in the container overnight.

Makes about 6 dozen small cookies—depending, of course, on how much cookie dough you eat. They are so thin that they don't travel well. That's okay, though, because if you take them to a party, people may underestimate their charms. These are not the beauty queens of the cookie world. Serve them warm from your oven to loved ones.

Poke holes in warm
cake and spread
Cake mix juice mixture over
the top. Let it soak
in several hours.

and bake at 350° for 25-30 min.
____, sugar + juice from 2 lemons.
__ out of oven, poke holes

Sharon married Robert Wayne Frey (1938-1992)
of New Edinburg, AR on Sep. 5, 1962. They lived
most of their married life in Georgia and had two
children -- Eric Todd Frey (Feb 13, 1967) and
Valerie Janese Frey Stone (Jan 15, 1969)
Sharon went back to school at age 40 and became a
nurse. She died of AIDS on Jan 18, 1993 after a
needle accident. She is buried in Athens, GA and,
as you know, her children live in the same town

Here's what's cookin' Apricot Delights serves ___
Recipe from the kitchen of Joy + Bella Cookbook
1 pkg (8oz.) Jello (any flavor)
1 cup sugar
1 can (1 lb. 4oz) apricots, drained
and puréed
½ cup chopped almonds or
(½ c. chopped walnuts)
Confectioners sugar
Combine Jello, sugar in saucepan. Stir in apricots.
Cook, stir over low heat until begins to boil, ___
clear and thickened. Remove from heat
(over)

Gag Photo -- Marjo___
Dahlon___

Chapter Seven

Sharing Family Recipes and Foodways

When I walk into my kitchen today, I am not alone. Whether we know it or not, none of us is. We bring fathers and mothers and kitchen tables, and every meal we have ever eaten. Food is never just food. It's also a way of getting at something else: who we are, who we have been, and who we want to be.—Molly Wizenberg, *A Homemade Life: Stories and Recipes from My Kitchen Table* (2)

Many heirloom recipe enthusiasts want to share their trove with family members. This chapter offers formats and options that make it easier to take that last step of pulling together or "packaging" your work for personal satisfaction but also to maximize its impact. Some suggestions will help personalize the recipes so that family members feel greater connections to them. Other suggestions will help you place recipes in a historical and cultural context, making them both more interesting and more useful to those beyond your family. Some suggestions can accomplish both.

Working Copies versus Archival Copies

A cookbook is usually a "workhorse" of a book. Unlike the novel that sits quietly on your bedside table and just gets picked up at restful parts of the day, cookbooks are handled frequently and used in messy conditions. If you create an heirloom cookbook, it will contain information that also makes it a family treasure, and therefore you want to take steps to preserve it for future generations.

My advice is to make two types of copies of your heirloom recipe collection— working and archival. With working copies, the version of your cookbook that you expect to be used often, a variety of office supplies and craft materials are perfectly acceptable—laminated pages, plastic sleeves, colored papers, or anything else that pleases you. This may be the version you share with most of the family. Do, however, create archival copies for yourself and a few conscientious family members. Archival copies of your cookbook will be intended to withstand the test of time, so paper and other supplies need to be stable—free of acids and harmful chemicals. Making an unbound version of your family recipe collection, photocopying it onto one side only of acid-free paper and placing it in an acid-free folder, is a good way to protect the information.

Another consideration is how many copies of a family cookbook you'll need. You may wish to offer copies to local libraries, archives, or historical societies for their collections (see donation details later in the chapter). When it comes to family, think about future generations, perhaps creating reserve copies for when today's young children become adults and new family members come along. Still another consideration is that when you choose who will and won't receive copies of your family recipes, you may inadvertently send a message, drawing a boundary between family and "not family." I created a kid-friendly cookbook for the children in my life. Some of the kids who got copies won't show up on my genealogy charts, yet they are people I am committed to loving and nurturing for the rest of my life. By giving these children favorite recipes woven with my family history, I am offering them greater understanding and a deeper connection. Similarly, my parents dying early meant I was gratefully "adopted" by a few families. I don't share DNA with these lifelong friends, but we have shared many years' worth of holiday celebrations and meals, so their recipes and foodways have become beloved traditions in my own life. I treasure the recipes they share with me.

Local Binding

Office Supply Bindings. Many of us tend to think on a grand scale, but there's nothing wrong with sharing a stapled stack of photocopied recipes. Report covers and binders are also possibilities, available in a variety of colors, sizes, and designs. With the aforementioned cookbook I created for my nieces and nephews when they were fairly young, I used a word processing program on my computer and inserted images into the text. Most of the recipes are followed by snapshots of the kids at work in the kitchen at various ages. After printing, I put the pages in plastic sleeves so spatters can be wiped away. A three-ring binder keeps each sixty-two-page volume together, and empty sleeves at the back allow the kids to add their own favorite recipes. The binders lie open easily, which is handy when you've got both hands full with cooking. I made sure to keep the recipes to one page or less, so the kids don't have to worry about flipping a page to finish a dish.

With fewer than a dozen copies to make, this format was useful, affordable, and kid friendly. I knew that if a book got damaged or lost, I could easily replace it. If you follow suit, be aware that some plastics (such as those on the covers of three-ring binders) may soften and lift off inks. Also, metal fasteners may rust in the moist conditions of the kitchen. However, almost seven years after I made those cookbooks, they have been used and are still going strong.

Scrapbooking. Professional baker Karen Vessels created small cookbooks using photograph binders and colorful scrapbooking craft supplies. Because she made copies just for her grown children, she handwrote all the recipes as a labor of love. "It means so much more when it is handwritten." She typed longer entries, however, so all the recipes fit on one page. Karen then added notes about freezing, storing, presentation, and serving. When she had finished, she made a photocopied version for herself. If this idea appeals to you, please see information about scrapbooking and archival practices in chapter 2.

Local Copy and Print Shops. Once cookbook creator Glenda Major put together family recipes and then added anecdotes, stories, poems, and quotes, she had 183 self-typed pages on her computer. After looking at many cookbooks for ideas, she chose to print double-sided pages on standard-sized paper (8½ by 11 inches) so that reformatting would not be needed, and she added a spiral binding that would allow pages to open flat during use. The finished product, mentioned previously, is titled *Hollyhocks and Old Maid Aunts* and has been well received by Glenda's family and friends. Several hundred copies have been sold to benefit her local archives.[1]

If you haven't been to a copy or print shop lately, you may be pleasantly surprised at the variety of options available for the working copy of a cookbook. In terms of paper, many shops offer not only acid free (which includes most current brands of copy paper) but also various colors, weights/thicknesses, and even background patterns. Sorting and stapling services can save you time and energy on your project, while cover lamination and index tabs may please your readers. Although some are sturdier than others, there is usually a wide array of binding options. Some shops offer help with clip art and layout design to add visual appeal.

Standard Commercial Binding

Several of the cookbook authors I talked to created their books with the help of a printing company that specializes in community cookbooks. Times are changing and options vary, but most result in the traditional comb-bound or spiral-bound books that are small in format, generally about 6 by 9 inches. Most companies require that you use their software, a formula approach that may be frustrating to creative authors yet a relief to those who want an easy, standardized final product.

One way to go about finding a suitable publisher is to find appealing community cookbooks and then ask if you can get feedback from someone who worked with the printing company. Or peruse websites for such companies online. Common search terms to find them include "make/print your own cookbook," "self-published cookbooks," or "fund-raiser cookbooks." Most companies put information about the publishing process on their website and will also send publishing kits to prospective authors. See the sidebar on pages 176–77.

Print-on-Demand Binding

Printing on demand can be a cost-effective and creative way to produce family cookbooks. The main difference between on-demand and traditional printers is that books are literally printed as needed; the author does not have to order a specific number of books in advance. Most publisher websites provide a cost-per-book price based on the number of pages and your design choices. Some charge fees for setup or other steps, however, so check the fine print on websites or in prospective authors' information packets carefully.

Services and options vary by company. In general, authors create books directly on the printer's website or using the printer's downloaded software, but some companies allow the uploading of book projects created with the author's own software. A variety of sizes, bindings, and color printing options are usually available. Most companies allow authors to upload their own images, and some offer a clip art library. In general, the author controls the design process to a large degree, although some print-on-demand companies require authors to use their templates. Some companies offer design packages specifically for cookbooks.

With most companies, authors can buy the books in bulk to distribute themselves, or they can allow others to purchase books through the company website or even through some online booksellers. (If selling through online booksellers is important to you, do some research. Some will only work with selected print-on-demand companies.) Find companies by using such search terms as "self-published book," "print on demand," or "custom book printing." You may also wish to add "cookbook" to your search terms, as some companies offer printing options tailored for recipes.

Organizing a Family Cookbook

There are many ways to arrange a cookbook. Perhaps the "classic" way is to organize everything by type of dish (soups, breads, and so on). But since this is a book to suit you and your family, you can decide the best order. Taking the extra step to create an index will help users find specific recipes regardless of where they appear in the book.

Chronological Cookbook. Chronological organization can take various forms. Some examples:

- Group the recipes by the decade when they were popular or when they entered the family's cooking repertoire.
- Create a seasonal cookbook that follows our ancestors' agricultural patterns of life; add recipes as they relate to planting and harvest times but also holidays, birthdays, and anniversaries.
- Focus on an individual's life, introducing chronological recipes from important occasions, milestones, and time periods. If you are focusing on a master cook from your family, you can follow the cycles of that person's cooking. (See appendix 3.)

Biographical Cookbook. Your project can focus on just the family's master cooks. Or you may want to create a large book that includes recipes grouped by family member, family unit, or generation.

⯈⯈ This list of considerations is designed to help you navigate selecting a press. Some concerns will be important to you, while others may not.

Costs

- Is there a price chart, and/or will the company provide you with a comprehensive list of fees and prices?
- Are there hidden fees or costs, such as purchasing a proof copy of the cookbook, shipping, additional printing, and/or mandatory company marketing?
- What are the payment terms, and is there a minimum order?

Templates

- Is there a template that each recipe must follow? If so, how much space does it allow for detailed recipes or personal notes?
- Does the template for the overall book contain all the parts that are important to you? (Think about cover, introduction, acknowledgments, table of contents, section dividers, index of recipes, index of contributors, and personal note pages for family information.)
- If there is an index, who will do the indexing?
- To help family members (and future researchers), will there be an easy-to-find publication date in the finished cookbook?

Recipe Collecting

- Does the company give you recipe templates to send out to family members?
- Can contributors deliver their recipes directly to the press online?
- If you do not wish to work online, will the printing company allow you to send in recipes on paper? If so, will the pages need to be typed?

Physical Attributes

- Is the cover soft, hard, or laminated?
- Does the company offer a binding that will work well as a cookbook (lie flat), and will there be a spine label to help find it on a shelf?
- What size will the finished book be?
- What colors are available for bindings, inks, pages, and covers?
- What weights of paper are available for the covers and inside pages? (Multipurpose copy paper is generally 20 pound, résumé paper 24 pound, and card stock 67 pound.)
- Is there a good choice of fonts? (You will want easy-to-read fonts throughout.)
- Can you add section dividers, printed on thicker and/or colored paper, and can they have tabs?

Archival Quality
- Are the pages acid free?
- Are the plastics or adhesives in the bindings harmful over time? (For archival copies of your cookbook, request a binding that is not glued and pages that are not laminated.)

Visual Appeal
- Can you add artwork or graphics?
- Can you add family photographs?

Production
- What is the normal production time?
- Will you be assigned a specific editor to work with?
- Do you get a proof or draft of the cookbook to look at before the rest of the copies are printed?
- Does the company automatically include cooking tips, nutritional information, and company advertisements, and can you forgo these if you don't want them?

Professional Concerns
- Who owns the copyright to the recipes and supplemental materials? This is an important question if you want to be fully in charge of who can buy a copy but also in case you ever want to reprint with another company or in a different format.
- Will the book have an International Standard Book Number (ISBN) to help with marketing?

Marketing
- If you want to make your cookbook available to the general public, does the company help with marketing?
- Can they make individual copies of your cookbook available on their website or via online booksellers?
- Is there a mail order page in the finished cookbook in case readers want additional copies?

Reprinting
- Can you reprint easily?
- Can you make changes before reprinting?

Geographic Cookbook. A cookbook arranged by geographic region makes a lot of sense for families that have moved often or have branches living in far-flung areas. For example, my mother grew up in Oregon but then moved several times while my father was in school or settling into his career—Montana, Indiana, the Georgia coast, and finally North Georgia. Her recipe box reflects each move with recipes from friends and neighbors in each location.

Even if your family stayed in one spot, a geographic cookbook can highlight locations such as the family's ancestral home place, familiar vacation spots, relatives' homes, and special travels—perhaps honeymoons or overseas journeys. Think about the foods that certain places evoke for you.

Indexes

A short cookbook can rely on a table of contents to guide users, but for larger volumes it is sometimes difficult to determine what category or section a recipe belongs in. That's where an index is a big help. To create one, simply read slowly through the final draft of the cookbook, making note of appropriate index entries along with their page numbers. You can create the list in alphabetical order, but if you are working by computer, most word processing programs will allow you to highlight your list and automatically arrange items in ascending order. "Sort" is usually the command for this feature, and it may be found in the Table menu. Consult the help guide for your word processing program if you can't find it.

Consider adding multiple entries to an index. Using my family's Teacakes recipe as an example, the index could hold an entry for the full title (Moseley Teacakes), for the simplified title (Teacakes), for the cook (Moseley, Ellen), and for the type of dish (Cookies or Desserts). You may also wish to add an entry for the recipe contributor if the recipe wasn't given by the original cook (Frey, Robert A., contributor).

Weaving in Family Facts and Materials

You could write down facts about your family and distribute the document to everyone during the family reunion, but would they keep track of it? Would they look at it again? Your chances improve if the information is woven in with your useful cookbook. These additions also give your cookbook greater visual appeal and highlight the importance of documents in historical research.

Original Recipes. Include scans of original recipes so users can see the unique handwriting of family members. Handwriting styles come and go, so reproductions can lend a historical feel to a cookbook. Including a line-by-line transcript of the recipe helps with difficult handwriting.

When my cousin Emily married, I made her a cookbook using the album-making feature of a popular online photo service. I scanned our grandmother's old recipe cards into image files, and these made up the bulk of the professionally printed book in all their homey, handwritten, and food-smudged glory. All I needed to add were some family photos both old (scanned) and new (digital) plus a few captions. The website's user-friendly interface meant I didn't need my own software or much expertise. Since the company saves project files (secured by a password), I am able to do a "save as" and instantly generate an identical cookbook that I can then tailor for other family members.

Family Charts. Names and dates can feel like a jumble to those who aren't genealogy buffs. Pedigree charts and family group charts organize the information and lend visual appeal. While they can be appendixes, they can also serve as endpapers or section dividers.

Family cookbooks created through an online photo website.

Biographical Information. A brief chronology or time line of a cook's life can be helpful and intriguing—birth, schooling, marriage, children's births, professional milestones, household moves, and other details. A description of the cook's personality, dishes, or kitchen by another family member is also a nice touch.

Photographs. Family photographs are an excellent way to intrigue readers and set a tone for the book. What will suit the tone of your cookbook best—formal portraits, casual snapshots, or a mixture? Consider adding photographs of family members at different ages or family groups over time.

Documents. Scans of documents such as a marriage certificate or a newspaper clipping adds information about the family. Excerpts from old letters or diaries (scans, transcripts, or both) can enliven a cookbook, especially if they pertain to cooking or celebrations involving food.

Familiar Details. Think about the colors and patterns that make a familiar kitchen seem dear—wallpaper, kitchen curtains, dish patterns. Capture these with your scanner or camera to add backgrounds, borders, or embellishments to a cookbook.

Giving Your Cookbook Character

Family cookbook author Glenda Major added some of her favorite poems, stories, anecdotes, and jokes to her cookbook. She said, "As a writer, I'm interested in all that. And I enjoyed poems growing up. I wanted something my grandchildren would read, not just look at for one recipe."

Family Quotes and Anecdotes. Add quotes or statements by the cook for each recipe or a "review" of the dish from family members. Short quotes can add humor and function like a quick story. One of the strengths of Major's cookbook is that she includes both old and new stories, tales about now-gone aunts but also an anecdote about a granddaughter exclaiming she had "bwain fweeze" after eating ice cream.[2] With that brief quote, Major taught her grandchild that everybody has stories. This weaves the generations together, helping younger ones see that they are part of a long line of family history. Also, Major has instantly made the cookbook even more interesting to that granddaughter's future children and grandchildren.

Jokes and Humor. In the cookbook I created for my nephews and nieces, I included several recipes from Grandma Frey, but I knew they wouldn't understand what a fun person she was just from tasting her Karo Nut Pie. I added a favorite photograph of her smiling softly, her face full of serene dignity. But I also included a picture of the two of us together when I was little. We were pretending to be princesses, so I have a mixing bowl on my head and she's wearing a tinfoil tiara. Finally, I added a classic image of what she called "pulling a mean ol' grammaw face," scowling deeply into the camera just to make her granddaughter smile.

Tiny Details. Because they are so interwoven into our lives, the family foodways we make the effort to save needn't be just those that are significant and traditional. Foodways can be small and warm. Grandpa Frey is remembered for his colorful vocabulary when it came to food. Cupcakes were always "cuppy cakes" and he talked to the fish in the frying pan, calling them "little dudes." Grandpa-related foodways include the fact that, aside from hymns at church, I only heard Grandpa sing in the kitchen, and he only sang one song. No longer clearly remembering Cab Calloway's classic "Minnie the Moocher," Grandpa stuck just to part of the chorus, and his version went something like "Heedee, heedee, hidey hoo" as he cooked. None of these details is a full story, yet can't you better picture my grandfather after reading them? A note or two can give your family cookbook charm.

Visual Appeal. Have the kids in your family create a cover, make artwork for section dividers, or illustrate recipes. Ask family members to take photographs of family artifacts or send scans of handwritten recipes to include.

Donating Cookbooks and Family Materials

Offering a copy of your finished cookbook to a local library, archives, or historical society is a generous gesture that benefits family and community members in the future. Most organizations have a collection development policy that determines what the staff can accept. If the institution would indeed like a copy, check to see what format or binding they would prefer. Many institutions place genealogy materials in "vertical files" (folders that gather loose papers and clippings on various subjects) and thus may prefer donations in an unbound format. An archivist can discuss these issues with you, and a helpful guide to donating materials can be found on the Society of American Archivists (SAA) website.[3]

Donating family materials is not only generous, but it also helps to preserve them for the future. All it takes is one household disaster or one person in a future generation deciding that family items aren't worth keeping, and everything you carefully collected could be lost. Archives are usually much safer for family materials than a private home, providing a security system, proper housing (containers), ideal climate control, and disaster planning. Another huge benefit is that family members then have equal opportunities visit the archives to use the materials, rather than everything being controlled by one person or one branch of the family.

Beyond a Cookbook

Keeping old food traditions alive gives a family a sense of identity and cohesion. Take your family foodways beyond written recipes and into daily life.

Family Gatherings. Create a monthly Yesteryear Recipe Night showcasing a single dish or offering a whole meal of dishes that are no longer typical family fare. This gives family members a reason to explore and work from old recipes, making the dishes familiar again. Some older recipes no longer fit our idea of healthy and may not be used regularly, but a special occasion gives you an excuse to bring them out. Or you now have a reason to try adjusting family recipes for modern tastes.

Try adding old-fashioned pastimes to the event. Games such as horseshoes, washers, checkers, cards, and the like became popular with families because they were inexpensive and fun. They still are. And tell a few family stories.

Make Your Own Butter. In our educational programs at the Georgia Archives, traditional butter making quickly became a favorite with kids and adults alike. It is a great activity for putting the family back in touch with agrarian, do-it-yourself roots.

Here are directions for making eight small servings of butter with the help of a group of people. (You can also make butter in a single 20-ounce container, but it will take longer.) Bring a pint of heavy whipping cream to room temperature. For flavor, you may wish to add about ⅛ teaspoon of salt and/or a sprinkling of dried herbs. Take eight small plastic containers with tight-fitting lids and fill them halfway with cream—about ¼ cup each. (The 4-ounce takeout cups that restaurants use for small side dishes work well.)

To speed up the process, add a clean glass marble or two to each container before closing securely. Wrap each container in its own paper towel to catch leaks and then pass them around for folks to shake for five to ten minutes. When the marbles no longer "thunk" the side of the container, this is because they are mired in thick cream. Shake a few minutes longer until you hear a sloshing, which means the liquid whey has separated from the butter. Drain the whey and wash the butter in very cold water. (When you have fresh butter, it's a good time to try the biscuit recipes in appendix 1!)

New Foodways. Practically any food-related activity can become a family tradition if you make an effort to repeat it. One of the most important foodways traditions in my family is our hors d'oeuvres Christmas Eve meal. When my parents were newlyweds, they realized they wouldn't be able to afford an elaborate meal when the holidays came. Thus they began to prepare several months in advance. If they had grocery money left over at the end of the week, they would purchase a jar of olives, a tin of smoked oysters, or a can of nuts to hoard in the cupboard. When the holidays finally arrived, they filled the table with a feast of small items.

Even after the family budget grew, we continued this tradition. Since my parents' deaths, my brother and I carry it on. The rest of America can have turkey and ham; I'd much rather see my table brimming with tiny gourmet items, from imported cheeses and elegant crackers to shrimp cocktail and stuffed mushrooms. A few details come and go—whether or not to use the red glass dishes or the fondue pot this year. Sometimes friends join us, adding their own favorite appetizers. But the tradition and the memories live on.

Family Cooking Website. A family recipe website means that everybody with Internet access can quickly find and use family recipes. Interviewee Annike Jones created such a site and reports it is a success.[4] She used a blog format so that new entries are instantly visible. Each recipe receives a label/tag/category (main course, breakfast, dessert) to help users find items quickly. There is also a label to help those wanting to find recipes that are quick or for beginners. Annike added clip art and family photos for visual appeal. An additional feature is that users can post comments or cooking tips about each recipe.

Annike notes, "I love having recipes that my grandma used to use, and some that I remember from my childhood. The same goes for my mom—she's posted recipes that were favorites in our house and from old friends from when I was young that I'm so glad I have. I love the way everyone includes a little note of explanation with each recipe. It makes me feel like I'm baking a bit of history!"

꙳ As this book project drew to a close, I made one more trip to New Edinburg, Arkansas. The night before Thanksgiving, Cousin Norma pulled a kitchen stool up to the counter for my young son. Just as she once taught me to make biscuits, she taught Eli to make pecan pie. They used nuts from the tree Grandpa Frey planted long ago. On that chilly November night, the two worked side by side in the same warm old kitchen where Grandpa and Grandma used

to work side by side. It is the same space where I long ago ate (or balked at eating) Squirrel Mulligan but also where I tried my hand at Ellen Moseley's Teacakes for the first time, fashioning them into little stars. All these years later, while the scent of toasted pecans and caramelized sugar wafted from the oven, Norma and I told Eli stories about other Thanksgivings, other pies, other people who once walked that kitchen floor. The sweet fragrance of the pie became a part of the afterglow.

Reader, wherever "home" is located, whatever "family" means to you, and whichever recipes you choose to preserve, I wish you just that sort of sweetness.

APPENDIX ONE

Exploring a Recipe

The Quest for the Extraordinary Biscuit

One of the saddest things is the sound of them whomp biscuits being opened in more and more houses these days.—Comedian Jerry Clower on canned biscuits

Digging Into a Recipe

Each chapter in this book has offered an organized collection of advice and tips on some aspect of working with family recipes. The appendixes take a different approach, giving you the chance to observe someone else's process—a bit like hanging out in the kitchen with Cousin Joe watching him cook.

This appendix focuses on adjusting a recipe. With a nod to Nathalie Dupree's classic cookbook *Southern Memories: Recipes and Reminiscences*, I call it my Quest for the Extraordinary Biscuit.[1] I realize this is a larger quest than you will probably tackle for an heirloom recipe, but treat this appendix like a covered dish supper. Partake of the information that is most helpful right now while keeping in mind what you might like to come back for later.

Chapter 3 discussed becoming an expert on the recipe you're tweaking. It doesn't have to be an overwhelming task. After collecting a base biscuit recipe from a family member, I searched for comparison recipes starting with my own cookbooks. A couple of evenings while my husband and I watched baseball, I surfed recipe websites. Then I set aside a quiet, rainy Saturday afternoon to plunk myself down in the library's cookbook section. Every time I came across a new insight into the how or why of a process or an idea for how to tweak a biscuit recipe, I wrote down my findings. Since it was for this book, I collected all types of biscuit know-how rather than just the specifics of how to tweak the recipe for my own needs. I also wrote out full explanations rather than merely jotting notes. Still, this appendix will give you a feel for the process.

Why biscuits? On a practical level, biscuits are inexpensive and quick—helpful for testing umpteen batches. They also taste darn good. What do we already know about biscuits? Say the word and it conjures up a small, round baked good that is somewhat bland, more savory than sweet. Picture golden and flaky on the outside but pale and fluffy on the inside.

Considered by many to be a breakfast food, biscuits nonetheless appear as miniature ham sandwich appetizers, a soup sidekick, or a layer in the strawberry shortcake. Some cooks add cheese or spices, while purists insist additions must only be to the finished biscuit—butter, preserves, perhaps an old-fashioned slathering of sorghum or cane syrup. Sometimes biscuits are smothered in various types of gravy. For a lucky few with the recipe, this can be Chocolate Gravy. (Don't worry. By chapter's end, you'll be one of the lucky few.)

But there is more than just frugality, taste, and creativity to recommend biscuits as a model for a book about preserving family recipes. They are, in the minds of many, quite southern—a regional icon. They evolved within a relatively short period of time, allowing me to dip into their history during visits to various archives. Biscuits are also very simple in theory—less than a half dozen ingredients and just a few steps. This makes it easy to see when historical recipes were becoming more akin to modern recipes. (See appendix 2 for the history of biscuits.) At the same time, their very simplicity highlights how complex baking can be.

Cookbook author Alton Brown states, "Standard everyday cooking is relatively forgiving. Baking is rarely so. In fact, baked goods are a great deal like cars: You can change the wheel covers, put in new mats, and change out the stereo, but if you're going to mess around under the hood, you'd better know what you're doing or you may wind up taking the bus."[2] After taking a close look at perfecting a baked good, a complex process, it will be easier for you to apply the process to simpler recipes.

The Beginning of a Quest

Still another reason I chose to study biscuits involves family. My grandma, Arlie Mae Reaves Frey, was the biscuit maker for her household after she married. A brain tumor in the mid-1950s, however, left her unable to manage the hand motions required for the biscuit expertise passed down from the mother she deeply loved and admired. Grandma and her mother wrote down many family recipes, but her handwritten notebook somehow got knocked into the kitchen trash can. Grandma saw her mistake as she emptied the trash into the burn barrel, but those heirloom recipes were instantly beyond saving. I'm trying to replace lost family knowledge.

By all accounts, Great-Grandma El Myra Trammell Reaves (1882–1950) was loving, yet sometimes described as "stern." That doesn't surprise me in a woman orphaned at fourteen who delayed marriage to help raise younger siblings. There was a soft side long remembered—helping her oldest daughter fill the house with flowers for teen parties, dresses sewn without patterns after seeing my grandmother's longing glances at shop windows, and indulging grandchildren with grape soda. I realize now that part of wanting to learn how to make appealing biscuits (as well as her signature gingerbread) is an attempt to catch a wisp of an intriguing family member that I missed out on meeting.

El Myra Trammell Reaves in her late teens, ca. 1900.

When I started my biscuit quest, Great-Grandma Reaves still had four living grandchildren old enough to remember her.[3] All spoke of her biscuits fondly, yet none knew specific ingredients or proportions. Only two months after my interview, oldest grandchild Sue died. Now I treasure her recorded reminisces. Through her eyes, I can see Great-Grandma Reaves using a corn shock mop and lye to scrub the wood floors around the wood-burning stove where the biscuits were made daily.

The second oldest grandchild, Buddy, remembered Great-Grandma's method was to shape biscuits in her hands rather than cut them out. He was an excellent cook in his own right, but now he is also gone. I'm glad that thanks to my family foodways research, I can click on my computer to hear his voice one more time. About his grandmother's biscuits, he admitted with true Buddy wit, "They were always smooth. And mine look like they've been shot out of a slingshot."

El Myra Trammell Reaves in her sixties, ca. 1946.

The next two grandchildren, Norma and Jimmy, were fairly young when their grandmother died and remember less. Still, both know a good bit about traditional southern cooking. In the absence of Great-Grandma's biscuit

Lovett T. Reaves (1882–1965) with his grandchildren, ca. 1945. From left to right, Norma, Jimmy, Sue, and Buddy.

recipe, I set out to gather whatever tips I could and made biscuits alongside Norma, Jimmy, and Jimmy's wife, Michelle. I hadn't made biscuits in a while. I soon remembered the sensuous, hands-on pleasures of soft flour and chilly buttermilk transformed into a hot comfort food.

Ready? Here we go.

A Note on the Extraordinary Biscuit

One of the many odd things about human beings is that we don't all like the same things. I suppose if we did, the world would be a boring place. In terms of the Extraordinary Biscuit, however, that means that when I'm ready to shout, "I've done it!" you may take a biscuit out of the same pan and decide it really should be a little more browned. Or flakier. Or taller. If you were in the kitchen with me during the baking, you might have muttered to yourself that I should have used cream rather than buttermilk. Such judgments are a matter of personal taste, yet they also reflect cultural and regional differences.

The curator of decorative arts at the Georgia Museum of Art, Dale Couch has a keen eye for cultural patterns across time. He spent his childhood in lower Aiken County, South Carolina, but his family was spread between Edgefield and Charleston. When I interviewed Dale about biscuits,[5] he spoke of a connection between biscuits and geography.

"In my background, there are an enormous variety of biscuits. Now, this is in part because we were on the Fall Line and our culture was a mixture of

Upcountry and Low Country," he said. "There were several dialects represented in my family—the people who said 'fah-tha' and the people who said 'far-ther.' The biscuits varied with that." His mother's roots were in the Low Country. Buttermilk biscuits were predominant, although his great-aunt Mat used sweet milk. His maternal grandmother Turner was known for her tall, fluffy biscuits. Meanwhile, on his father's side of the family, Aunt Myrtis's biscuits were "about three inches in diameter and were thin and crackerlike."

Also on the paternal side of Dale's family, beaten biscuits sometimes appeared at the table. He noted, "Towards the 1970s, they became more of a cocktail thing used in households as a teatime sort of food." In addition, they ate cathead biscuits, hand-formed biscuits usually described as large and somewhat lumpy, and his aunt Liziella on his father's side made angel biscuits, a hybrid between a biscuit and a roll that called for mayonnaise in the dough.

With such a variety of biscuit recipes, just choosing what type to try first is a major decision. And then there is actually tweaking the recipe. To showcase the know-how I gathered, I arranged information by ingredient and cooking variable. A few tips couldn't be transferred to other biscuit recipes, but I organized the rest of my findings below to give you, the potential biscuit cook, clues on how to find your way to your own Extraordinary Biscuit.

There are, however, three basic ground rules that apply to any biscuit you're going to make:

1. *Select fresh, quality ingredients.* They don't have to be expensive, just good quality. Biscuits rely heavily on chemical reactions, so make sure your leavenings are fresh and up to the task. Biscuits also depend on fats, which change in taste and sometimes consistency as they age.

2. *Properly handle dough.* In his book *Classical Southern Cooking*, Damon Lee Fowler explains: "When quick biscuit dough is overworked, the fat melts and the glutens are excited into action. The final result is heavy, greasy, and tough. However, biscuit dough must be worked some after it is mixed, or the bread will be uneven and crumbly. The secret is a light, judicious, and preferably cool hand."[6] How do you know when your handling is just right? That question brings us to the final rule.

3. *Practice.*

Foundation Recipe for the Search

Before beginning to compare or tweak recipes, you must have a basic knowledge of the crucial ingredients. For biscuits, these are some form of flour, leavening, salt, fat, and liquid. Various techniques will transform these ingredients into biscuits.

For my quest, Cousin Norma was the first to share her time-tested recipe.[7] I recorded it so that it could become my starting point. She learned to make biscuits from watching relatives cook, converting the process over time to suit her own needs and to make use of new products such as nonstick cooking spray and the toaster oven. In her recipe, the flour, leavening, and salt are already combined in the self-rising flour. The fat, in this case oil, also contributes toward the liquid requirement.

Norma Reaves McCoy's Quick Biscuits

1⅔ cups self-rising flour (with extra for working the dough)
¾ cup 2 percent milk
2 tablespoons canola oil or bacon grease
Nonstick cooking spray

Stir first three ingredients in a bowl with a spoon until just mixed. Put extra flour into a second bowl and turn dough out into it. Roll dough in the flour until just coated. Spray nonstick spray into small (9 x 9) baking pan. Pinch off some dough the size you wish your biscuit to be and pat it into the pan. (For this amount of dough, four to six biscuits is a good goal.) Give each biscuit a bit of room in the pan. Spray the tops of the biscuits with cooking spray or rub with extra bacon grease. Bake in regular oven at 425° or toaster oven at 325°F. If using toaster oven, you may need to move temperature to 350° at the end to ensure brownness. Baking time is simply until golden brown and varies by size of oven and size of biscuits. Expected baking times are 12 to 15 minutes for the regular oven and 20 to 25 for the toaster oven.

One of the first things I learned when beginning to compare this recipe with others is that oil-based biscuit recipes are less common than ones calling for shortening or butter. Recipes with solid fats usually require an extra step when mixing—first blending the dry ingredients with the fat, and then adding and mixing in the liquid.

Myra Reaves with her granddaughter Norma in the mid-1940s.

General Notes on Ingredients

As stressed earlier in this book, using proper measuring techniques for all ingredients is important. Another aspect to keep in mind with the ingredients is that a blend often works well. Mississippi native and longtime food editor for the *New York Times* Craig Claiborne remarked that the biscuits from Mrs. Wilkes' Boardinghouse, a restaurant in Savannah, were "one of the greatest things, ever, to happen in my life."[8] Mrs. Wilkes's recipe calls for both shortening and butter (or margarine) as well as a blend of buttermilk and whole milk.[9] Claiborne's own recipe for Southern Biscuits calls for a blend of baking powder and baking soda.[10]

Notes on the basic ingredients follow below in the order in which they are used in most biscuit recipes.

Flour. Wheat flour provides the basic structure for your biscuits.

Food writer Robert St. John notes that adding more flour will result in a denser biscuit.[11] Aside from simply the amount, flour's protein (gluten) content varies widely and also greatly affects your results. Hard wheat is higher in protein content than soft wheat, and this makes for a stiff or elastic texture in dough. The flours highest in protein, generally 13 percent or more, are used in making pastas. Bread flour is also high in protein. All-purpose and self-rising flours generally range from 12 to 9 percent protein. Low-protein flour, between 9 percent and 6 percent, is usually sold as "pastry flour" or "cake flour." Mid to low protein content is recommended for biscuits.

Culinary historian John Martin Taylor writes, "The perfect biscuit is largely in the choice of flour," and "Anyone can make a good biscuit with soft southern flour."[12] The problem, however, is that most bags of flour don't list the protein content or origin, so you may stand in the grocery store baffled about what to buy. Georgia cooking expert Mrs. S. R. Dull offered one criterion, but it requires getting your hands in the bag: "To test for pastry flour, squeeze tight a handful of flour and if it clings together and shows each finger print and wrinkle, it is a pastry flour."[13] The table in Shirley O. Corriher's *CookWise* is quite helpful at the purchasing point, giving protein contents of major brands.[14]

Since southern flours tend to be lower in protein, I quickly became loyal to White Lily. A worrisome note, however, is that White Lily, produced since 1883 in Knoxville, Tennessee, was purchased by a northern company in 2007 and soon began producing flour at two plants in the Midwest. According to a 2008 newspaper article, the company has promised bakers "won't know the difference."[15] In my kitchen it is "so far, so good." If you cannot find your preferred brand, perhaps you can take a tip from the *Cook's Illustrated* recipe for Fluffy Biscuits and use half all-purpose and half cake flour.[16]

Aside from protein content, there are other flour choices. Bleached flour usually has chemical whiteners, so my personal choice for all-purpose flour is unbleached even though my biscuits are not quite as pale inside. I wanted to learn to make classic biscuits, so I steered away from whole-wheat or non-wheat flours, but your research and testing may come up with successful biscuits using these alternates.

Leavening. Baking powder or soda, through a chemical reaction created by heat and moisture, produces bubbles of gas to create texture within the structure-giving flour.[17]

One of the first batches of biscuits I made on my own after beginning The Quest turned out horribly—bland and gluey. I had been so intent on following the recipe exactly that I didn't notice how few ingredients there were. When Cousin Norma told me "flour," she meant self-rising, while I took it to mean all-purpose. It was a good lesson on the importance not only of leavening but also of clarified recipe writing! To substitute all-purpose, suggestions vary from adding 1¼ to 1½ teaspoons of baking powder and ⅛ to ½ teaspoon of salt per cup.

Does more leavening mean a lighter biscuit? In *Bill Neal's Southern Cooking* the author warns, "Extra leavening will not compensate for lack of technique: in excess, baking powder tastes bitter and discolors the finished product."[18] Virginia cookbook author Edna Lewis found that some commercial baking powders leave an aftertaste regardless of amount. *The Gift of Southern Cooking*, a cookbook she coauthored with Atlanta chef Scott Peacock, provides a recipe for making your own using cream of tartar and baking soda.[19] It may also help to look for a brand of leavening that does not contain aluminum.

There are a few additional leavening tips to keep in mind. The leavening in self-rising flour may age more quickly than isolated leavening in a sealed container. *Joy of Cooking* authors Irma Rombauer and Marion Becker suggest replacing unused self-rising flour more often than all-purpose.[20] They also note that if your leavening isn't well distributed, brown spots may show on the surface of the baked biscuits.[21]

Salt. This ingredient provides flavor.

When biscuits are made with butter, cream, or milk, it can be particularly important to balance out the sweetness of the dairy with salt. When adjusting the amount of salt in a recipe, don't forget "hidden" salt that may already be in your butter or self-rising flour. As for particular types of salt such as sea or kosher, I never found a recipe that called for anything special, but you may wish to experiment.

Fat. "Fat" has become a word to be avoided in our society, but the fact is that this ingredient provides crucial moisture and texture in biscuits. The word "shortening" is now used most often for plant-based fats but can also mean lard or other animal fats, although usually a rendered fat rather than dairy based.

In the past, southern biscuits were usually made with pig fat. I must admit that contemplating making my own batch with lard was difficult. Quite frankly, I felt as though my arteries might harden on the spot, and I also couldn't get the image of a pig carcass out of my head. The latter reaction is rather amusing, considering how much bacon I've eaten in my life and also the fact that my generation is likely the first in centuries never to witness the slaughtering of a hog. However, after Georgia biscuit master Bonnie Crowley made me a batch, I had to agree with John Martin Taylor when he said, "The flakiest biscuits are made with fresh lard."[22]

Today, most recipes use vegetable shortening, butter, or a combination. A few use oil. Bacon grease is sometimes used in combination with other fats or to coat the finished biscuits and will impart a distinctive flavor. When substituting fats in a recipe, oil and butter will slightly reduce the amount of liquid needed, as oil is a liquid itself and butter contains more moisture than most shortenings. As for margarine, it can be made with a variety of ingredients and often has high water content, so it may take some work to adjust a biscuit recipe for this type of fat. Using only the stick form of margarine formulated for baking should help. Personally, I always lean toward butter because of the flavor, melting quality, and nonchemical nature.

My mother's old standby, *Betty Crocker's Picture Cook Book* from 1956, has a recipe for Stir-N-Roll Biscuits that promise to be quick to make and easy to clean up.[23] This recipe uses oil, a liquid fat, allowing all the ingredients to be mixed together at the same time. The easy biscuits do taste good. But, again, personal preferences vary and I found myself gravitating toward butter for added flavor. I also have come to agree with contemporary cooking guru

Martha Stewart that adding extra butter to the recipe makes fluffier biscuits.[24] One of the tips a friend gave me long ago is that frozen butter can be dispersed into dough in small, easily softened bits by using a fine cheese grater.[25]

Liquid. Liquid lends moisture to the biscuit dough, which helps to activate other ingredients and creates steam.

Milk, buttermilk, and water are the typical liquids called for in southern biscuit recipes. One of the tips Cousin Norma gave me about liquids is that

biscuits with buttermilk don't rise quite as much as ones containing milk, yet it does give a good flavor. To give milk a taste more akin to buttermilk, you can alter it with a kitchen acid. A 1936 cookbooklet for Arm & Hammer Baking Soda suggests placing a tablespoon of white vinegar or lemon juice in a cup and then adding ¾ cup milk to create "soured" milk.[26] Altering the acid/base balance (pH) of your recipe, however, may change how it rises.

A mixture of more than one liquid often works well. Fannie Farmer included two baking powder biscuit recipes in her 1896 cookbook—the lard version calls for half milk and half water while the butter version calls only for milk.[27] And there are alternatives. The Flying Biscuit Café in Atlanta uses light cream in its wonderful biscuits.[28] Damon Lee Fowler's Soda Biscuits recipe calls for either buttermilk or all-natural yogurt.[29] When it comes to liquids, necessity truly can be the mother of invention. One day I discovered my fridge was devoid of dairy completely— except for my husband's leftover vanilla milkshake. It worked like a charm and gave a nice flavor too. I found reconstituted powdered milk will also do in a pinch, although most powders are nonfat, so you may need to adjust your recipe accordingly.

I mentioned that liquids in biscuit dough will create steam. Some recipes recommend piercing the biscuits with a fork dipped in flour before baking to allow excess steam to escape.

Sugar. The occasional biscuit recipe calls for sugar, which not only provides flavor but also can serve as a tenderizer and a browning agent.[30] The most sugar I've seen in a regular biscuit recipe is about two tablespoons per batch of six biscuits.

The Hybrid Biscuit and the Creative Biscuit

There are many variations on the biscuit that call for unusual ingredients. Angel biscuits usually contain yeast and are something of a cross between a biscuit and a roll. In my Arkansas family, these popular baked items are called Buddy Biscuits since Cousin Buddy found the recipe in the newspaper and shared it with his siblings.[31] Cream biscuits and drop biscuits may be more traditional, the former made with cream as the liquid and the latter created with a softer dough, yet some recipes contain eggs, yeast, or even cooked potato.[32]

Some biscuits use flours other than wheat. A 1918 cookbooklet from the Royal Baking Powder Company, *Best War Time Recipes*, contains recipes that reduce or eliminate traditional flour by replacing it with oatmeal, barley, or rye.[33]

The relatively bland taste of biscuits makes a good base for a variety of creative flavors added to the dough—sausage or bacon crumbles, cheese, cooked sweet potato, raisins, spices, or herbs, for example. Interestingly, during an interview in my grandparents' county, a woman named Norma Jean Hensley told me her neighbor made biscuit dough in which he substituted the usual liquid with juice (pot liquor) from cooked turnip greens. "First you have to get over the color. They're kinda green. But they will taste like real buttermilk, a sort of sour taste."[34] (When I tried this in my own kitchen, my kindergartener would only eat the biscuits while holding his nose. They tasted like buttermilk biscuits but smelled like greens.)

Adjusting Aspects of a Biscuit

The ingredients are only part of the equation for creating a pleasing biscuit. The next step is examining techniques. Rather than present a hodgepodge of tips, I found it more sensible to organize them in terms of how they affect various aspects of the finished biscuits. You can then choose the aspects most important to you and zero in on methods to help create your extraordinary biscuit.

Temperature. In his book *Gracious Plenty*, John T. Edge points out that biscuits should be served hot.[35] Heat means more fragrance, softer texture, and steamy moisture—a pleasure to hold in the hand and savor in a bite.

Diameter. When it comes to size, unleash your imagination. I used to use the inside circle of a donut cutter to make biscuits just slightly over an inch across that my family called Thimble Biscuits. (This name is also used sometimes for thick biscuits with a nest for jam cut out of the top with a small cutter.) Similarly, the Carriage House Restaurant in Natchez, Mississippi, is known for "itty-bitty" biscuits the size of silver dollars.[36] On the other size of the scale, when I was growing up in Athens, Georgia, there was a small grocery store called Thrasher's that sold homemade biscuits rumored to be cut out using the rim of a coffee can, about five inches in diameter. You needed both hands to eat one.[37]

There are some general considerations when adjusting biscuit size in a recipe. In general, you'll need a denser, more substantial dough for larger biscuits, particularly if they are rolled and cut. Baking time will increase with size. Also, size affects the ratio of exterior and interior. As cookbook author Nathalie Dupree stated, "Personally, I don't want too big a biscuit, because I enjoy the brown outside as much as the inside."[38] With all due respect, I have to admit I prefer the soft inside to the brown outside, so making larger biscuits appeals to me.

I own a variety of biscuit cutters both new and antique, but hand-forming is perhaps the easiest way to make larger biscuits. The best full description I've found of large "cathead" biscuits can be found in Joseph E. Dabney's book on Appalachian cooking.[39] Basically, this type of biscuit is pinched off rather than cut out, so the size is left up to the cook's preference.

If you are in the process of tweaking a biscuit recipe, hand-formed biscuits can be problematic; it is difficult to be specific about dough size when writing recipe notes. For example, the primary biscuit recipe in *Charleston Receipts*, a Junior League cookbook that has been popular for more than half a century, reads, "Take a good forkful of dough . . ."[40] Keeping track of how many biscuits your hand-formed batch makes will help, but you can also measure the average height and diameter.

Of course, the largest biscuits of all take up the whole pan. Cousin Buddy recalled when Great-Grandpa Reaves made breakfast on early mornings before going hunting. "He'd make biscuits, but he'd just make up his biscuit dough and not roll them out. He'd pour it all into the pan. He'd make one big biscuit and we'd sit down and break off a chunk of it."[41]

Height. *Betty Crocker's Picture Cook Book* informs us that "'Southern' type biscuits are thin and rich; 'Northern' types are thick, plainer biscuits."[42] I'll leave it up to you to decide if this is true. I've certainly eaten some lovely, tall southern biscuits. However, according to Nathalie Dupree, "Too thick a biscuit requires too much baking powder to reach an appealing height, and a strong taste of baking powder can ruin a biscuit."[43] I've eaten the sort of biscuit she's talking about and agree with her. After many taste tests, I have decided that texture and flavor are more important to me. There are, however, additional methods to increase biscuit height.

Interviewee Dale Couch recalled his grandmother Turner's belief in the temperature of ingredients affecting biscuit height. "She made a fluffy biscuit but always put ice in the buttermilk she was going to add. I remember she insisted that everything should be cold and worked quickly. That affected the rising of the biscuits. And they were huge things—taller than life and fluffy." He added, "If you pulled them apart, you usually could butter the top third, the middle, and the bottom. You could butter them in two places. It was like a sin! I mean, you put butter on all that flour and lard! I'd lie to tell you there was anything better."

Many recipes stress cold ingredients. *Home Helps*, a cookbook produced by a now-extinct brand of shortening called Cottolene, even recommended chilling the shortening.[44]

Interviewee Greg Jarrell, raised in the foothills of the Appalachians by his grandparents, also talked about tall biscuits, but his family used another method to achieve them. "If we wanted tall biscuits, we would roll them thin and then stack them in three layers. You would roll out your biscuits, cut them out, put them in your pan. Then you'd roll out another layer, wetting it with

buttermilk and stack the layers that way. When you baked it, it came out real tall and fluffy and it would very easily pull apart in layers." Family cookbook author Glenda Major included a recipe for Aunt Marguerite's Alabama Biscuits that contained yeast but were also rolled, cut, and stacked (two layers) before baking.[45]

Jarrell also noted that his grandmother (born ca. 1897) owned various-sized tin cans with the top and bottom cut out that she used as biscuit cutters. While cookie bakers of the past often used a drinking glass for cutting circles out of dough, biscuit cutters were a common kitchen tool to solve multiple problems arising with thick, tender dough. The ideal biscuit cutter is open or has holes in the top, allowing a finger or kitchen tool to dislodge stuck biscuits but also keeping air pressure inside the cutter from compressing the dough. In addition, a cutter should be sharp enough to cut cleanly. Several recipe sources warned that cut-out biscuits may not rise as high if a blunt cutting edge seals the sides of the dough. Many recipes also warn cooks not to twist the cutter for the same reason.

Interior Tenderness. A large number of cookbooks cite overhandling of the dough as a cause of tough and dense biscuits. (Purists will not reuse scraps of dough from cutting out biscuits for this reason.) Food writer Molly O'Neill states that tenderness "is a result of how quickly the liquid is added to the butter and flour meal. The faster it's done, the less gluten develops and the more tender the result."[46] Interviewee Paula Eubanks wrote in her family cookbook about mixing biscuits:

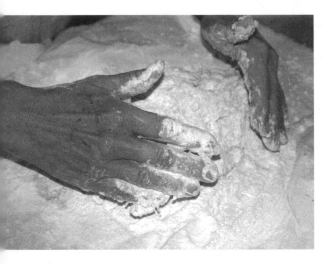

Paula Eubanks preparing to knead the biscuit dough, 2008.

Knead very lightly; it should be soft and delicate. Too much handling and the biscuits will be tough. If the dough feels too hard, if you push down and it pushes back, you can compensate by letting the finished, uncooked biscuits sit for an hour or so before baking. Flour has gluten in it that gets all tense when you mix it after liquid has been added. Letting the biscuits rest lets the gluten relax so the biscuits won't be tough and hard— reminds me of people who get really mad and after awhile relax and forget about it. Aunt Merle, a home economics teacher, explained the scientific end of all this to me when she spent time with us during her summers off. Undermixing will yield very soft, tender biscuits that crumble when cut in two. The ideal is a biscuit that is tender inside, crisp on the outside, that holds together when cut but melts in your mouth.[47]

The World War II–era *Favorite Recipes for Country Kitchens* put out by General Foods stated that uncooked biscuits resting briefly after being cut out will spring into a more even shape.[48] The amount of liquid in the dough and the heat of the area where the uncooked biscuits are waiting will affect how much of the leavening is activated before the oven. Professional bakers measuring how well dough can withstand a delay before baking call this "bench tolerance."[49]

Sifting is also a key to adjusting tenderness. After reading the recipe for Soda Biscuit in *Mrs. Hill's New Cook Book*, published just after the Civil War, I decided to see if the author was right about sifting making a lighter biscuit.[50] She was. Many modern recipes call for double sifting—once for just the flour and a second time after the addition of other dry ingredients.

This sifter was marketed to readers of the *Boston Cooking School Magazine* in May 1909.

Interior flakes and layers are often mentioned as optimal results in biscuits. According to *The Joy of Cooking*, "A light hand in kneading gives the treasured flaky result."[51] James Villas, in his book *My Mother's Southern Kitchen*, echoes this idea when relaying his mother's directions for making biscuits. At the point of cutting the shortening into the flour, she instructed him in making gentle strokes, saying, "Don't crush those lumps so much! They're what makes the biscuit flaky."[52]

But perhaps Dale Couch's grandmother was onto something with her idea about cold ingredients. Food writer Molly O'Neill states that the key to "optimum flake" comes from "quickly incorporating *very* cold butter—it can be chilled in the freezer—into the dry ingredients with the skill and alacrity usually reserved for making a perfect pie crust."[53] *The Encyclopedia of Appalachia* similarly states that "the shortening and liquids used should be icy cold and the oven very hot during baking. It is the juxtaposition of temperatures that causes the shortening to explode between the layers of dough, giving good biscuits their airy and flaky texture."[54]

Still other sources suggest mechanical methods to ensure layers. *Southern Living* magazine printed a buttermilk biscuit recipe that explained a layer-building technique in which the rolled-out dough is folded several times "as if folding a letter-size piece of paper."[55]

Exterior Crust. Early twentieth-century cooking expert Mrs. Dull warned not to crowd biscuits in the pan.[56] As much as I respect this late, great lady, I have to disagree! She sought uniformly golden biscuits, whereas I think biscuits bumped up next to each other in the pan have wonderfully soft sides. I even managed to find a six-sided biscuit cutter capable of creating a pan of biscuits loosely fitted together like a honeycomb.[57] And a biscuit scrunched up against its neighbor will also rise up rather than spreading out, according to cooking expert Shirley Corriher.[58]

Many recipes for baked goods—including Craig Claiborne's for Southern Biscuits—call for baking on a shiny surface.[59] A dark or matte-texture pan tends to create biscuits with darker and thicker bottoms. With my preference for a soft crust, I use a very thick, shiny, restaurant-grade aluminum baking sheet. If you don't have such a pan, lining a dark one with white parchment paper may help a little.

"Anointing" the tops of the biscuits is another way to affect the biscuits' exterior. Mrs. Dull suggests biscuits can be brushed with milk before baking to give them a sort of glaze.[60] For a softer finish, quite a few recipes recommend brushing the tops with butter when the biscuits are still warm.

Flavor. Several sources pointed out the common sense of using ingredients with more flavor to make a more flavorful biscuit. Buttermilk has more flavor than milk or water. Butter or bacon grease has more flavor than shortening or oil. Multiple sources also stated that while self-rising flour is fine for the dough, flouring your work surface with plain flour will prevent sharp flavors from excess salt and leavening on the crust of the biscuits.

Additional Biscuit Methods

There are some biscuit techniques that affect the entire biscuit rather than a certain aspect. I have grouped these below by step.

Mixing Dry Ingredients with Fat. Fannie Farmer in 1896 instructed cooks to use their fingertips.[61] Mrs. Dull approved of this method as well, yet also indicated it was fine to "chop in" shortening with a spoon.[62] Once I changed from using oil in biscuits to butter, I started using a pastry blender. But I soon switched to my fingers. Although fingers can bring unwanted warmth to dough if you aren't quick, I can feel the texture better this way. (And it pleases the childlike part of myself that once adored making mud pies.)

Speaking of texture, Mrs. Wilkes and many others often describe the properly mixed fat/dry combination as like course cornmeal.[63] Although I find the consistency more akin to grits, my biscuits got better when I paid more attention to texture. At first I thought I might be overmixing at this step, but found a Tennessee recipe that calls for about eighty strokes with a pastry blender, indicating this is a longer process than I originally thought.[64]

Professional chef and cookbook author Scott Peacock points out that at this stage the mixture can be set aside for many hours. He will mix biscuits to this point and refrigerate them so that it is quick and easy to finish the biscuits just before a meal.[65]

Adding Liquid. Once the liquid is added to the other ingredients, *The Joy of Cooking* recommends, "The time for stirring should be a scant ½ minute." After turning the dough out onto a floured surface, it further recommends handling the dough for another scant half minute, "just long enough so it is neither knobby or sticky, and the riser is well distributed."[66] Mrs. Wilkes helpfully states, "Knead by picking up the sides of the dough away from you while pressing down with the palms of your hands and pushing the dough away. Repeat 6 or 7 times. Work the dough into a large ball while kneading. Keep your fingers dry by frequently dipping them in dry flour."[67]

With a few of my first batches of biscuits, I was so wary of overhandling dough that I barely touched it after adding the liquid and ended up with biscuits that fell apart. A kitchen visit with local biscuit master Bonnie Crowley helped me be a little bolder about kneading (see appendix 2). Bill Neal, author of *Bill Neal's Southern Cooking*, warns against overhandling, yet adds, "You will knead slightly, however, to give this unsupported dough enough stretched gluten to maintain its shape and height."[68]

Cutting Dough. My great-grandmother and many other cooks in the Arkansas family, past and present, formed biscuits with their hands. I'm not very good at making them uniform in size, however, so I always reached for my rolling pin. After I saw interviewee Paula Eubanks spread biscuit dough by simply patting it with her hands, I now have one kitchen utensil fewer to clean. Patted-out dough still works well with a biscuit cutter.

After watching a friend in Texas use a set of nesting stainless steel biscuit cutters, I had to find my own—one of the most useful souvenirs I've ever brought home. I don't have to worry about rust and have a choice of four sizes. Normally I use the larger cutters, although for parties where biscuits are served as appetizers, I use the smallest. The small cutter is also good for using up tiny patches of uncut dough for biscuits that instantly appeal to kids.

Dough can be spread to any thickness desired, of course. Rombauer and Becker suggested ¼ inch for plain biscuits.[69] According to the restaurant's cookbook, the biscuits for the famous Mary Mac's Tea Room in Atlanta are cut from dough an inch thick.[70] The majority of cut biscuit recipes like Jessica B. Harris's in *The Welcome Table: African-American Heritage Cooking*, call for ½ inch thick dough.[71]

Hand Shaping Dough. There are quite a few ways to shape biscuits, and the names for the methods can vary widely. I once watched a heated argument between two southern cooks about whether a "cathead biscuit" is the same as a "drop biscuit." (One said cathead biscuits were lumpy and flour dusted while drop biscuits were smooth. The other said the finished texture was irrelevant.) Fist biscuits are another type. Someone somewhere will probably argue hotly about whether this means the dough is rolled into a log so that individual biscuits can be pulled away in the cook's fist or whether the dough is rolled into balls and mashed flat with a fist. Kathy Starr, in *The Soul of Southern Cooking*, gives a recipe for the former, describing forming the dough into a long roll "until it resembles a rolling pin."[72]

Heat. Some sources say the oven should preheat for a half hour to ensure even temperature throughout the cooking space. Temperatures are generally quite hot for biscuits, but recommendations vary. *The Joy of Cooking* offers recipes that range from 400° to 475°F, depending on the ingredients.[73] Louis and Billie Van Dyke, authors of *The Blue Willow Inn Bible of Southern Cooking*, recommend 475° for their buttermilk biscuits.[74] Scott Peacock recommends 500° for his recipe.[75]

Baking temperature and baking time may both need to increase as the size and thickness of the biscuit increases, and also as the density of the dough and size of the oven increases.

Cleanup Tricks. Cutting out dough does mean a floured countertop to clean up, but the edge of a pancake turner or spatula works very well to scrape up the flour and crumbs. A plastic ice scraper intended for a car windshield works well too; I have a clean one I bought just for that purpose. Working on a silicone mat is a way to avoid messy countertops altogether. And because it can go directly into the oven, making biscuits with the mat may mean you can handle the dough less.

When cleaning up, remember that heat causes the protein particles in flour to bind to each other. If you're ready to wipe down a floury countertop or rinse a floury bowl, using cold water at first will make the job easier.

A Few Unusual Biscuit Sidekicks

When I discussed biscuits with others, I began to hear about interesting toppings and recipes connected with them. These tips and tricks are examples of endearing family foodways, yet they may slowly disappear now that biscuits are not an everyday item for most households.

Speckled Hen. This simple topping for biscuits came from Georgia interviewee Rachel O'Neal, who learned it from her Smithville, Tennessee, grandfather: "Get a glob of butter, pour molasses over it, and mash it with a fork until it looks good." The mixture resembles the feathers of a multicolored chicken.

Orange Glaze. Carole Cohen of Savannah shared a cooking tip she learned as a bride in the Georgia Low Country: You'll need a couple of tablespoons of frozen orange juice concentrate—do not add water, but do allow it to thaw. One at a time, dip sugar cubes into the melted concentrate and place one atop each biscuit just before putting the pan into the oven. The biscuits come out with a flavorful glaze. (The hot glaze may run, so use a pan with an edge.)[76]

Chocolate Gravy. My cousin Joe Robert McClellan and his wife, Louise, both from south-central Arkansas, shared this regional recipe:[77]

¼ cup cocoa
¼ cup self-rising flour
⅓ cup sugar
1½ cups water or milk (plus a little extra)

Mix dry ingredients well, then add a small amount of water or milk to make a paste. Stir well, then add 1½ cups of water or milk. Cook in a saucepan over medium heat, stirring often until thick.

Author's note: This recipe using milk makes a mild chocolate flavor. If darker gravy is desired, use water instead of milk and Dutch-process cocoa instead of regular. For thick, pudding-like gravy, simply cook it longer. Spread or pour over split biscuits.[78]

What to Do with Leftover Biscuits

Biscuit Toast. Paula Eubanks's biscuit recipe states, "If any are left over, which is unusual, then you can cut in half, butter, and toast them for breakfast. This is 'Biscuit Toast' which some people think is better than the biscuits."[79] Grandpa Frey had a small, round cast-iron griddle that was flat except for edges that sloped gently upward.[80] That old griddle had a permanent home on one side of his stovetop, and every day he used a little butter to toast leftover items including biscuits, rolls, and cornbread. (I highly recommend trying this with a slice of homemade pound cake.) The griddle was lost for many years after his death, but then turned up in my brother's camping gear. Now a prized item in my kitchen, the griddle quickly rekindled the joy of slow-warmed toast.

Robert A. Frey's stovetop with toasting skillet.

Coffee Soakee. Several interviewees mentioned this simple dish of leftover biscuits soaked in coffee and eaten with a spoon. Cream and sugar are optional.

Biscuit Pudding. Interviewee Greg Jarrell spoke about his grandmother's biscuit pudding:

> During the week, we always had a paper grocery bag in the refrigerator for leftover biscuits. On Saturday afternoon, right about the time that supper was going to be prepared, the biscuits would be brought out and crumbled into a big bowl. Then mix in two or three eggs, depending on the size of the eggs, and sweet milk, vanilla, and sugar. Mix it up real good, bake it in the oven. Sometimes if there were lemons on hand, you'd make a lemon sauce to go with it. But we didn't have lemons in the house that often.

Cush. Interviewee Eleanor Sullivan of Greensville, North Carolina, shared this recipe:

> My mother made the dish called Cush. It was made of home-canned tomatoes, and she always made homemade biscuits with flour and everything. She would use the homemade biscuits as a thickening in the stew . . . it was like stewed tomatoes with day-old homemade biscuits in it. That was the way of using leftovers from a large family.

With Eleanor's permission and further input, I developed a basic recipe:

6 large, fresh garden or heirloom tomatoes, or about 5 cups canned
1 to 2 medium-sized day-old biscuits, crumbled (¼ to ½ cup crumbs)
2 teaspoons granulated sugar
½ teaspoon salt, or to taste
Herbs and spices to taste (optional)

Blanch and skin the tomatoes if using fresh. Stew the tomatoes, crumbs, sugar, and seasonings in a medium thick-bottomed pot on low heat, stirring often enough to prevent scorching. Cook for at least 20 minutes for fresh tomatoes, 10 for canned. Longer cooking time makes for softer tomatoes and allows the flavors to blend better.

Lazy Gal Pie. Interviewee Bonnie Crowley's grandmother, born in 1870, had a special way of using leftover biscuits during the apple season:

> She used to take the biscuits she would have left over from breakfast and toast them a little bit. And she'd make me go out to the apple tree and get all those apples. . . . I would go and gather the apples and she would peel them and stew the apples down. And then she would put a layer of those biscuits and a layer of those apples, all the way up. It would be so juicy, you know. My granddaddy loved that and he always teased her that that was Lazy Gal Pie.

Mrs. Crowley noted that her grandmother put cinnamon in the stewed apples. The biscuits were split before toasting.

Chocolate Cake in a Bowl. Mamie Pipkins contacted me with some recipes after hearing about my book project. She kindly gave me permission to print the following recipe.

> I grew up in rural Echols County of South Georgia in the 1940s and 1950s when times were very hard. Food was very seldom thrown away . . . either because there was just enough to feed the family or it was served as leftovers. The leftovers often came back to the table in a little different form, and one of those dishes created by my mother is what I want to pass on to you. Somewhere along the way it became known as Chocolate Cake in a Bowl.
>
> When we were young, Mama made biscuits at least once and often twice a day. If one or two were left over, she would wrap them up to save them. . . . After a few days she would have 10–12 saved up, so she would make some chocolate "frosting" to pour over them. I never saw my mother measure any of the ingredients when she made it, and I never measured either. However, I have tried to come up with some amounts that will work.[81]

2 cups sugar
½ cup cocoa
1 cup milk
1 teaspoon vanilla
8 to 10 biscuits (medium size)

Mix sugar and cocoa together in a medium saucepan. Add milk and vanilla, and bring to a boil over medium heat. Cook about five minutes. Crumble biscuits into a bowl, and pour chocolate over. Stir well.

The Frey Extraordinary Biscuit and the End of the Quest

At the beginning of The Quest, I assumed I would learn a handful or two of tricks and then develop my own recipe. Instead I learned enough about biscuits that I recognized appealing recipes when I read through them; it was simply a matter of narrowing down. I now use two basic biscuit recipes. For a quick batch using ingredients I always have on hand, I rely on Cousin Norma's recipe. At other times I turn to the Boardinghouse-Style Biscuits recipe found in *Mrs. Wilkes' Boardinghouse Cookbook*.

I met Mrs. Wilkes several times while living in Savannah—a kind lady who always seemed to be smiling. Mrs. Wilkes died in 2002, but her family carries on the restaurant bearing her name. For this book, I interviewed her granddaughter Marcia Thompson, who told me about the beginning of the published biscuit recipe:

> We'd take a two- or three-week vacation and drive somewhere. This was in the 1950s and 1960s, when I was a little girl. And on the vacation, Mama [Mrs. Wilkes] would tell the recipes and we would write them down. And then we put them into that cookbook and Mother published it. And I thought and she thought and Mama thought that we'd sell a few of those cookbooks and that would be it. But that is the same cookbook we're basically selling today. And she sold over 300,000 of them herself before she died.

Marcia kindly granted permission to include the biscuit recipe here:

Boardinghouse-Style Biscuits

2 cups self-rising flour
½ teaspoon baking powder
1 teaspoon sugar
2 tablespoons shortening
2 tablespoons butter or margarine
⅓ cup buttermilk
⅓ cup whole milk
1 tablespoon plus 1 teaspoon water

Preheat the oven to 450°F. Grease an 8-by-8-by-2-inch baking pan well. Sift the flour, baking powder, and sugar into a bowl. Cut in the shortening and butter until the mixture resembles coarse cornmeal. Make a well in the center of the flour and pour in the butter-milk and milk. Mix lightly and quickly with your hands to form a dough moist enough to leave the sides of the bowl. Turn onto a lightly floured surface. Knead by picking up the sides of the dough away from you while pressing down with the palms of your hands and pushing the dough away. Repeat 6 or 7 times. Work the dough into a large ball while kneading. Keep your fingers dry by frequently dipping them in dry flour. Pinch off portions of dough for desired size biscuit. Press lightly to make the biscuits look flat on the pan. Make sure the biscuits touch each other. Bake for 15 minutes. Yields about 8 boardinghouse-sized biscuits.[82]

With two good recipes and the techniques I learned from The Quest, I can actually turn out biscuits that fit my definition of extraordinary. What is somewhat baffling is that my head is full of biscuit knowledge, yet I can tell my skills diminish if I don't bake biscuits often. Even more baffling, I'm still not sure I've baked my Best Biscuit Ever. I suppose that's a good thing. It gives me something to look forward to. And now on to Great-Grandma Reaves's gingerbread . . .

Exploring Recipe History

The Evolution of Biscuits

Cooking's not a science captured in formulas and rules, but a creative and personal art that's fueled by innovation and imagination—and even memory.
—Lynnmarie P. Cook, "Mama Faye's Biscuits"

Recipe Background

As with appendix 1, this section is designed to give you a hands-on experience with family recipes—this time how you might better understand historical background. As an archivist, I've helped researchers with food-related searches. While some in the world might scratch their heads, we genealogy and history buffs relish the thrill of the information chase. Exploring food history and foodways can be a fascinating journey, giving you a clearer picture of the culture and daily lifestyle of your ancestors. And perhaps you have a recipe of particular importance—either on an emotional or practical level. Of the people interviewed for this book, eight had already earned money through heirloom recipes or products created with them; the more you know about a recipe, the better you can develop or market it.

You'll probably want to start with secondary sources, writings of historians and food experts. Basic information about many foods is compiled in works like *The Oxford Companion to American Food and Drink* or the online *Food Timeline*. These and many more are available at your public library. Reference librarians (as well as the Suggested Reading and Bibliography sections of this book) can guide you to additional sources.

You may very well find out all you wish to know by using such secondary sources. On the other hand, perhaps the information has spawned additional questions or further nudged your curiosity. Next comes a search using primary sources—original materials in family records, archives, or elsewhere. In previous sections of this book, we discussed finding similar recipes for comparison purposes, allowing you to gather cooking ideas and adjust family recipes. Now you'll be looking at similar recipes with a historian's eye. The idea is to search out earlier and earlier versions, looking ever backward in time to build a picture of how a dish or recipe evolved. It isn't just a search for the earliest known recipe for a dish. Ultimately, you want to learn how relevant dishes, recipes, and ingredients were affected by changes in farming practices, social patterns, or technology.

I'll be honest. Of all the tasks related to family recipes, this may be the most complex. How do you know when you've gathered enough information? How can you be sure you didn't miss anything? Most of all, because the information needs context to be truly useful, how do you connect the pieces you find with each other or with general knowledge about the past so you can draw some conclusions? Food historians make a career out of drawing such conclusions, and their expertise is based on a great deal of reading and original research. If that sounds daunting, know that in order to be successful, professional researchers also have to come to peace with the idea that the past is finished and yet not static. Their understanding of history (and ours) constantly changes and grows with new discoveries. Yes, playing the part of an amateur food historian is tricky, yet it often has rich rewards even beyond the thrill of the chase.

In terms of your own heirloom recipes and family foodways, I encourage you not to be afraid to dabble. Once you hit the point of primary document research, online resources and reference request services may make it surprisingly easy to learn interesting bits and pieces about the background of an important heirloom recipe. In addition, many people who love genealogy make research trips to various libraries and archives; it is easy to add a few minutes of historical food research to your "to do" list. And while you are traveling, visit historic homes or farms in regions where your ancestors lived and look for knowledgeable docents who can tell you more about foodways in the past for various members of society.[1] A clearer picture of how a favorite dish evolved and how your ancestors ate increases your enjoyment of a family recipe. Please read on.

⋅⋗ When it comes time to begin research using original documents, fortunately some are now available online, and this "low-hanging fruit" is a good next step. If you're relatively new to family research, conduct an online search to see what archives and historical societies are located in the geographic region(s) significant to your family. Find out if they offer scans or transcriptions of their archival materials that are viewable online. Otherwise, if you can't travel, look into the institution's policies on reference requests. Although such searches are usually limited and involve both fees and patience, an experienced and efficient staff member conducting foodways research on your behalf can turn up rich information.

Now that you have a bare-bones understanding of the research process, let me show you how an information quest unfolded for me. My Quest for the Extraordinary Biscuit turned into a desire to understand how these little bites of bliss came about. In addition to turning you into a true biscuit expert (and perhaps helping you win Trivia Night at the local pizza parlor), the following account will hopefully teach you more about primary-source research as well as how interviews preserve vanishing kitchen techniques.

The Historical Progression of the Southern Biscuit

For well over a century, it has been easy to find recipes for the type of biscuits I described in appendix 1. In fact, the chemical leavenings so important to modern biscuit recipes—baking soda and baking powder—were available to southern cooks before the Civil War.[2] In addition, by the 1880s the price of wheat flour was reasonable for more than just wealthy southern households.[3] Also during the mid- to late 1800s, cooking technology and advances in manufacturing meant that more homes had wood-burning stoves.[4] Cooks no longer had to rely on the labor-intensive methods of baking in ash-covered Dutch ovens or the rare brick oven. So when did these advances come together for the sake of biscuits?

According to dictionaries, "biscuit," from the Latin *bis* (twice) and *coctus* (cooked), originally indicated a small cake that was cooked two times.[5] The Old French *bescuit* or *bescoit* and the obsolete English *besquite* or *bisket* share a family resemblance with the modern French and English word *biscuit*.[6] And the biscuit as we know it is at least a distant cousin of scones, biscotti, Irish soda bread, and cookies, as well as crackers and the exceedingly hard baked creations that were once mainstays for soldiers and sailors—hardtack or sea biscuits.

As you will find if you do your own exploring, the evolutionary lines of a recipe are often indistinct and difficult to trace. In her notes for *Martha Washington's Booke of Cookery*, historian Karen Hess examines various recipes for "biskit" found in that handwritten manuscript, noting that most early biscuit recipes may be Italian in origin and that older English cookbooks contained recipes for certain types of biscuits.[7]

When I discussed the murky earliest origins of biscuits with a colleague, southern material culture specialist Dale Couch, he pointed out the research of historian David Hackett Fischer on the southern backcountry, largely the Shenandoah River Valley.[8] Elaborating on Fischer's work, Couch speculated that American southern biscuits may have developed when the hearth breads of English and Scottish colonists met up with Germanic stoves in an area favorable for wheat production.[9] Whatever the exact origin, the humble, lumpy biscuit likely reflects the increasingly multinational nature of the Western World following the Age of Exploration!

Secondary sources from historians are fascinating, but there's nothing like digging through early cookbooks and manuscript recipe collections yourself. With the Biscuit Quest, for example, instructions for rusk, drop cakes, and sugar biscuits—when read with a baker's eye—show innovation popping up here in this source and then a few years later popping up again over in that source. Using available ingredients, various cooks sought to make individual-serving baked goods that suited their needs at the moment: sweet or savory, small or large, soft or crisp, quick-and-fresh or long-lasting, melt-in-your-mouth or hardy enough to survive a journey. They were formed in the hand, by dropping onto a hot surface, by placing in molds, or by cutting from a sheet of dough.

Some recipes for individual baked goods, through either disinterest or carelessness, vanished forever—variations that never made it as far as becoming a prototype. Others slowly faded, dropped from new editions of cookbooks or simply not passed down to younger generations learning the ways of the kitchen. Yet some forms pleased enough tasters to be repeated, perfected, passed along, and popularized rather than dying out. I can only be thankful that some lines of evolution led to such treasures as the teacake, the cracker to crumble in soup, and that fragrant, flaky, blissful creation known to Americans today as the biscuit.

Beaten Biscuits

During the time when the United States was a new nation, the word "biscuit" meant the same thing here as it did to folks in England—what we now call a cookie. Consult Hannah Glasse or other early cookbooks, and biscuit recipes call for significant amounts of eggs, sugar, and spices and thus would not create a biscuit such as we know today.[10] Hess notes that "For the English, a biscuit was to remain a flat round crisp cake, what we Americans might call a cookie, a cracker, or a rusk, depending on type."[11] By the time Amelia Simmons introduced what many call the first American cookbook in 1796, at least a few branches of individual baked goods were evolving in a new way.[12] She uses the word "cookies" to describe small, sweet baked treats, while the recipe she calls Biscuit still calls for an egg, but the sweetener is gone.[13]

> *Biscuit*
> One pound flour, one ounce butter, one egg, wet with milk and break while oven is heating, and in the same proportion.[14]

I consulted Mary Randolph's 1824 work *The Virginia Housewife; or, Methodical Cook.* Her recipes for Naples Biscuit, Drop Biscuit, and Tavern Biscuit still seem cookie-like despite their names, but then I found her recipe for Apoquiniminc Cakes:

> Put a little salt, one egg beaten, and four ounces of butter, in a quart of flour—make it into a paste with new milk, beat it for half an hour with a pestle, roll the paste thin, and cut it into round cakes; bake them on a gridiron, and be careful not to burn them.[15]

Apoquiniminc Cakes are bland rather than sweet and use the same ingredients as Simmons's Biscuit, only with the addition of a little salt.

Simmons and Randolph both leave out leavening, if you look at the recipes with a modern eye. The leavening, however, hides in the verbs. Simmons uses the word "break" and Randolph uses the word "beat." Both recipes are what many food historians feel are the ancestors of modern biscuits—the beaten biscuit leavened by repeated, prolonged beating or folding of the dough. Once the stiff dough appeared blistered, it retained tiny air pockets that made the finished products softer to the teeth. To the modern palate, they are something of a cross between biscuits and crackers.

Beaten biscuit recipes are quite labor intensive and thus often associated with slavery and labor inequality in the South. Food writer Susan Puckett described the process of testing the beaten biscuit recipe from novelist William Faulkner's mother for the book *A Cook's Tour of Mississippi*: "I was beating them and beating them and beating them. My arm was about to fall off." And the result? "They were like hockey pucks!"[16] Cookbook author and food writer Damon Lee Fowler, however, points out that "beating the dough is a fine way to take out your frustrations."[17]

With the Quest for the Extraordinary Biscuit veering into yesteryear, my path took me to the Root House, a small white Greek Revival–style house built in Marietta, Georgia, around 1845.[18] It is now a house museum standing quietly amid its gardens while modern traffic from the Atlanta bedroom community roars by. One misty spring morning, now-retired curator Maryellen Higginbotham granted me an interview and tour that included the functional separate kitchen building. There on a side table was the wooden treasure I had

Biscuit brake at the Root House Museum. *Photo by the author; permission courtesy of Cobb Landmarks and Historical Society, Inc.*

come to see—the "beating brake" or "biscuit brake" (also spelled "break").

The handmade device, about the size of a boot box, has wooden sides as well as rollers that make it look like an old-fashioned clothes wringer. The closest relative in the modern-day kitchen would be a pasta maker. A removable crank on the side of the brake turns the rollers so that the biscuit dough can be repeatedly passed through. "You beat them three hundred times if you're going to serve them to family and five hundred times if you're going to serve them to visitors," Higginbotham said, paraphrasing the words of long-ago cookbook author Eliza Leslie.[19]

Beaten biscuits from the Root House Museum. *Photo by the author; permission courtesy of Cobb Landmarks and Historical Society, Inc.*

The biscuit brake was invented in the 1870s by a woman from New Jersey.[20] In his book *Southern Food*, John Egerton writes, "Like the cotton gin, this Yankee invention swept through the South, and for another half-century or more, it not only saved beaten biscuits from extinction but actually made them smoother, prettier, and more popular than before."[21] Mrs. Henry Lumpkin Wilson, charged with compiling a cookbook of important regional recipes to share with the world for the 1895 Cotton States and International Exposition, included a recipe for beaten biscuits, and when Mrs. S. R. Dull published her landmark *Southern Cooking* in 1928, it contained several beaten biscuit recipes as well.[22] Many contemporary cookbooks also include beaten biscuit recipes—most adapted to modern devices such as the stand mixer or food processor. While beaten biscuits are quaint to most, there are still southerners who would prefer never to eat cured ham without them.[23]

A Matter of Leavenings

According to *The Oxford Companion to American Food and Drink,* soft biscuits began appearing on American tables in the early 1800s and were common by midcentury.[24] Perhaps this was true earlier in the wheat-producing "bread basket" states than in the corn-dependent Deep South, but the increasing popularity of home-baked goods containing flour was also dependent on easier leavening.

A visit to Colonial Williamsburg's period kitchens in Virginia and discussions with staff members Barbara Ball and Dennis Cotner helped

BROWNIES

1 cup sugar	2 eggs
½ cup butter	½ cup flour
2 squares chocolate	½ cup chopped walnuts

Beat egg yolks. Add sugar. Add chocolate and butter melted together. Next add stiffly beaten egg whites and lastly the flour and nuts. Bake until it leaves the edge of the pan. When nearly cold cut in squares.

Recipe from *Picnic Time*, published by the Lydia E. Pinkham Medicine Co. of Lynn, Mass., ca. 1917. Many modern brownie recipes call for leavening, but some still achieve cake-like texture with whipped eggs. This century-old recipe requires the extra step of separating the eggs, an echo of cakes from long ago.

clarify eighteenth-century baking for me.[25] Yeast and eggs were the main two leavenings. Most breads were achieved with yeast (a biological leavening) and cakes with whipped egg (a physical leavening). Cotner stated, "To make a good cake like your pound cake, you're separating your yolks and egg whites. You put your egg yolks into your beaten sugar and butter. Then you froth your egg whites. By alternating whites and flour, you get that blended in. It's as light as any pound cake you're making today." The beaten biscuit process was closer to soft biscuits but still required a physical process on the part of the cook. The real breakthrough was chemical leavening.

Blending an alkali with an acid in the presence of moisture and heat creates carbon dioxide bubbles—a chemical leavening that causes dough to rise and have a springy texture.[26] Early alkali was usually potassium carbonate, called pearlash, also written as "pearl ash." This was refined from potash (pot ash), processed lye from the burnt remains of certain types of plants including tree wood.[27] As for the acidic side of the chemical leavening equation, cooks used ingredients such as buttermilk, wine, or citrus.

When do chemical leavenings begin to pop up in recipes? I searched nineteenth-century cookbooks and archives' recipe collections, keeping my eye out for any recipe that seemed closer to the soft, alkali-plus-acid modern biscuit. At the end of the eighteenth century, Amelia Simmons mentions using pearlash as a leavening.[28] Similarly, the Georgia Historical Society holds a 1828–32 recipe book of Savannah's Anna White that contains a Cider Cake recipe blending pearlash with cider and vinegar. White's Short Cakes recipe, however, dictates that the dough be rolled out three times—a form of the beaten biscuit despite the fact that she understood the use of pearlash in the kitchen.[29] Closer, but not there yet.

As the Industrial Revolution chugged forward, alkali chemical leavenings from both organic and mineral sources became more available to home cooks and thus appeared as ingredients in recipes. Sodium bicarbonate was (and still is) commonly referred to as soda, while some older recipes call for saleratus, a leavening with a name taken from the Latin *sal aeratus* (aerated salt) and usually referring to either sodium bicarbonate (soda) or potassium bicarbonate.[30]

I started scanning recipes for mention of alkali leavening. White's recipe book includes instructions for Soda Cakes that contain flour, butter, and a tablespoon of soda, but then the recipe also dictates adding half a pound of sugar and baking the cakes in a mold.[31] Close, but not a biscuit. In 1840 *The Southern Gardener and Receipt Book* by P. Thornton of South Carolina recommended using pearlash in cooking recipes, while the soda was used to get the wash clean.[32] Sarah Rutledge included saleratus in some recipes in the 1855 edition of *House and Home; or, the Carolina Housewife*, but none is very biscuit-like.[33] At the Library of Congress, I had the pleasure of reading through the recipe book of Issa Desha Breckinridge of the politically prominent Kentucky family. Various individual-serving cookies and cakes from the 1850s volume require soda paired with acids such as buttermilk or soured milk, but none of the finished baked goods would have resembled biscuits.[34] Research-wise, the nineteenth century was half over and, although I'd learned much about biscuit evolution, I hadn't found the type of recipe I was ultimately looking for.

Knowing that unless someone is sharing recipes with a new cook or out-of-region visitor, the common everyday recipes stand less chance of being written down than novel or unique ones, I began to wonder if I actually would find a pre–Civil War soft biscuit recipe. Thus I cheered when I finally came across an 1859 (and admittedly Yankee) pamphlet that offers the following recipe:

> *Soda Biscuits.*—To one quart of flour, add two tea-spoonsful of cream of tartar, one of soda, and a piece of butter the size of an egg. Sift the cream of tartar into the flour; rub the butter thoroughly into the same; dissolve the soda in two-thirds of a pint of sweet milk, or warm water, and mix quickly; bake immediately in a hot oven.[35]

That is a true biscuit. But was it an *extraordinary* biscuit? Early chemical leavenings were not without their challenges.

Baking Soda versus Baking Powder

An interesting note that gives clues about the evolution of the biscuit is found in the 1844 edition of Lydia Maria Child's household guide. Of prepackaged leavening, the author says:

> Those who are fond of soda powders will do well to inquire at the apothecaries for the suitable acid and alkali, and buy them by the ounce, or by the pound, according

to the size of their families. Experience soon teaches the right proportions; and, sweetened with a little sugar or lemon syrup, it is quite as good as what one gives five times as much for, done up in papers.[36]

Advertisement for Mrs. Lincoln's Baking Powder, from *Boston Cooking School Magazine*, May 1909.

Aside from the cost, one of the problems Child alludes to is that the proper blend of alkali and acid was elusive both with homemade components and with commercial soda or saleratus. An undated cookbooklet produced by the Rumford Baking Powder Company explains the problem in its pitch to homemakers, trying to wean them away from the "old fashioned" use of soda and dairy as leavening: "it was not possible for the home cook to gauge accurately the amount of lactic acid present in the sour milk and consequently to know equally accurately the amount of soda to be added in order to form a perfect combination."[37] When the balance of acid and alkali is not achieved, finished baked goods have an off taste and perhaps even yellow-green streaks.[38]

Mrs. S. R. Dull, cooking columnist for the *Atlanta Journal* for many years, suggested the formula of a half teaspoon of soda per cup of buttermilk.[39] But moving to a standardized chemical acid was thought by many to be an easier and more reliable method. Cream of tartar (bitartrate of potassium), an acid originally derived from grapes during the winemaking process, became a more dependable partner for the soda.[40] Alkali and acid powders were first packaged separately. But then the idea of blending the two—along with a starch to prevent lumping—caught on, and the result came to be known as baking powder.[41] This product was increasingly accepted as it opened possibilities for lighter, more varied baked goods. Cookbooks from the 1880s and several decades forward carried recipes for both soda and baking powder biscuits (indeed, many still do), but the latter quickly became more popular.

At the time that baking powder emerged, the age of chemistry in commercial foods was picking up speed. To the casual consumer today, the likes of phosphates and aluminum in a leavening may be confusing, but at least today we have legislation to help protect us from unsafe food additives. In the nineteenth century, some baking powder manufacturers shared shady practices with their corporate neighbors the patent medicine producers, and baking powder became one of the products linked in the public's mind with unappealing fillers and sham ingredients. Even with legitimate products, some companies used more effective blends than others. The Pure Food and Drug Act of 1906, however, helped to sweep away some of the less successful and more offensive products.[42]

An Explosion of Biscuit Recipes

After the uproar of the 1906 act, companies were eager to have consumers trust their products. One of the happy results for recipe lovers is that surviving manufacturers embraced the trend of product-promoting cookbooklets. Few were as earnest (or wordy) as the baking powder companies. In the 1911 cookbooklet *Royal Baker and Pastry Cook*, the words "Royal Baking Powder is Absolutely Pure" appear at the bottom of each page, and the back cover is crammed with testimonials from twenty chemistry experts.[43]

Even beyond the 1906 act and the resulting product testimonials that paved the way for cookbooklets, written recipes became more widespread. As a biscuit pilgrim reading my way through historical sources, to me the latter half of the nineteenth century meant metaphorically coming away from the soft scratch of ink-dipped pen to paper. Ever-speeding technology brought the clank of the printing press on finally inexpensive paper, the roar of trucks over the interstates transporting factory-processed ingredients, the computer beep alerting that a new recipe has been posted on a Listserv, and the Food Network broadcasting in high definition.

I see the march of progress reflected in foodways in general and in the humble biscuit in particular. I'm not alone. Of examining history through the kitchen, Root House former curator Maryellen Higginbotham said, "We have found that the foodways theme is a significant one. Everybody likes to eat, so that is a good way to connect with visitors of all ages and nationalities." The Root House developed an educational program for school children in the early 2000s that used the biscuit as a common denominator. It compared biscuits over time from procurement of ingredients to the presentation of the finished baked good—from the 1850s days of beaten biscuits up through the introduction of commercial leavenings, the 1931 invention of Bisquick brand mix, the rise of the canned biscuit, and the current reliance on fast food.[44] "Now you can go to McDonald's to get your chicken biscuit. You don't even need to cook," Maryellen pointed out.

Biscuit Artifacts and the Dough Bowl

The Root House was not mistaken that biscuits are deeply ingrained in the history of the South. Artifacts such as the biscuit brake show that even at a time when kitchens had far less equipment—tools, utensils, appliances, and furnishings—at least some cooks spent time or money on implements dedicated to biscuits. From museums to antique stores, one can find biscuit cutters in both homemade and factory versions. Many cutters were promotional items, stamped with the names of flour, leavening, and shortening companies. Dale Couch shared his knowledge with me about biscuit tables.[45] These heavy-duty furnishings, sometimes with a limestone or marble top, often had a hood to keep pests and dust away from the work surface when not in use.

MAGIC COVER

Magic Cover for Pastry Board and Rolling Pin; chemically treated and hygienic; recommended by leading teachers of cooking. By mail 60c.

Table cover for rolling dough marketed to readers of the *Boston Cooking School Magazine*, 1909.

For me, one of the most intriguing methods for making biscuits is reflected in another artifact—the wooden "bread tray," "biscuit bowl," or "dough bowl." These kitchen implements were usually oblong and hand carved. Nathalie Dupree's *New Southern Cooking* describes such an item owned by the grandmother of food writer Shirley Corriher. Flour was distributed throughout the elongated bowl, but biscuits were made at one side. "She worked the shortening into the flour and then added the buttermilk, making a big wet puddle of dough in the one end of the bowl. Then she dusted her fingers with flour heavily, picked up biscuit-sized pieces of the gooey wet dough, and rolled them in the flour at the other end of the bowl."[46] In later years it wasn't uncommon to have a round bowl, created more quickly by lathe. Basswood was a popular material because it is light and does not crack easily, but maple and other woods were also used.[47]

Many of the people I interviewed remembered seeing grandmothers, mothers, or aunts make biscuits with such a bowl. Arkansas interviewee LouElla Thompson, born in 1916, used to make biscuits in this fashion and was able to describe it to me rather well:

> My mother had an oblong one about [two feet] long. I have a round one [about a foot and a half] around. That's what I made my bread in. Instead of emptying out that flour every time you made the biscuits, you just placed it in a container to keep the flour within the bowl. You just sifted that flour each time you made bread. You just dipped the sifter in and sifted the top of whatever flour was in the bowl. We had more flour than we used each time, of course.

Biscuit dough bowl belonging to the household of the author's great-great-grandfather John Henry Frey (1831–1890), which was chewed on by rats while in storage. *Photo courtesy of Amberlee Fletcher, Lilac Lens Photography.*

You'd make a little hole in the flour—we called it a duck's nest—that we put our milk and our shortening in. I don't believe we had self-rising flour back when I was growing up, so we had to use salt and baking powders to add to it, you know. And I used my hands to work up. A lot of people didn't do that. A lot of people used a spoon, but I found you could do it a lot better with your hand. Then you work it over just right and pinch it off. You learn to make your little biscuits out like that.

It is the fact that flour remains in the bowl once the biscuit dough is done that truly intrigues me—a prime example of cooking sensibilities developed by master cooks. When I asked LouElla how she knew she had enough flour mixed in, she said, "You just know this by experience. If it's too soft, your biscuits will just sprawl out, you know. But if you get it just right, they stay just the size you make them out."

At the Mossy Creek Barnyard Festival in Perry, Georgia, I came across a handmade bowl. Delighted, I told the wood-carver about the Quest for the Extraordinary Biscuit as he wrote up my sale. He stood back for a moment, rubbing some wood chips out of his flowing beard and wiping a hand on his stained overalls before he said, "I can tell you how to make biscuits with this thing. You tuck it under your arm like this," he began. I leaned forward to listen. "Then you open up the fridge, grab one of those tubes of canned biscuits, and knock the can on the lip of this here bowl to pop it open."[48]

Humph.

Bonnie Crowley with her wooden dough bowl in 2008.

I now had a proper bowl but no way of learning to use it. Mrs. Thompson lived more than six hundred miles away and had not used her dough bowl in years. Then I interviewed Bonnie Crowley of Athens, Georgia.[49] Known for her biscuits, she baked as many as four hundred over Christmastime for family, friends, and neighbors.

My grandmother taught me how. Secretly. She would tell me, "I want you to make a dough for pie crust. I can't make a stiff enough dough to make a pie. Mine is so soft that it tears up." She had been cooking for years and years and years, but that was her excuse. So I, the crazy thing, thought that I would do it better than she could. But all she was doing was teaching me how to make biscuits. I'd make it up and she'd say, "Aw, that's okay. Just do it up like biscuits and we'll make us a pie another time." And so that's how I learned to cook biscuits.

Then I asked Mrs. Crowley if she had ever made biscuits with a wooden bowl. She looked surprised and said, "That's the only way I've done them. I've still got my tray." I was delighted. She soon showed me the wooden bowl she got when she got married, now more than sixty-five years ago. How does she know how much flour to leave behind in the bowl?

I just know. I just take my lard and put it in there and work it up. If it doesn't look like it's going to be enough, then I pour a little more milk in there till I think it's enough. You know, I just keep working. When I think it's enough, I stop.

Verbal directions obviously weren't going to be enough. I returned for a cooking visit with Mrs. Crowley, my brother in tow for help.[50] While I pulled out my kitchen scale, audio recorder, and camera, Mrs. Crowley pulled out her ingredients—White Lily brand self-rising flour, Kroger grocery store brand cultured low-fat buttermilk, and a mound of lard long since removed from its commercial container. The lard was pure white, glossy, and soft despite being refrigerated. I took up my camera and began dictating notes to my brother while Mrs. Crowley preheated her electric oven to 500 degrees.

Since I had access only to an older kitchen scale without a tare button, I weighed the bread tray empty. Three pounds, eight and a half ounces. She sifted a mound of flour into her tray, and when she was satisfied, we weighed it again. She'd added two pounds one ounce of flour. Next we weighed the lard and put the buttermilk in a measuring cup so I would be able to see how much she used.

Soon her hands were busy over the dough bowl, which she placed perpendicular to her on the countertop. Her left hand rested on the edge of the bowl to steady it while her right hand dipped into the ingredients. Rather than working in the common two-step biscuit method—combining dry ingredients with fat before adding the milk—Mrs. Crowley added fat and liquid at the same time.

"I work it with my hands," she told me. "Some people spoon their dough, but I don't have time for that." Mrs. Crowley's way of "working it up" requires a consistent and rather elegant counterclockwise motion of her spread fingers followed by a loose fist and upward movement of the thumb—a practiced motion that I captured on video. In this manner, just a skim of flour is blended in with each cycle, allowing the dough to remain smooth. Meanwhile, the wettest part of the dough at the interior of the ball is pressed up and out through the space between Mrs. Crowley's first finger and thumb as her hand contracts at the end of each stroke. That's important for keeping the dough circulating. "You ought to have seen my grandmother make biscuits," Mrs. Crowley said with a smile. "She'd stand here and do this."

Bonnie Crowley "working it up."

The dough started off quite wet, a puddle resting atop the dry flour. Five minutes later, Mrs. Crowley changed tactics. She took about thirty seconds to draw the dough together, pulling up the bottom edges of the dough toward the middle. The motions reminded me of swaddling a baby in a blanket. When she pulled back from the task to clean some of the dough from her stirring hand, the dough was a ball with a few flour-coated creases and held its shape.

"I need to get it more stiffer. So I knead it," Mrs. Crowley remarked at this point. The kneading process was a different motion than either mixing or drawing together the dough. She repeatedly lifted the top of the dough farthest from her and brought it toward the middle, folding it in half. Every five to six folds, she would turn the dough counterclockwise. Watching my video clip afterwards, I counted seventy-one kneads.

Next Mrs. Crowley placed an old Tupperware plastic pastry mat on the countertop, dusted it with flour from her bread tray, placed her biscuit dough in the center, and then used a wooden rolling pin with deft motions. Using the ruler attachment of my brother's handy-dandy Swiss Army knife, we ascertained the rolled dough was three-quarters of an inch thick. Mrs. Crowley showed me a biscuit cutter that her husband helped her make more than sixty years ago from a Vienna sausage can with the lid removed and holes punched in the bottom for air to escape. That cutter was now largely retired, though. Instead she used a commercial cutter, a three-inch open metal ring with fluted

Her homemade biscuit cutter.

edges that she twisted when making each cut. She made fourteen biscuits and then rerolled the dough to make six more. Scraps of dough left from the second cutting were thrown away.

The raw biscuits were placed on a greased steel cookie sheet, now dark brown with age, and placed on the center rack of the oven. Just over fourteen minutes later she slid the golden-brown finished biscuits onto a large white platter. Disregarding the fact that the biscuits were too hot to comfortably touch, much less eat, my brother and I each grabbed one. The exterior was golden and flaky. The interior was pale and fluffy. Truly an extraordinary biscuit.

For those of you interested in trying Mrs. Crowley's method, her ingredients were one pound plus one-fourth ounce self-rising flour (about 3⅔ cups or 460 grams), which includes some used from the tray to lightly dust the rolling surface), four ounces of lard (about ½ cup or 113 grams), and one and one-half cups of low-fat buttermilk.[51]

◈⧗ Making biscuits with Mrs. Crowley brought my historical research on biscuits full circle in my mind. From manuscript recipes and period cookbooks to knowledge passed down by grandmothers, what does all this add up to in terms of the Quest for the Extraordinary Biscuit? Thankfully, I heard something along the way that made a lot of sense about where to go from here. Sitting outside the historic Peyton Randolph house one sunny summer morning for our interview, Colonial Williamsburg hearth cook Dennis Cotner said, "I think it's very important not to dwell in the past with foodstuffs, because those things will always evolve and change, but to have a fairly good working knowledge of where we used to be so that you know how to change things as you go down the line." An excellent sentiment.

Exploring a Cook's Legacy

Tradition is a guide and not a jailer.—W. Somerset Maugham, *The Summing Up* (223)

When Anton Ego, a famous and caustic food critic, threatened to ruin the reputation of a particular chef, comfort food saved the day. With one bite of the simple vegetable dish, the elderly critic was emotionally transported back to his childhood kitchen and saw the smiling face of his mother. The experience erased the long years and forever changed his sour outlook. The fact that Ego is an animated figure in the Pixar film *Ratatouille* and ate food cooked by the paws of a rat is beside the point. The audience gets it. Food can be a powerful reminder of good times and warm places, of home and love. In the ultimate sense, that is what this book is all about.

What is particularly striking about this scene from *Ratatouille* is that a powerful food memory brought the character back to his own personal wellspring. Although my family's cooking legacies are scattered across a double handful of cooks, in the course of research for this book I met many people for whom heirloom recipes primarily point back to a single kitchen, a single cook. Sometimes the master cook is a confident leader who envisions what the family foodways should be and then teaches members to follow it. On the other hand, that master cook might be an unassuming person who simply inspires by remarkable cooking skills. Sometimes master cooks appear and disappear in singular form, while sometimes they descend from a great cook and/or spawn a handful of equally great family cooks.

Regardless of demeanor or intent, master cooks leave a long shadow over family kitchens—sometimes for generations. I spoke with many people who wanted more than to save heirloom recipes and use them effectively. They wanted to somehow keep an unusually good family cook's "magic" from completely disappearing. This desire may even tie into your own legacy; if much of your kitchen knowledge originated with one person, then the story of that master cook's foodways journey is also the story of yours.

If your family is currently graced with a master cook, this book can help you work together to preserve recipes, know-how, and lore. But what if the master cook is now gone? Just as working with orphaned recipes offers additional challenges, so does trying to piece together the legacy of a deceased master cook. Lest the task seem bigger than the tools given in previous chapters, this appendix takes a closer look at the problem.

Freida Miller Thomas

Although my mother and grandparents were important cooks in my past, there was yet another figure who taught me much about cooking—my next-door neighbor growing up, Freida Miller Thomas. A passionate lifelong cook, she planned to write a cookbook after she retired. Only she didn't live long enough.

Many of Freida's recipes are alive and well in my kitchen. And probably every party I've ever put together benefited from her know-how. I've collected my own family's history and recipes for years, but thinking of Freida made me wonder what would it be like to start with just recent memories and a few recipes. When I voiced this to the Thomas family, they graciously gave me the chance to explore the process and share it with readers.

Across the span of a few months, I sifted through Freida's recipe and cookbook collection, looked at some of the family's documents, and interviewed her husband as well as her three grown sons.[1] It was a fascinating and sometimes surprising journey. Although there are biographies available about celebrity chefs, stories focused on the development and legacy of a home cook are rare. My research revealed truths about home cooking, heirloom recipes, the role food plays in our lives, and how we may pass on personal or generational knowledge. The resulting document allows you to compare and contrast family experiences as well as glean research ideas. It may even inspire you to think about what you'd like your cooking legacy to be.

A Surrogate Aunt and Cooking Mentor

One of the keys to genealogy is to start with what you know. This is also good advice for setting out to preserve a legacy, so I wrote down what I knew about Freida and my experiences with her cooking.

My family moved next door to the Thomases in 1971. Freida was a homemaker during most of my childhood. Her husband, George, was a sociologist until his retirement, and then he returned to his love of painting. My brother and I are interwoven age-wise with their three sons, Brian, Zack, and Dominic. Through shared neighborhood, school, and social activities, Freida's philosophy of hospitality and the importance of food shone brightly. The Thomases hosted more parties than anyone else on the block, and kids were welcome to perch on kitchen stools to watch—and learn from—the preparations. Birthday parties gave my mother a headache, but Mrs. Thomas seemed to thrive on them.

Mrs. Thomas and my mother shared trips to the u-pick farms during the summer, Dominic and I exploring rustling tunnels of corn or endless rows of peach trees. A couple of hours later, lovely smells and taste tests coaxed us to visit back and forth between the two kitchens. This is how we learned that ingredients have wide potential and cooks have different styles—sweet creamed corn and peach jam in one house, herbed corn chowder and pickled peaches in the other.

For most kids, there comes a time when merely watching gives way to the adults letting you help. Once I was old enough to reach the countertop by step stool, I was allowed to help snap peas or wash carrots not just at my own house but at the Thomas house as well. On afternoons when my mother served as Cub Scout den mother for the neighborhood boys, Mrs. Thomas suggested I come to her house. I usually arrived to find supplies for some kitchen craft spread out on the table—wooden spoon puppets, apple dolls, dough ornaments, and the like.

One-on-one time with an adult made quite an impression, but it was also my first real taste of the lure and satisfaction of the creative process. Mrs. Thomas never said, "Okay, here's how you do step one." Instead, it was: "How do you think we could preserve an orange so it smells good for a long time?" She coaxed me into thinking aloud about ways to save fruit before mentioning that spices could help preserve them. "How could we add spice to uncut fruit?" After perusing the spice rack, we decided to press whole cloves all over our orange.

George Thomas painted this portrait of his wife, Freida, in 1999. *Courtesy of George Thomas.*

The Thomas family in 1976. Brian is nine, Zack eight, and Dominic three. *Courtesy of George Thomas.*

Freida Thomas made figurative birthday cakes. Bendable drinking straws form the legs of this spider-shaped cake from 1973. *Courtesy of George Thomas.*

Although years later it was a small blow to my ego to learn that some nameless person in the Middle Ages was the true creator of the clove orange pomander, I loved Mrs. Thomas's teaching methods. Brainstorming as well as question-and-answer helped me think more effectively and truly understand the project. I've employed a similar creative process ever since whether teaching kids about primary documents, learning to make decent biscuits, or writing a book.

After the Cub Scout days were done, projects with Mrs. Thomas happily continued. Out of the blue one day she announced she was going to teach me to make pralines, directing me to copy down the recipe while she got out her pans. When the confections were done, we invited my mother over for a tea party using the good china. By high school, Mrs. Thomas led me through planting an herb garden. Frey-Thomas tea parties could now feature a homemade mint brew. "Going next door to play" became tea and conversation.

The Expanding Cooking Mentorship

During my college years, Freida's influence was such that I grew chives on my doom room windowsill even if I just added them to canned soup. After my mother died, Freida was the one I called most often in those uh-oh-the-lasagna-burned-and-company-is-almost-here situations. Freida's policy of always welcoming one more to the table was much appreciated during visits to town during my single years. One of the best things she did for me, however, was address me as an equal in the kitchen despite the fact that this was far more a courtesy than a reality. Many mentors make the mistake of never acknowledging when their apprentices move up a level or two. Freida, however, discussed cooking with me and occasionally asked for my recipes, granting a sense of accomplishment and pride.

Through food, I came to understand something special about Freida. In the winter of 2000, a period when I stayed with the Thomas family for a month while job hunting after graduate school, I recorded the following passage about Freida in my journal:

> She said understanding the components and flavors of a dish was a deep joy. Food at a restaurant is a puzzle to be unlocked. "All my cooking around here isn't just about feeding people's mouths." And then with even deeper passion, she spoke about the flavors, the cuisine of her Cajun ancestors and family. Preserving the culinary arts of the Louisiana French is a responsibility, a duty—and a passion. I told her how I feel when a journal entry nails down exactly how I feel or what I experienced—deep personal exhilaration. And she said that's how she feels when she turns out perfect pralines.[2]

During the Christmas of 2003, Freida didn't feel very well. Her cooking tasted just as good, but there wasn't as much of it. In the early spring she received a cancer diagnosis, and she lived just a few more months. Freida's kitchen after her funeral felt odd and yet comforting, the smell of Cajun food cooked by her oldest son still in the air as I looked through her Rolodex of recipe cards one by one. When those recipes were later scanned and shared among the brothers, I received a copy as well. Reading through it is a stroll down memory lane of meals and gatherings at the Thomas house. It holds recipes from

Freida's recipe Rolodex contains clipped recipes and ones from friends but also original recipes clearly marked and dated. *Photo by author; courtesy of George Thomas.*

some of my neighbors and schoolteachers. I also found recipes that came from me, my mother, and my grandmother. It was too late to say it to Freida, but I saw that our kitchens—and our lives—were more linked than I realized.

Exploring a Legacy

Writing down my memories of Freida was cathartic. It felt good, too, to share my writing with her family and know that the grandchildren too young to have memories of Freida may someday see her through someone else's eyes. But what did I really know about this woman who had been in my life so long I couldn't even remember meeting her? It was time to add interviews.

Fiercely determined that people in general and women in particular be judged by their accomplishments rather than their age, Freida never revealed her birth year. Let's just say she was old enough to experience the World War II home front but too young to remember much about it. She was born in Reddell, a small town in south Louisiana where her parents owned a store. Everyone knew about her roots because she took great pride in her Cajun culture; Freida was the first cook I knew to showcase a particular cuisine. Our family also witnessed her progression from homemaker and community volunteer to elementary gifted education Teacher of the Year. (Her students who met their goals were often rewarded with treats from her kitchen.)

For a better picture of Freida's skills and how she developed them, I first turned to her husband, George. During his first year as a widower, he wrote "The Story of the Lives of Freida Miller and George Thomas," an unpublished portrait of two individuals and a thirty-eight-year marriage that contains family photographs, letter transcripts, and family artwork. Despite how long I'd known George and Freida, I began to see them with different eyes through reading it. The same was true about interviews.

One of the first things George talked about was his wife's cooking sensibilities. "Her sense of smell was so acute and her sense of taste was so acute. Without a doubt, a gifted chef or cook—these are the tools of her trade." He continued with an anecdote about a trip the couple took to Amsterdam. While taking a stroll one afternoon, Freida suggested they eat because she smelled something interesting cooking. She then led them to a restaurant, but one that wasn't nearby. "She was following her nose *two blocks*."

Freida Miller at age thirteen. *Courtesy of George Thomas.*

Freida created this stitched landscape of her hometown for the fiftieth wedding anniversary of her parents, Cleophas and Belle Miller, in 1969. *Courtesy of Dominic Thomas.*

The Miller store in Reddell, Louisiana, ca. 1949. *Courtesy of George Thomas.*

It calls to mind what famed twentieth-century food writer James Beard said about extraordinary kitchen talent in his book *Delights and Prejudices*: "The ability to recall a taste sensation, which I think of as 'taste memory,' is a God-given talent, akin to perfect pitch, which makes your life richer if you possess it." Beard also states, "And naturally good chefs and cooks must depend upon memory when they season or when they are combining subtle flavors to create a new sauce or dish."[3]

Life Cycles of a Cook

How did those extraordinary kitchen skills develop? George outlined what he called Freida's "life cycles" as a cook. Although her knowledge grew through the years, Freida's resources and the demands on her fluctuated, greatly affecting her cooking.

"Bachelorette" Days. Freida was the youngest of eight children, raised by older parents who had reached stability in their lives. Her father was a locally prominent businessman and her mother a homemaker. Of the Miller family, George wrote, "All of Freida's siblings, and many of their offspring, are superb cooks and possess a wonderful collective sense of humor. I have never been in the presence of a group with such a high appreciation for good times and good food."[4]

Young Freida had plenty of opportunity to be in the kitchen, and her mother, Belle, was reputed to be an excellent cook. About his wife, George mused, "It was very clear to me that she learned to cook at Mother's knee."

Freida once wrote that by the tender age of eight she could already make better French drip coffee than anyone else and once served it up to Earl Long when he was passing through her father's store on the gubernatorial campaign trail. "I suppose that's why I've always thought of myself as a success in the culinary arts—I had a reputation to maintain from a very early age."[5] A college degree in home economics, missionary work in the Yucatán that included teaching nutrition, and two jobs as a home economics agent for the state of Louisiana prepared her well for the kitchen.

George and Freida met at Tulane University, both pursuing graduate studies in social work. Food figured into the relationship from the beginning. When asked if Freida's approach to food was different from his when they first married, George began to laugh loudly. He then described himself and his friend Jim as bachelor roommates. They rented a furnished apartment because "What would we have had otherwise? We would have been sitting on two orange crates!" As for the kitchen, "I knew we had forks and knives, but that was all I could vouch for. I never looked. Honestly."

Freida offered to cook supper one night and came by early to take stock. "She opened up the refrigerator and inside was one curled-up package of bologna, a half a loaf of Wonder Bread, and two six-packs. I think we may have had a bottle of mustard too. . . . I hear some rattling and looking through the drawers, picking up the pans and whatnot. Then she says, 'Well, I have to go out for a little while, do a little shopping.'" She came back with French bread and ingredients to make spaghetti with sauce from scratch. "I watched all this at an angle from the sofa in the living room. I was entranced. And how long was this meal going to take? I mean, a bologna sandwich would have been twenty-two seconds." His final take on the situation, however, was "It was an excellent meal." And it was just the beginning.

Early Marriage. The couple married in 1965 and immediately moved to Madison, Wisconsin, for George's career. The first baby was soon on the way. George notes, "For that period of time, she was cooking up all these fandango dishes—Cajun things. Partially I think it was because she was living in such a foreign environment. She was homesick, really, and that was combined with pregnancy." At the end of the first six months of marriage, he weighed more than he ever had in his life. "If you were feeding a hog for market, you couldn't have done a much better job!"

George and Freida married in 1965. *Courtesy of George Thomas.*

They had no money to eat out, but it didn't faze Freida. "This really was not a challenge to her. Coming out of her background, you could make endless good things out of virtually nothing. Now *that* is a cook." George repeated an old saying, "A Cajun will eat anything that doesn't eat him first," and then noted, "When she cooked a chicken gumbo, she went and got the oldest, the most rubbery hen that the butcher had to offer. And sometimes she'd send him into the back [for an older one]. Back then, it wasn't always in cellophane. You could get the whole chicken. He'd come out holding one by the neck and she'd say, 'No, go back and get the toughest old bird that you can find.' She'd tell me, 'You cannot make a real chicken gumbo without getting the oldest, most rubbery hen that you can get.' Then you just boil it to death, bones and all to get the flavor. . . . That really was a hallmark of her cooking. And it would take hours."

Motherhood. Within a few years, the Thomases moved to Florida and son Zack joined the family. After a second move to Athens, Georgia, the family increased by third son, Dominic. George's career standing and the family finances also increased. During this period, George encouraged Freida to choose more expensive ingredients. "Now, no doubt the finished meal was quality, but it kind of offended me. I said, 'If you're going to make a stew, go out and get some sirloin steak and chop it up. Get some really good chickens.' And I said that enough that she did move in that

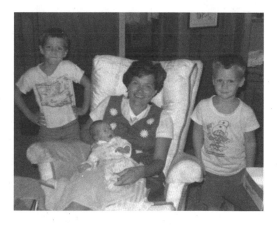

By 1972 the family of five was complete. *Courtesy of George Thomas.*

Contemplating dinner while the baby plays on the kitchen floor, 1973. *Courtesy of George Thomas.*

direction in subsequent years. Somehow or another, thinking back on it now, in her mind it probably lost something. The actual outcome of the meal may have lost something."

After these admonishments, Freida "spent lavishly on food." George came home from the office one day in the early 1970s to find Freida sitting at the table, looking nonplussed. "I could see she had been sitting there with some of the other women from the neighborhood because of the empty coffee cups, but they had left." Freida reported the neighbors were feeding their families for around $250 to $300 per month. She spent around $800.

While the grocery bills expanded somewhat comfortably, there were other challenges to raising three children. "Her cooking style changed again at that point without any question. It went to pretty mundane, regular middle-class American meal preparation for any number of years because it had to be quick. Otherwise the natives would rebel." Indeed, Freida had three young boys with pedestrian tastes to feed. "It got to the point that what would pass for seafood in the house was fish sticks." George reported, "That was a good ten-year period there of lost time in terms of the fine art of cooking."

Culinary arts were reserved for holiday gatherings. "Nothing, nothing, in terms of her cooking, ever pleased her more than a minimum crowd of ten, preferably fifteen or eighteen. And so on holidays, she would make sure that we would have a number of people there. There were relatives, neighbors, anybody she could drag in off the street." Sometimes her efforts were not appreciated. George told of a dinner of Crawfish Étouffée for his office staff, most with little culinary experience. "Hardly any of them ate it." He overheard guests questioning each other about the "bugs" (crawfish) in the stew.

Freida and her three sons in 1975. *Courtesy of George Thomas.*

Over the years, Freida proved proactive when it came to satisfying her culinary creativity. When she first moved to Athens, she was so homesick

A picnic-on-the-floor crawfish party at the Thomas house in 1979. *Courtesy of George Thomas.*

for her Cajun roots that she looked through the phone book for French names. In this way she found a good friend and kindred Cajun cook in a woman named Nancy Couvillon. The two rounded up at least twenty couples with ties to southern Louisiana, and the group met regularly for potluck suppers for more than a decade. George noted, "Believe me, they were, one among the other, their harshest critics. If a thing didn't get a rave notice, it was the equivalent of being condemned." Freida found peers and what her husband called her "outlet for cooking her authentic or original meals."

Revitalization and the Empty Nest. George happily noted, "Surprisingly enough, when the kids got to be teenagers, they were indoctrinated with Cajun food because we visited down there. When Freida got back to it, they would eat the gumbos and the fricassees and so on. And from there on out, she'd cook again."

George then spoke about life after their sons left home. "Now you get to another element of the life cycle. Then you end up as—and I hate this term because I never felt this way—an 'empty nester.' This is the wrong term to describe this stage of living. This was fantastic!" He laughed. "But it was back to just two people. You don't cook a gumbo for just two people." Freida relied heavily on the freezer as an overflow spot for leftovers. "And that freezer was always so packed that you didn't know what was in there. . . . She'd go into that freezer and come out smiling. 'Hey, look what I found! We can have this tonight!'"

But this period was also a very busy one for Freida, working toward National Teacher Certification and pouring herself into various school projects. There were many late nights and working weekends. This is when I often heard Freida dream out loud about creating her own cookbook once the work was finally done.

The Next Generation

My next step was to interview Freida's sons. The three are now scattered geographically—Washington, D.C., Seattle, and Boston—but all enjoy cooking and make it a regular part of their lives. It was gratifying to see how Freida's foodways are visible in her children even years after her death. Still, each recalled his own cook-mentor relationship with his mother in ways that often surprised me.

When it comes to siblings, comparisons are almost impossible to avoid. Middle brother Zack laughed and said, "Don't you love how everybody in a family will say, 'I'm the quiet one'? I stopped saying that years ago because you can say that to somebody and then hear your brother saying that to somebody." But each of the brothers has his own manner of cooking, and all three seem to agree on descriptions. Of his siblings, oldest brother Brian said, "They won't be anywhere near as upset if it doesn't turn out as I might be."

Youngest brother Dominic tends to focus on the social aspect of food. Middle brother Zack is less easily labeled. "Everybody has their own way," Zack said. "For [Dominic], it is about everybody coming over. Brian has moved towards the high-end gourmet. 'What is the *best* seafood gumbo?' He's going to die trying to get it just right, but it's going to be absolutely perfect. I don't know where I fall in that." He does describe himself, "at least in my memory," as "the most unpicky" eater growing up, sharing concoctions like Cream of Wheat with added wheat germ with his mother while his brothers would decline. Preferences aside, all three brothers love cooking.

Cooking Lessons. I assumed that the way Freida taught me to make orange pomanders or pralines was the way she taught her sons to cook. I was wrong. My lessons with Freida focused on problem-solving techniques, and I was guided hands-on through the entire process. Conversely, all three brothers stated that they learned by watching first and foremost.

Zack said, "She never pushed the food thing. . . . I guess we learned by osmosis." Brian stated, "My mom didn't have other people helping her out unless she trusted somebody. She wouldn't let just anybody cook with her. . . . She'd have me chop stuff. But I didn't touch any kind of main ingredient." Of her method of guidance, he added, "She wouldn't drag us into the kitchen, but if we were watching, she'd start explaining stuff. But it wasn't like a class." Dominic agreed: "I was a sous-chef at home in high school and middle school, so I would help cut up things, but I was clearly the underling." Brian described this as "You can chop this, but you can chop it *my* way."

Moving toward becoming a cook in the Thomas house happened relatively late, and it meant following directions. In their separate interviews, all three brothers brought up learning to make roux, the heated fat and flour mixture that forms the basis of many Cajun dishes. Dominic described it this way: "There's a family roux-stirring technique that on pain of death, Mom said, 'You cannot share this.' There's a special technique. It's not brain surgery. It's really pretty obvious, but maybe that's because I'm so used to it. She taught me that, but she wouldn't teach me anything else about gumbo or the other things until I did that roux-stirring for a good long time. This was in high school. Couldn't start the roux-stirring until I was in high school. Couldn't do other things until after doing the roux."

How important is the technique? Zack said, "All those complex recipes say only that—'make a roux.' And there are about fifty different ways that can happen. It's definitely the trickiest part."

The description of the Thomas Roux Rite of Passage brought to mind Norman Maclean's novella *A River Runs Through It*. In this autobiographical story, the narrator states, "My brother and I would have preferred to start learning how to fish by going out and catching a few, omitting entirely anything difficult or technical in the way of preparation that would take away from the fun. But it wasn't by way of fun that we were introduced to our father's art."[6] The young Maclean boys were drilled on a casting rhythm based on a count of four, sometimes precisely measured by metronome as they practiced. Later in the story, both brothers grow up to be fine fishermen, but the narrator's younger brother pulled away to develop techniques of his own. Similar patterns unfolded in the Thomas household.

Dominic reported that Brian eventually broke from the roux technique, a career in science leading him to reason that a glass dish in the microwave would work better. "I don't think Mom was too happy about that at first. Later she would sometimes cook it in the microwave and such for expediency, but you'd never hear her say that she would not teach or use [the old] technique ever again." Dominic himself experimented with roux, eventually even creating a gluten-free version for family members with food sensitivities.

Trust was part of the learning process, said Dominic. "You had to be willing just to sit in the kitchen and be guided in a sense. You can't be a pushy, fidgety kid or you'll get thrown outside." So Freida may have been waiting for her sons to mature to the point where they were easier to work with and had a greater capacity for understanding. Or perhaps autonomy was foremost for Freida, as her kitchen was, in some sense, an artist's studio.

Zack said of his later years cooking with his mother, "Because I never struggled with my mom about how things should be made, she accepted me in the kitchen." He tells about when some members of his mother's family came

Zack Thomas making a cake in 1978. *Courtesy of George Thomas.*

to visit, they all wanted to cook. Although she loved them dearly, her solution was to put a line of tape on the floor that they were not allowed to cross. "They'd be standing at the line, trying to look in there and see what my mom was doing. It was incredibly adolescent, but it was smart too. My mom was the youngest, so they all had things to say and advice to give on how it should be cooked. But I helped Mom make those meals. Me and Mom were in the kitchen and she knew I wasn't going to say anything."

Why the difference between the way Freida taught me and the way Freida taught her sons? With a laugh, Dominic offered: "I don't remember her posing questions. Maybe I asked so many questions myself that she could never get to that. It was more shutting me up. That was the challenge, probably." Brian said, "I think in that regard maybe she felt that you were interested and she was willing. I mean, she was definitely a teacher. Whereas I guess when you're the child of your mother, you feign indifference." Brian and I discussed how running a household is a busy occupation, that teaching one child is often easier than teaching three, and that with your own child, perhaps it always seems there will be a better time.

Rejecting Mediocrity. Perhaps Dominic summed up the boys' growing-up years with regard to food by saying, "I didn't learn proper techniques. What I learned was to touch food—to feel it, taste it, love it, enjoy it." Advice attributed to French author and aviator Antoine de Saint-Exupéry seems relevant: If you want to build a ship, don't drum up people to collect wood and don't assign them tasks, but rather teach them to long for the endless immensity of the sea. In a similar way, Freida prepared her sons to become cooks by instilling in them a deep love of good food and showing them that mastery was possible. For all three, leaving home (and entering a world where food was commonly mediocre) served as a catalyst for embracing cooking.

Interested in continuing to eat well, Brian began cooking on his own in college. During that time and the years thereafter, he often turned to his mother for cooking information, writing down both recipes and notes. A strong interest in food in general and Cajun food in particular continues. Brian invited me to dinner for our interview. He served Cheese and Spinach Soufflé as a forerunner to Bean and Mushroom Soup with French bread, a hearty meal for a cold winter's night. It was excellent.

Brian cooked in the kitchen he and his wife renovated after buying their home. Brian admitted particular attention went into selecting a stove and designing the space for optimum workflow. Wife Micha noted that Brian's love of food is pervasive. "Brian can remember meals he ate three years ago." Brian replied by mentioning his mother's cooking: "She liked it to turn out well, so she didn't just toss stuff off. She was focused on what she was doing. She had a passion for it, and I think I picked that up."

For Zack, the college cafeteria during his freshman year in Portland, Oregon, awakened his desire to cook. "It was terrible. So I started calling my mom immediately asking for stuff, and she put together a blue vinyl notebook with some recipes in it and sent them out to me." Soon there were frequent calls home for additional cooking information and recipes.

Burned out on school for a time, Zack took a year off and moved to Florida. "I got really into cooking then. . . . Me and my friends would stay in when we weren't at our jobs. We'd buy all this food and then come home and cook and cook and cook."

The friends learned cooking techniques from each other, but this period is also when Zack began an eight-year odyssey working in various restaurants that helped him develop skills, build confidence, and form cooking sensibilities. "I really got into the sautéing aspect because it's tricky and I had enough experience that I could do it pretty well. . . . you just get a feel for if you're going to cook these three meats, you have to throw that one on first. That one has to go on the hotter part. It is a nice feeling—being able to understand it all. Without having to consult books or worry, you just launch into action."

As for Dominic, he cooked for special occasions during high school, but it was in college that he learned to embrace socializing through food. At Brandeis University he worked in the dining hall and in off-hours began baking with his buddies. "The bread-baking was this fellowship we had around food and wanting to enrich that fellowship. It was enough to create these wild breads with each other and just taste them and savor them. We weren't drinking. No booze. We were just eating bread and water and playing cards. That was enough. Then in junior and senior year I got involved with student events. I would throw the Thanksgiving party."

It was on a trip to visit him at school near Boston in November of 1993 that I first witnessed Dominic as a social cook. He had bent coat hangers dangling from the heating vent in his dorm room so that he could suspend a pan of bread dough where the yeast would rise more quickly. One never knew what color of finished product would come from that pan—bright yellow turmeric bread, rosy paprika bread, or herb bread with its greenish cast. All breads came in handy that year for a potluck designed to introduce international students to an American holiday while also integrating their food heritages.

I watched Dominic combine his mother's cooking and hosting skills with his hands-on training from the dining hall; he suddenly could orchestrate volunteers while boiling potatoes and icing cookies. The Indian puri bread set off the smoke alarm, and he had to make calls to Freida for turkey advice, but Dominic came into his own as a cook.

Adaptability of Technique. One of the many kitchen lessons I learned through exploring Freida's legacy was adaptability.

Of his mother's cooking, Brian stated, "She was not a formal cook in the sense that she never went by the letter of any recipe. She took what was at hand and made it anew every time. That was the biggest thing I got from cooking with my mom. She was always doing something a little different—not for the sake of doing something different, but to adapt to whatever was going on recipe-wise. If there was an ingredient missing, then she'd work around it. She came up with some pretty consistent results."

All three sons look back in wonder at the poor quality of many of Freida's kitchen tools, which forced her to work around the limitations of her cookware. Brian recalled, "That was one of the amazing things about her because, in my opinion, she had a miserable kitchen." He mentioned low-quality pots, a contractor-grade electric stove, and cheap knives. "She had some iron pots.

Those were the only good tools she had. Considering the kind of stuff she cooked with, it was pretty amazing."

Further along in his interview, Zack surprised me by revealing the degree of Freida's flexibility. Of the coveted and secretive roux process, he stated, "I can turn out a roux that is pretty good, I guess. I don't want to cheat at making a roux. So I try to get it brown the way that you're supposed to, slightly burning the flour as you go along. . . . But my mom, she didn't mind cheating on that kind of stuff." He described a store-bought browning and seasoning sauce and said, "Sometimes she'd just make it right with that."[7]

Zack continued, "There was none of this notion of, 'Oh, I've got to run to the store to get a fresh batch of organic tomatoes.' It was, 'Oh, I need this or that flavor to make this happen. What do I put in there?' It doesn't have to be an extraordinary ingredient. I really like that notion. What you're shooting for is what people will eat and what tastes really good as opposed to that you're going to brag on your ingredients that so many are into these days. We're all into that in Seattle. I do get fresh and local stuff at the farmers' market because I believe in that. I think my mom would have been into that. But it wouldn't have been what decided it. That was not going to be the top criteria."

Adaptability of Tradition. Freida's adaptability went beyond ingredients and cooking utensils. Zack moved back to Athens after college with his future wife, Stephanie. Unknowingly echoing his father's experience with Freida's newlywed cooking, Zack said, "There had been no one around, so my mom just started feeding us like she was getting us ready for the kill. We put on so much weight. . . . Finally, it was Easter, I think, and we went over there. And Mom had made these huge steaks. It was just *waaaaay* too much."

The couple talked after the meal and decided to switch to a vegan diet. "That, uh, didn't really sit too well with Mom. The whole not-eating-meat thing was fine, but the not-eating-seafood thing? It was really hard. And it got to a point where Mom was looking at me like she didn't know who I was."

Eventually Zack chose to compromise. "I decided I would eat whatever Mom cooked, because it wasn't worth losing that relationship with her. Because it was kind of clear that I was going to be estranged to some point over the whole food thing. But then, Mom had also decided that she would meet me halfway. So she started inventing recipes that were vegetarian Cajun style like Vegetarian Red Beans and Rice. She started making vegetarian gumbo. But then also if she made a jambalaya, I would just eat that. And anytime she would make a regular Red Beans and Rice, I would eat it even with ham in it."

Zack reported that Freida also became more flexible about holiday celebrations. "Who's going to question the authority that we're going to have the big meal at Mom's house?" Zack asked. But Freida freely let the celebration move to other venues. "I think she wound up bringing the turkey over, so basically she cooked the meal anyway." He laughed and added, "But it was a time for the relaxing of the culinary dictatorship. And letting it be a little more open. The shock of the meal being away from her kitchen, that helped that progression a lot."

Reproducing the Favorite Dish—Pralines. In my interviews, roux-based Cajun dishes weren't the only culinary creations mentioned by all four members of Freida's family. Pralines also hold a special place in her legacy. George noted that she usually made the pralines for special occasions—Thanksgiving, Christmas, Easter—and she would make them only when the weather was right. "The pressure would be on, leading to those holidays." In the South, you need a cool, crisp day. "Because she wouldn't do it otherwise."

Discussing her process, he continued: "This was horrible to me because I loved to eat those things. She would pull a pan out that looked perfectly respectable to me, or as soon as she poured them out of the pan onto the waxed paper, she'd say, 'No, they're not going to cool correctly and form correctly.' I'd say, 'How can you tell that?!' And she'd say, 'I can just tell.' And then it was always the same old story. Within five seconds, she'd just take that whole pan, a dozen or fifteen of 'em, right over to the garbage can and *pssshhht!*" He mimicked tipping a pan into the trash. "I always thought, 'Hmm. At midnight I can come back in here . . .'"

George then told a praline story already familiar to me. Brian wanted to make some for the meal at home following Freida's funeral service. "He asked me, 'What's the combination? I know its something about the humidity and temperature. If they're not right, then the pralines will just crystallize, frost up. If they don't look smooth, light brown, and so on . . .' And I said, 'I don't have any idea.'"

George paused for a moment in the interview, pointing toward Freida's recipe collection sitting in the other room. "I don't know if there's a recipe in there, but if there is, it is a prosaic one and it wouldn't have her touches in it and it wouldn't have anything about the humidity or anything of that sort."

It was true. Brian tried the recipe file, Freida's collection of cookbooks, and her back issues of cooking periodicals. But Freida didn't write in her cooking materials very often, she had a huge collection to choose from, and she took such good care of her materials that one couldn't tell by stray food spatters which recipes had actually been used.

At some point during the time of the funeral, I heard that Brian was looking for his mother's praline recipe. I still had my copy and hurried to my files to share it. Meanwhile, Brian had turned to his mother's friend Nancy Couvillon for help with the pralines as well. Thanks to these sources, Freida's praline tradition continues. It is Mrs. Couvillon, however, who may have added the crucial piece. She gave the sons confidence.

Zack reported, "After Mom died, Mrs. Couvillon came over. I had never made pralines before. I'd always just gotten them through Mom. But Mrs. Couvillon brought some pralines over and I thought, 'Man, I've missed my chance to learn to make pralines.' And she said, 'Oh, don't worry about that because I couldn't make pralines either until my mother died.' And then she said, 'All of a sudden, I could make pralines! I could get those to set up and they worked fine, so don't even worry about it.'"

One significant lesson from the praline story is that important missing information was actually held by someone outside the family. As discussed in chapter 6, when gathering recipes, it often pays to expand your search. A second significant note is that trial and error was a part of Freida's method. I am comforted to think that even with one of her signature dishes, this master cook's food didn't always turn out perfectly the first time. Sometimes temporary failure and multiple batches are just a part of the process.

Reproducing Other Dishes. I asked the Thomases which dishes that Freida made were their favorites and whether they were able to reproduce them. Youngest son Dominic brought up the roux-based Cajun dishes first. He admitted, "There have been many places where I've been stumped." After searching his recipe files, he turns to the cookbooks his mother preferred.

While he doesn't usually turn to his brothers, he will occasionally pose questions to his mother's sisters or his godmother from the Miller side of his family. Mrs. Couvillon has also been a help. But he notes that turning to other cooks—even ones who knew his mother well—can be problematic. "They have such different ways, I guess." He acknowledges Mrs. Couvillon's considerable kitchen skills, yet says that "she has a different feel for things. She's Cajun, but it's not the family recipe. There are actually some differences."

Middle brother Zack's heart still belongs to his mother's Red Beans and Rice. "After she died, there was a bunch of Red Beans and Rice in the freezer, and I just went through systematically and ate all of it for myself, which was kind of greedy, but it was my last chance. I feel terrible saying that, but on the other hand I really don't feel that bad because I got to have the pleasure of that food.

I guess I really miss that. I've been meaning to make Red Beans and Rice myself, but I haven't eaten Red Beans and Rice since Mom died."

Zack does have a recipe for the dish. "But a lot of those recipes are 'salt to taste' or 'chop up some green peppers.' I guess it's the kind of recipe for people who know what they are doing. There's some underlying consistency to your food, your culinary culture there. So when you say a few simple sentences, then people know what that means and what you're supposed to be doing without going into all the nitty-gritty 'heat the pan to exactly this heat' or that kind of stuff."

Of his mother's cooking process, Zack said, "It probably tasted different every time she made it, you know. But she had a certain taste she was shooting for." Zack compares his mother's Red Beans and Rice to his own Fried Tofu, developed from his days working at the popular Athens restaurant The Grit, and well loved by his son, Oakley.[8] Zack notes that, like his mother, he adjusts his signature dish according to variances with each batch of ingredients. "So when I start making that, it's going to be different every time. Down the road, Oakley may never be able to replicate it because there's something in my mind that's the ideal of what that dish should be like. I'm aiming at it and I'm not using a recipe—it's just the way that I make it. So he'll be stuck at tofu just like I'm stuck at Red Beans and Rice."

Zack continued, "Even if you made it taste exactly like Mom's, I just don't think you'd think it did. How much of it is just this figment of imagination? You invented the whole thing in your mind about how great it was. How are you going to know if it was as good or not?" After thinking for a moment, Zack added, "Maybe that's, with the Red Beans and Rice, why I haven't eaten it. I mean, nobody else in my [household] eats it, so I don't mind it being the end of the line with me. It is an important thing to me, and I'm fine with it staying that way."

When asked about reproducing favorite dishes, oldest son Brian immediately brought up gumbos. "And she made a really good Shrimp Creole and Étouffée. But she was pretty good at most main dishes." Can he reproduce these dishes so they taste just like his mother's? "No," he admitted. "Sometimes I wish I could turn out things the way my mom did, because she was undoubtedly the better cook, but I'll never learn anything if I just follow a recipe slavishly. Plus, things change. There are things she could get a hold of but I can't and vice versa now. It's the whole recipe ingredient thing—whatever you've got at hand is what you've got to cook with."

Like Zack, Brian is at peace with not being able to exactly reproduce his mother's dishes. "I think that was almost intentional on my mom's part. She didn't

At the author's wedding in 2007. Left to right, Elizabeth and Dominic with son Theodore; George; Valerie and new husband Brian; Zack with Dominic's oldest son, Maddock; Brian Thomas. *Courtesy of Nipper Photography.*

want anybody to cook like her. She wanted us to cook well. But cooking is like writing—you find your own voice. You can copy somebody else's recipes and try to cook like them. Maybe you're successful. But she really meant that if you're going to cook, you should try to cook the way *you* cook."

Freida's Cucumber Sandwiches

Freida's note: "Recipe created for Val on October 17, 1993, for her first tea party."

2 long cucumbers (the English variety with the small, tender seeds)
4 big green onions
½ cup almond pieces, or ¼ cup almonds and ¼ cup walnuts

Tony Chachere's Original Creole Seasoning, to taste
Salt and pepper, to taste
1½ tablespoons real mayonnaise
One loaf very soft white bread, frozen
½ cup butter, softened

Peel cucumbers and cut into chunks. Pulse in food processor with onions, nuts, and seasonings. Run through cheesecloth to drain away most of the juice. Put in bowl with mayo and stir. Make sandwiches with frozen bread slices, putting the cucumber mixture on one slice and a layer of butter on the opposite slice. Cut away crusts. Allow bread to thaw and serve slightly cool or at room temperature. To keep sandwiches from drying out, store in refrigerator with layers of waxed paper between and on top of the sandwiches, placing a slightly dampened tea towel over the top.

Crawfish Stew (to serve 45)

20 lb. peeled crawfish, or
        10 lbs. crawfish
        10 lbs. shrimp
        2 cans crab fingers

Roux: 7 cups flour } brown to dark copper
       5 cups oil }   color

Add: 20 med. onions, cut finely
        3 bell peppers, chopped finely
       10 ribs celery, chopped finely
Cover to smother the vegs. —
Let simmer until fat rises, stirring often.

Add: 3½ quarts hot water. Stir to mix.
Let simmer about one hour (cover on pot).

Season with 1 cup salt
              1 qt. chopped parsley
              2 T. red pepper
              seafood seasoning
              Tabasco to taste

Now add the seafood ^ crawfish + shrimp — Simmer
about 20 min. Add more
water if too thick.

(Just before serving:

    Add crab fingers,
      and crab peices

Reheat.

Creamy Pralines

This is the recipe Freida had me copy in the early 1980s.

3 cups packed light brown sugar

¼ teaspoon cream of tartar

⅛ teaspoon salt

1 cup milk or cream

2 tablespoons butter

1 teaspoon vanilla

2¼ cups pecan halves

Barometric pressure must be 30 inches or above. Combine sugar, cream of tartar, salt, and milk. Stir over low heat until sugar dissolves. Wipe crystals from side of pan with cloth or rubber spatula. Cook to 236–238 degrees. Cool to 220 degrees. Add butter, vanilla, and pecans. Beat until creamy. (Do not use electric beater.) Drop in spoonfuls onto a buttered sheet of waxed paper or Formica. Yield: 1½ to 2 dozen.

These are the questions I posed to the Thomas family during my interviews. They may give you ideas about what to ask in your own interviews.

1. Which recipes/dishes do you feel were Freida's best? Do you have written recipes for them? If so, are you able to cook them so that the food turns out just like hers?
2. What do you know about how she learned to cook?
3. What were some distinctive aspects of Freida's approach to cooking?
4. Tell me some of your food memories about Freida.
5. What were some dominant features of her kitchen—favorite cooking tools, organization methods, favorite ingredients, etc.
6. Do you think of Freida as a southern cook? Do you think of yourself as a southern cook?
7. What did you learn from your mother about cooking that you don't think you would have learned elsewhere?
8. How many written recipes do you have that belonged to your mother?
9. What advice would you have for a family wishing to preserve the foodways of a strong cook?

Acknowledgments

I am deeply grateful to Eric Frey, Norma Reaves McCoy, and Carl Stone. They tirelessly helped me track down often strange and far-flung bits of information. They were also generous with their time and resources, accompanying me on history adventures and generally lending a hand. I'm also indebted to those listed in the bibliography who granted interviews. Many of them shared recipes, tracked down missing details, or even allowed me into their kitchens so I could watch them work. (As this book goes into production, eight of them are now gone and fondly remembered.)

Other individuals kindly served as consultants or helped me with images: John P. Albert, Danielle Green Barney, Evelyn Morgan Bowen, Janet Clark, Martha Cook, Amberlee Fletcher of Lilac Lens Photography, Diana Harton, Mandi D. Johnson, Mildred Childress Miller, Joe Robert and Louise McClellan, Jimmy and Michelle Reaves, Lydia Stone Rensch, Marci Greene Severson, and Shelia Bowen Towery.

I would like to thank, especially, the home cooks who gave their input on chapter 4: Nadya Belaya (Ukraine and England), Isabel Chys (Belgium), Birgit Debeerst (Belgium and South Korea), Nicoleta Herinean (Romania), Julissa Ilizaliturri-Keenan (Mexico), Andrew Kim (South Korea and Hong Kong), Hadley H. Koo (South Korea and Germany), Ezequiel Korin (Venezuela), Suruchi Gadkari Krieglstein (India), Lina Nazar (Afghanistan and Pakistan), Leslie Browning Pourreau (France), and Mahnee Shawananoak Titus (Shoshone Tribe and England).

Many individuals provided contacts or shared recipes and research materials. A big thank-you goes to Eddie Bennett, Jane Bridges, Carole Cohen, Tom and Jean Dirksen, Charles Durant, Martha Eubanks, Carol Feeney, Dawn Fowler-Hamilton, Jennifer O'Neal Frey, Naomi Gold, Randy Gooden, Carolyn Hall, Susan Hoffius, Jim Jordan, Suzanne Kantziper, Kaye Kole, Diane Kuhr, Matiel Leffler, Bobbie Levy, Jim and Sarah Liebold, Judy Cowles Magee, Gillie McDonald, Harriet Meyerhoff, Kaye Minchew, Anna Marie Soper-O'Rourke, Betty Oliver, Mamie Pipkins, Janice Rhoden, Jean J. Rowe, Luciana Spracher, Bobbie Jean Causey Teague, Elizabeth Adams Thomas, Heidi Anne Thomas, Jennifer Vessels, Arden Williams, and Georgene Cowles Wickstrand. I wish I had been able to mention every recipe and resource, but please know that even materials that didn't appear in the finished book helped build background knowledge.

My proofreading and recipe testing team was invaluable: Bryan Alexander, Beth Bailey, LeEllen Chandler, Isabel Chys, Alli Phillips Connorton, Anna De Jaeger, Paula Eubanks, Amber Henson, Debbie Hernandez, Steve Hoffius, Caroline Hopkinson, Amy Pontzer Jones, Annike Jones, Debbie McCann, Jennifer Niven, Penelope Niven, Monica LaBelle Oliver, Tamara Patridge, John Preston, Elizabeth Adams Thomas, Heidi Heiner Thomas, Jennifer Vessels, Mary Wickwire, and Janet Wright.

In addition, I would like to thank several people for research help: Marylène Altieri (Schlesinger Library, Radcliffe/Harvard), Maribeth Bohley, Laura Botts (Mercer University Library Special Collections), Yvonne Carmicheal (Clayton County [Georgia] Public Library), Laura Carter (Athens Clarke County Library), Steve Cotham and Sally Polhemus (McClung Historical Collection), Judith Gray (American Folklife Center), Gail Greve (Colonial Williamsburg Foundation Special Collections Library), Caroline Hopkinson (Armstrong Atlantic University Library), Barbara Janson and Judith Lowney (Johnson & Wales University Library), Alison Kelly and Laura Kells (Library of Congress), John Kupersmith (University of California Library), Marian Hart, Kim Norman, Lindsey Rackett (University of Georgia Poultry Research Center), Mary Evelyn Tomlin (National Archives Southeast Region), Sue Verhoef (Atlanta History Center), and Pamela Whitenack (Hershey Community Archives). Many colleagues from the Georgia Archives were invaluable for their support and expertise, including Elizabeth Barr, David Carmicheal, Dale Couch, Steve Engerrand, Greg Jarrell, Amanda Mros, Tina Mason Seetoo, Anne Smith, and Christine Wiseman.

As I was beginning to study genealogy, several people generously shared their hard work and know-how, including William G. Frey, Mary Stewart Frey, Aubrey Huddleston, Clyde Marks, R. Lovett Reaves, and Barbara Trammell. You have my deep appreciation.

My research road led to many historic sites that were invaluable for helping me better understand historical kitchens and foodways: Ash Lawn–Highland, Berkeley Plantation, Colonial Williamsburg Foundation (particularly Barbara Ball, Dennis Cotner, and Deborah Mitchell), Cyrus McCormick Farm, Fort King George Historic Site, Foxfire Museum and Heritage Center (particularly Robert Murphy), Historic Jamestowne, Jamestown Settlement, Jarrell Plantation Historic Site, Jimmy Carter National Historic Site and Boyhood Home, Mingus Mill and Oconaluftee Mountain Farm Museum, Monticello (Thomas Jefferson Foundation), Museum of Appalachia, Root House Museum (Cobb Landmarks and Historical Society), Tullie Smith Farm (Atlanta History Center), and Wades' Mill.

A deep thank-you to the University of Georgia Press for their guidance on this project, particularly Regan Huff, Ann Marlowe, Erin New, and Laura Sutton. Special appreciation goes to my editor, Pat Allen, who warmly nurtured this project from start to finish.

I want to thank my muses. Being "Aunt Val" is one of the deepest joys of my life, reminding me of why it is important to preserve history for the next generation. My love goes to Graham, Trevor, Erin, Emma, Colin, Margaret, Daisy, Shane, Maddock, Theodore, Clarke, Samantha, Claire, and Tom. And of course I also wish to thank Eli, my beloved boy (and favorite sous-chef), who kindly made his appearance after his due date so I could get the first phase of this project squared away.

My love and admiration also belongs to my parents and grandparents, who provided a fantastic childhood and then also the gift of their friendship when I became a young adult. I will always miss you.

Last but certainly not least, I wish to thank my ever-supportive husband, Brian. From stopping at yet one more archives to helping take notes when my hands were covered in flour to proofreading, you were always there. You made the journey even more fun. My love and thanks forever.

Notes

Introduction. Comfort, Revulsion, and Cultural History—Served Up in a Single Bowl

1. I was already working with family recipes, but this particular one was my choice for a recipe-collecting assignment for Dr. Genelle Morain's Folk Literature in the Curriculum class (EEN 713) at the University of Georgia in the spring of 1993.

2. Robert Alvin Frey, letter to author, May 1993.

3. Brillat-Savarin, *Physiology of Taste*, 85.

4. Hess and Hess, *Taste of America*, 32. *Dining at Monticello*, a book about Jefferson's foodways edited by Damon Lee Fowler, doesn't contain specific squirrel recipes, yet it does discuss wild game.

5. Ziemann and Gillette, *White House Cookbook*, 108.

6. Kurlansky, *Food of a Younger Land*, 112–13.

7. Ibid.; Sokolov, *Fading Feast*, 75–82; A. Smith, *Oxford Companion*, 58, 396, 553.

8. Proust, *Swann's Way*, 48–51.

9. Bertha Ashley interview, 22 May 2008.

Chapter 1. Setting a Course

1. Theophano, *Eat My Words*, 6.

2. Moffat, *Times of Our Lives*, 12.

3. Hauser, *You Can Write a Memoir*, 3–4.

4. Recipe created by the author in honor of her brother, Eric T. Frey. He is a veteran of the Marines and stated that creating a box to warm food inside an engine is an old military trick.

5. Zinsser, "Writing Family History," 17.

6. Ibid.

7. Paula Eubanks is working toward publication of her recipe collection, "The Family Table."

8. Robert A. Frey, New Edinburg (column), *Cleveland County (Arkansas) Herald*, 11 October 1993–23 October 1996.

9. See Bianchi, Robinson, and Milkie, *Changing Rhythms*; Aulette, *Changing Families*; Volo and Volo, *Family Life*.

10. Kivnick, "Remembering and Being Remembered," 50.

11. Ibid.

12. Williams, *You Say Cuisine*.

Chapter 2. Organizing and Protecting Your Materials

1. Microfilm at the Arkansas History Commission, Little Rock. The Account Books of A. Madenwald (Medenwald) range from 1865 to 1910 and contain information for Champaign City and Odin, Illinois, as well as Dardanelle, Arkansas.

2. Willene O'Neal uses MasterCook software to organize her recipes.

3. Jane Bridges interview, 13 February 2008.

4. Major, *Hollyhocks and Old Maid Aunts*, 183.

5. Paula Eubanks and Martha Eubanks joint interview, 2 December 2007.

6. Dorothy "Dot" Louise Slappey Eubanks (1922–1990) of Bibb County, Georgia.

7. See Theophano, *Eat My Words*; Tye, *Baking as Biography*.

8. Kummer, "Half a Loaf."

9. Ostmann and Baker, *The Recipe Writer's Handbook*, 212.

10. See the United States Copyright Office website at www.copyright.gov.

11. On the Society of American Archivists website, www2.archivists.org, the Publications section offers several online brochures including a guide to copyright and unpublished material.

12. Although procedures and safeguards vary somewhat from institution to institution, these are standard working procedures recommended at archives. They are gleaned from field literature as well as my work experiences at the Calvin M. McClung Historical Collection (Knoxville), the Library of Congress Manuscripts Division (Washington, D.C.), the Georgia Historical Society (Savannah), the Savannah Jewish Archives, and the Georgia Archives (Morrow). I also received training in 2002 at the National Archives and Records Administration (NARA) Modern Archives Institute in College Park, Maryland. Additional information can be

found online. My favorite source is the NARA preservation page, www.archives.gov/preservation.

13. Cotton gloves are available from archival supply companies. I prefer Gaylord, Light Impressions, and Hollinger Metal Edge.

14. Robert W. Frey and Sharon L. C. Frey, personal letter to Robert A. Frey and Arlie Mae R. Frey, 25 February 1969.

15. If you need to ask for this type of pen by brand name, the most common manufacturers include Fiskars, Abbey Publications, and Nikken.

16. I order most often from the companies listed in note 13.

17. An Internet search for "emergency preparedness" and "preservation" will turn up useful information from reputable sources such as the Library of Congress, the American Library Association, and Heritage Preservation: The National Institute for Conservation. Another helpful Web search is "mold and mildew" along with "preservation."

18. Williams and Jaggar, *Saving Stuff*. An online search for "museum care guide," "museum handbook," or "artifact care guide" will turn up Internet pages or books from reputable sources such as the National Park Service or large museums.

19. Kathryn McNerney and Linda Campbell Franklin are two authors who have written helpful books about kitchen objects.

Chapter 3. Adjusting Recipes

1. Author's journal, 14 December 1990.

2. Flinn, *The Kitchen Counter Cooking School*, 36.

3. For most common ingredients, an Internet search for "[ingredient name] cup to grams" or "[ingredient name] cup to ounces" will turn up various conversion charts and calculators. These are not standardized, so amounts given may vary from site to site by a few grams/ounces. And which measurement system should you use? This is, of course, personal choice. There is a nice symmetry of using ounces with American recipes, yet I find that because grams are a smaller unit, the clarified recipe usually doesn't need decimal points to be accurate. Most scales handle both grams and ounces, so cooks with scales can handle either measurement system.

4. Evelyn Morgan Bowen, descendant of the Frey family, kindly allowed me to scan items from her recipe collection. The Vanilla Wafer Cake was on a page that had come loose from an unknown community cookbook. Based on the amounts of other ingredients and comparisons with similar recipes, I estimated that yesteryear's 25-cent package was around 6 ounces (170 g).

5. Ostmann and Baker, *The Recipe Writer's Handbook*. A comparable source is *Recipes into Type: A Handbook for Cookbook Writers and Editors*, by Joan Whitman and Dolores Simon.

6. I would like to thank the following interviewees in particular for sharing their recipe modification know-how: Jane Bridges, Doris Koplin, Norma McCoy, Gillie McDonald, Hoyt Oliver, Willene O'Neal, Tamara Patridge, Michelle Reaves, Luann Sullivan, and Janie Thomas.

7. The Smith-Lever Act of 1914 established this service. Expertise varies from county to county, but local agents have access to a large network of experts. A Web search for "Cooperative Extension" together with the name of your county can connect you to more information.

8. My interview with Dennis Cotner of Colonial Williamsburg on 25 July 2007 sparked more research into this concept.

9. Paula Eubanks interview, 26 April 2008.

10. Lincoln et al., *Home Helps*.

11. Other books that touch on this concept include Sue Shephard's *Pickled, Potted, and Canned* and David Kamp's *United States of Arugula*.

12. Beeton, *Mrs Beeton's Book of Household Management*, 328. In just one example of a proportion-based older recipe, Mrs. Beeton's recipe for "Spongecakes, Small" calls for "the weight of five eggs in flour" but also "the weight of eight in pounded loaf sugar."

13. Schenone, *Thousand Years*, 85.

14. Zimmer, *Robert E. Lee Family Cooking*, 99.

15. Ibid., 94–96.

16. Ibid., 113.

17. Hess's commentary in her edition of *Martha Washington's Booke of Cookery* and in Abby Fisher's *What Mrs. Fisher Knows about Old Southern Cooking* is excellent, yet tends to be at the expert level. *The Taste of America*, the book she penned along with her husband, John L. Hess, helped me get a better feel for her culinary point of view and made her historical cookbook commentary more readable for me.

18. My interview with Dennis Cotner on 25 July 2007 particularly helped me understand the effects of cooking speeds and methods.

19. Doris Koplin interview, 12 July 2007.

20. Norma McCoy interview, 8 September 2007.

21. The recipe originated with *Betty Crocker's Picture Cook Book, Revised and Enlarged*. There are actually two recipes to use—filling on page 370 and crust on page 343. A guide called "How to Measure to Be Sure of Results" appears on pages 8–9 of this cookbook, but my mother did not use the method recommended for flour. One U.S. cup of all-purpose flour should be close to 125 grams, but my mother's "cups" were more like 160 grams.

22. Tamara Patridge interview, 18 July 2007. Similarly, folklorist Diane Tye discusses "flavor principles" in *Baking as Biography*, 61.

23. Anna Santiago Robinson interview, 13 May 2008.

24. Susan Puckett interview, 12 May 2008.

25. Eddie Bennett interview, 25 July 2007; Zack Thomas interview, 8 March 2008.

26. Doris Koplin interview, 12 July 2007.

27. Utah State University Extension posted an ingredient substitution list by Dr. Georgia C. Lauritzen in 1992 that I find more extensive and helpful than most. It has since been updated by Ann Henderson, Susan Haws, and SuzAnne Jorgensen. See http://extension.usu.edu/files/publications/publication/FN_255.pdf.

28. Eddie Bennett, Robert Curry, Willene O'Neal, and Zack Thomas all mentioned this concept in their interviews. See also Beard, *Delights and Prejudices*, 8–9.

29. Jacobsen, *American Terroir*.

30. Major, *Hollyhocks and Old Maid Aunts*, 25.

31. Glenda Major interview, 31 January 2008.

Chapter 4. Working with Regional or World Recipes

1. The Dutch name for what Birgit calls "mouse poop" is *hagelslag*, literally "hailstorm." Popular brands include De Ruÿter, Jacques, Kwatta, and Venz.

2. The Bradley County Pink Tomato Festival has been around since the mid-1950s.

3. These products by a company called Dr. Oetker are increasingly marketed in the United States in larger grocery stores. They are available online through various sellers.

Chapter 5. Interviews and Cooking Visits

In 1890 Laura Russell (1827–1904) of Plymouth, Massachusetts, wrote down reminiscences of her life and family history including details about foodways. She did not include any recipes. Her writing is now held by the Pilgrim Society.

1. Dusty Gres was a project director for *Key Ingredients: America By Food*, a traveling exhibition mounted by the Smithsonian and sponsored by the Georgia Humanities Council from 2008 to 2010. I served as consultant for that exhibition. Dusty kindly agreed to be interviewed on the spot and later contributed the recipe. Dusty told me the recipe "was just in her head and in her hands. . . . She had magic hands. I don't know any other way to put it." It is not known which cookbook contained the original recipe.

2. Gillie McDonald on 24 March 2007 and Bonnie Crowley on 9 October 2008 both laid tables filled with home-cooked foods that could feed (and deeply please) an army.

3. Bonnie Crowley interview, 27 March 2008. Bonnie learned to cook from her grandmother Carrie Judson Wynn Thackston, born in 1870 in Oglethorpe County, Georgia.

4. Doris Koplin interview, 12 July 2007.

5. The thoughtful donor was Willene O'Neal in January 2014.

6. Tamara Patridge interview, 18 July 2007.

Chapter 6. Orphaned Recipes and Conducting Research

1. Robert Alvin Frey lived from 23 October 1911 to 14 June 2000. I recorded the recipe for Teacakes in my journal on 14 December 1990.

2. John William Frey (1860–1929) and Hepsey Jane Mosley Frey (1860–1947) both lived in Cleveland County, Arkansas, all their lives and had fifteen children. (Hepsey's tombstone records a different spelling of her maiden name than her parents' graves.) John was the son of John Henry Frey (1831–1890), who populated the area with eleven children. These families helped swell the ranks of Frey reunions.

3. Susan Marks's *Finding Betty Crocker* and Laura Schenone's *A Thousand Years Over a Hot Stove* are two helpful sources that discuss the home economics movement and its impact on written recipes.

4. Hess and Hess, *Taste of America*, 104.

5. A. Smith, *Oxford Companion*, 352, 365.

6. www.foodtimeline.org.

7. Spelling changes are gradual and may in fact take many decades, but looking at old cookbooks reveals the trends.

8. This is the only recipe thought to survive from El Myra Trammell Reaves (1882–1950).

9. Sperry, *Reading Early American Handwriting*; Stryker-Rodda, *Understanding Colonial Handwriting*; T. Thornton, *Handwriting in America*.

10. Robert Curry and Susie Curry interview, 28 April 2008.

11. Ina Shipley manuscript recipe scrapbook, ca. 1851–1956, collection of the author. Purchased 6 June 2007.

12. Although perhaps odd to us now as a paper fastener, straight pins are fairly common in archival collections from the early twentieth century and before.

13. "Doughboy" is an outdated slang term for American soldiers, particularly during World War I. To locate the origin of the article, I searched newspaper databases using strings of text from the recipe and commentary. A copy of this newspaper article appeared in the *Pittsburgh Press* on 8 February 1919 and was written by Mary Damont. According to the Salvation Army website, every June there is Salvation Army Donut Day. A recipe is included but is also available elsewhere on the Internet.

14. See British Library Board, "Learning: Books for Cooks" and "Learning: Dictionaries and Meanings" for more information.

15. Moritz and Kahn, *Twentieth Century Cook Book*; Kander, *Settlement Cookbook*.

16. Ferris, *Matzoh Ball Gumbo*.

17. Moritz and Kahn, *Twentieth Century Cook Book*, 53.

18. General Foods, *Betty Crocker's Picture Cook Book*.

19. I am particularly grateful to George Thomas and Katie Smith for going above and beyond to share my mother's recipes.

20. Cleveland County Cooks, *Cleveland County Herald*, Rison, Arkansas.

21. Edge, *Gracious Plenty*, 2–3. Researcher Anne Bower also writes about community cookbooks.

22. Roahen and Edge, *Southern Foodways Alliance Community Cookbook*, xiii.

23. The 1963 volume was previously owned by Arlie Mae Frey's older sister, Ollie Isabel Reaves Livingston (1909–1969), and the notations inside gave me clues about the preferences and cooking habits of another long-gone family cook.

24. Bobbie Jean Hopson Causey Teague kindly gave me her copy of *Crossett Cook Book* by the Crossett (Arkansas) Congress of Parent-Teachers. It was first compiled in 1931, and Bobbie Jean helped with revisions for the 1959 edition. Her mother was Robert A. Frey's elder sister Alma Frey Childress (1906–1989).

25. Among the main community cookbook publishers are Cookbook Publishers Inc., Morris Press, and Fundcraft.

26. Egerton, *Southern Food*, 352–72.

27. The organizations listed in the text have been some of the most proactive in recent years about preserving and celebrating regional foodways, but additional important organizations include American Folklife Center (Library of Congress), California Foodways, Cultural Conservancy Indigenous Health/Native Circle of Food, Foodways Texas, Folklife in Louisiana, Fresh Forty Nine (Alaska), Georgia Mountains Foodways Alliance, Greater Midwest Food Alliance, Indiana Foodways Alliance, National Caribbean-American Foods and Foodways Alliance, Northwest Folklife, Pine Mountain Settlement School (central Appalachia), Sabores Sin Fronteras (University of Arizona), and Smithsonian Center for Folklife and Cultural Heritage. Other books that highlight regional foodways in the United States can be found in the bibliography: J. Anderson, *American Century Cook-Book*; Barile, *Cookbooks Worth Collecting*; Camp, *American Foodways*; Cook's Country, *America's Best Lost Recipes*; Edge, *Foodways*; Egerton, *Side Orders*; Kamp, *United States of Arugula*; Long, "Culinary Tourism"; Lynn and Pelton, *Early American Cookbook*; McWilliams, *Revolution in Eating*; Shindler, *American Dish*; Willard, *America Eats!*

28. Glenda Major interview, 31 January 2008.

29. This recipe came into the family repertoire through my maternal grandmother, Marjorie Eileen Greene Cowles McPherson (1920–2003), who spent much of her life in Rainier, Oregon.

30. In early 2009, Judy Cowles Magee told me about this Pillsbury recipe made by her maternal grandmother, Dessie Jane Weekley Greene (1888–1958). I would like to thank my mother's siblings—Judy Cowles Magee, Russell L. Cowles, and Georgene Cowles Wickstrand, for their generosity with family stories, pictures, and recipes.

31. An Internet search for "recipe website" will turn up many recipe collections with varied features. Unless you think a lost recipe may have come from a specific

publication or product label, your best bet may be to seek out websites that encourage home cooks to post recipes. My personal favorites are Allrecipes.com, Cooks.com, and A Taste of Home.

32. www.hungrybrowser.com.

33. Sue McClellan interview, 8 September 2007.

34. Lloyd "Buddy" Reaves interview, 2 July 2008.

35. www.foxfire.org; www.folkschool.org; www.history.org. If you need reproduction kitchen utensils and fittings, there are various Internet sources, including Historic Housefitters (New Preston, Conn.), Jas. Townsend & Son (Pierceton, Ind.), Smoke and Fire (Waterville, O.), and USHist.com (Shingletown, Calif.).

36. www.alhfam.org.

37. Spaulding and Spaulding, *Civil War Recipes*, 26–40.

38. Rutledge, *House and Home*, 165.

39. Household Department column by Mrs. Wm. N. White, *Southern Farm and Home* 1, no. 6 (April 1870): 214. Because of the heavy spices, this recipe may have been intended for use as a relish or chutney. Please note that consuming large quantities of nutmeg or mace can cause temporary physical symptoms such as dizziness, headache, or a numb tongue.

40. This story came from my grandmother Arlie Mae Reaves Frey (1917–2000) and involved my great-grandmother El Myra Trammell Reaves (1882–1950). Both lived in Cleveland County, Arkansas, throughout their lives.

Chapter Seven. Sharing Family Recipes and Foodways

1. Troup County Archives, LaGrange, Ga.

2. Major, *Hollyhocks and Old Maid Aunts*, 137.

3. www2.archivists.org. Online brochures available through their Publications section include a guide to donating materials to a repository and a guide to deeds of gift (transfer of ownership).

4. The family prefers not to make its blog address public.

Appendix 1. Exploring a Recipe

The epigraph quote from Clower is in Grizzard, *Don't Forget to Call Your Mama . . . I Wish I Could Call Mine*, 69. "Whomp" is the sound of a refrigerated can of biscuits being hit against a surface so that it will pop open.

1. Dupree, *Nathalie Dupree's Southern Memories*, 60. It was toward the end of writing this appendix that I came across Dupree's phrase "quest for the perfect biscuit" and experienced one of those moments of serendipity where you realize there are kindred spirits out there sharing similar fascinations.

2. A. Brown, *I'm Just Here for More Food*, 6.

3. Sue Carolyn Reaves McClellan (1935–2007), Lloyd Wilton "Buddy" Reaves (1937–2011), Norma Faye Reaves McCoy, and Jimmy Ray Reaves, all of Cleveland County, Arkansas.

4. Quoted in Rogers, *Hungry for Home*, 160.

5. Dale Couch interview, 28 April 2008. Details clarified in an e-mail to author, 21 November 2008.

6. Fowler, *Classical Southern Cooking*, 328.

7. Norma McCoy interview, 8 September 2007.

8. Quoted by John T. Edge in Wilkes, *Mrs. Wilkes' Boardinghouse Cookbook*, 9.

9. Wilkes, *Mrs. Wilkes' Boardinghouse Cookbook*, 136.

10. Claiborne, *Craig Claiborne's Southern Cooking*, 252.

11. St. John, *Deep South Staples*, 198.

12. Taylor, *New Southern Cook*, 220. Southern flour was difficult for me to find while living in northern California. I sometimes substitute part cake flour.

13. Dull, *Southern Cooking*, 153.

14. Corriher, *CookWise*, 6.

15. Dewan, "Biscuit Bakers' Treasured Mill."

16. *Cook's Illustrated*, 1 May 1993.

17. Figoni, *How Baking Works*, chap. 13.

18. Neal, *Bill Neal's Southern Cooking*, 34.

19. Lewis and Peacock, *Gift of Southern Cooking*, 230.

20. Rombauer and Becker, *Joy of Cooking*, 547.

21. Ibid., 632.

22. Taylor, *New Southern Cook*, 220.

23. General Foods, *Betty Crocker's Picture Cook Book*, 85.

24. Stewart, "Where to Find Martha: Radio."

25. A thank-you goes to the quiet lady who worked many years at the eastside Winn Dixie in Athens, Georgia, when I was growing up. I never knew her name, but she always had a smile and a cooking tip.

26. M. Anderson, *Successful Baking*, 25.

27. Farmer, *Original Boston Cooking-School Cook Book*, 70.

28. Champion, *Flying Biscuit Cafe Cookbook*, 18.

29. Fowler, *Classical Southern Cooking*, 329.

30. A. Brown, *I'm Just Here for More Food*, 55–56.

31. Unfortunately, our family cannot find the source of this recipe, but there are many angel biscuit recipes like it in cookbooks and online.

32. M. Brown, *Southern Cook Book*, 215.

33. Royal Baking Powder Company, *Best War Time Recipes*, 5.

34. LouElla Thompson interview, 9 September 2007. The informant's daughter, Janie Thompson Hensley, joined the interview for the last few minutes.

35. Edge, *Gracious Plenty*, 37–39.

36. *Southern Living*, "Mississippi's Best Biscuits," 47.

37. For information about Thrasher's Grocery, located at 217 Hiawassee Avenue, I thank Laura Carter of the Athens Clarke County Library and Eric Frey.

38. Dupree, *Nathalie Dupree's Southern Memories*, 60.

39. Dabney, *Smokehouse Ham*, 115.

40. Junior League of Charleston, *Charleston Receipts*, 191.

41. Buddy Reaves interview, 2 July 2008. Details clarified in a later phone conversation.

42. General Foods, *Betty Crocker's Picture Cook Book*, 82.

43. Dupree, *Nathalie Dupree's Southern Memories*, 60.

44. Lincoln et al., *Home Helps*, 11.

45. Major, *Hollyhocks and Old Maid Aunts*, 27.

46. O'Neill, "Jam Session," 59.

47. Eubanks, "Family Table," 12.

48. General Foods, *Favorite Recipes for Country Kitchens*, 6.

49. Figoni, *How Baking Works*, 295.

50. Hill, *Mrs. Hill's New Cook Book*, 228.

51. Rombauer and Becker, *Joy of Cooking*, 632.

52. Villas, *My Mother's Southern Kitchen*, xii.

53. O'Neill, "Jam Session," 59.

54. Abramson and Haskell, *Encyclopedia of Appalachia*, 917.

55. McGahey, "Our Best Buttermilk Biscuits," 166.

56. Dull, *Southern Cooking*, 154.

57. My hexagonal biscuit cutter was made by Ateco and purchased at Dean & Deluca in 2008. I was unable to find a Web presence for Ateco, but their products are available in various kitchen shops, baking supply stores, and restaurant supply companies.

58. Corriher, *CookWise*, 153.

59. Claiborne, *Craig Claiborne's Southern Cooking*, 253.

60. Dull, *Southern Cooking*, 154.

61. Farmer, *Original Boston Cooking-School Cook Book*, 70.

62. Dull, *Southern Cooking*, 154.

63. Wilkes, *Mrs. Wilkes' Boardinghouse Cookbook*, 136.

64. Williams, *You Say Cuisine*, 94.

65. Peacock, "Mini Prep," 7.

66. Rombauer and Becker, *Joy of Cooking*, 632.

67. Wilkes, *Mrs. Wilkes' Boardinghouse Cookbook*, 136.

68. Neal, *Bill Neal's Southern Cooking*, 34.

69. Rombauer and Becker, *Joy of Cooking*, 632.

70. Lupo, *Southern Cooking*, 225.

71. Harris, *Welcome Table*, 192.

72. Starr, *Soul of Southern Cooking*, 140.

73. Rombauer and Becker, *Joy of Cooking*, 632–33.

74. Van Dyke and Van Dyke, *Blue Willow Inn Bible*, 151.

75. Peacock, "Biscuits."

76. Carole Cohen, phone conversation with author, 30 October 2008.

77. Joe Robert McClellan, e-mail to author, 14 August 2008.

78. John T. Edge writes about chocolate gravy and shares additional recipes, including one alternately called Sopping Chocolate that incorporates bacon, in *The Southern Foodways Alliance Community Cookbook*, 25 (bacon recipe), and *A Gracious Plenty*, 243 (plain chocolate).

79. Eubanks, "Family Table," 12.

80. An Internet search for "round cast-iron griddle" will turn up several new examples for purchase. Grandpa's, made by the Martin Stove and Range Company of Florence, Alabama, is nine inches in diameter and has a smooth surface.

81. Mamie Pipkins, e-mail to author, 6 November 2007.

82. Wilkes, *Mrs. Wilkes' Boardinghouse Cookbook*, 136. More information about the restaurant and cookbook can be found at www.mrswilkes.com.

Appendix 2. Exploring Recipe History

1. To find educational locations, try the local chamber of commerce or an online search for "agritourism" or "house museum" and the state or county you wish to know more about.

2. Egerton, *Southern Food*, 217.

3. Edge, *Foodways*, 123.

4. Fowler, *Classical Southern Cooking*, 7.

5. Shephard, *Pickled, Potted, and Canned*, 56.

6. O'Neill, "Jam Session"; Hess, *Martha Washington's Booke of Cookery*, 335.

7. Hess, *Martha Washington's Booke of Cookery*, 335.

8. Fischer, *Albion's Seed*, 728–29.

9. Dale Couch, e-mail to author, 1 October 2008.

10. Glasse, *Art of Cookery*.

11. Hess, *Martha Washington's Booke of Cookery*, 335.

12. Hopley, "American Cookery."

13. A. Smith, *Oxford Companion*, 109.

14. Simmons, *First American Cookbook*, 38.

15. Randolph, *Virginia Housewife*, 139–40.

16. Puckett, *Cook's Tour of Mississippi*, 27. Susan Puckett interview, 12 May 2008.

17. Fowler, *Classical Southern Cooking*, 330.

18. The Root House Museum, built circa 1845 by William and Hannah Root, is located at 145 Denmead Street NW in Marietta, Georgia.

19. Maryellen Higginbotham interview, 14 May 2008; Leslie, *Miss Leslie's New Cookery Book.*

20. Egerton, *Southern Food*, 219.

21. Ibid.

22. Mrs. H. Wilson, *Tested Recipe Cook Book*, 46; Dull, *Southern Cooking*, 155–56.

23. Egerton, *Southern Food*, 218–21. John Egerton's *Southern Food* provides an in-depth look at beaten biscuits, including their link to ham.

24. A. Smith, *Oxford Companion*, 53.

25. Barbara Ball unrecorded interview, 7 September 2006; Dennis Cotner interview, 25 July 2007.

26. Figoni, *How Baking Works*, 287–301.

27. A. Smith, *Oxford Companion*, 109.

28. Ibid.

29. A. White, Anna Mathews White Paper.

30. A. Smith, *Oxford Companion*, 109.

31. A. White, Anna Mathews White Paper.

32. P. Thornton, *Southern Gardener and Receipt Book*, 90, 139.

33. Rutledge, *House and Home*, 158.

34. Breckinridge, Issa Desha Breckinridge Recipe Book.

35. Andrews, *Breakfast, Dinner, and Tea*, 303.

36. Child, *American Frugal Housewife*, 20.

37. M. Wilson, *Rumford Southern Recipes*, 7.

38. Dooley, *Heritage Cook Book*, 169.

39. Dull, *Southern Cooking*, 153.

40. Figoni, *How Baking Works*, 288.

41. A. Smith, *Oxford Companion*, 109.

42. Ibid., 228.

43. Royal Baking Powder Company, *Royal Baker and Pastry Cook.*

44. J. Anderson, *American Century Cook-Book*, 175.

45. Dale Couch, e-mail message to author, 2 October 2008.

46. Dupree, *New Southern Cooking*, 211.

47. Page and Wigginton, *Foxfire Book of Appalachian Cookery*, 188.

48. Author's journal, 22 April 2007.

49. Bonnie Crowley interview, 27 March 2008.

50. Bonnie Crowley interview, 9 October 2008. Eric T. Frey assisted.

51. More information and pictures along with videos can be found via the author's website, www.valeriejfrey.com.

Appendix 3. Exploring a Cook's Legacy

The epigraph from Maugham is quoted in McWilliams, *A Revolution in Eating*, 55.

1. An additional avenue of research would be to interview Freida's surviving siblings in hopes of learning more about their mother's kitchen as well as Freida's early cooking.

2. Author's journal (studio book), 19 February 2000.

3. Beard, *Delights and Prejudices*, 8.

4. Thomas, *Story*, 5.

5. Ibid., 340.

6. Maclean, *River Runs Through It*, 2.

7. Zack didn't know the name of the brown cooking liquid. Brian reported in an e-mail on 4 November 2008 that it was Kitchen Bouquet.

8. Greene and Hafer, *Grit Cookbook*, 8.

Suggested Reading

Writing Guides

Goldberg, Natalie. *Writing Down the Bones: Freeing the Writer Within*. Boston: Shambhala, 1986.

Hauser, Susan Carol. *You Can Write a Memoir*. Cincinnati: Writer's Digest Books, 2001.

Lamott, Anne. *Bird by Bird: Some Instructions on Writing and Life*. New York: Pantheon, 1994.

Moffat, Mary Jane. *The Times of Our Lives: A Guide to Writing Autobiography and Memoir*. 3rd ed. Santa Barbara, Calif.: John Daniel, 1996.

Pressfield, Steven. *The War of Art: Break Through the Blocks and Win Your Inner Creative Battles*. New York: Warner, 2002.

Woolf, Vivienne, et al. *Capturing Memories: The Art of Reminiscing*. London: Vallentine Mitchell, 2002.

Zinsser, William. *Writing about Your Life: A Journey into the Past*. New York: Marlowe, 2004.

Autobiography and Reminiscing with Recipes

Berkeley, Ellen Perry, ed. *At Grandmother's Table: Women Write about Food, Life, and the Enduring Bond between Grandmothers and Granddaughters*. Minneapolis: Fairview, 2000.

Caldwell, Patsy, and Amy Lyles Wilson. *Bless Your Heart: Saving the World One Covered Dish at a Time*. Nashville: Thomas Nelson, 2010.

Darden, Norma Jean, and Carole Darden. *Spoonbread and Strawberry Wine: Recipes and Reminiscences of a Family.* Garden City, N.Y.: Anchor, 1978.

Edge, John T. *A Gracious Plenty: Recipes and Recollections from the American South.* New York: G. P. Putnam's Sons, 1999.

Farr, Sidney Saylor. *More Than Moonshine: Appalachian Recipes and Recollections.* Pittsburgh: University of Pittsburgh Press, 1983.

Foose, Martha Hall. *Screen Doors and Sweet Tea: Recipes and Tales from a Southern Cook.* New York: Clarkson Potter, 2008.

Lewis, Edna, and Scott Peacock. *The Gift of Southern Cooking: Recipes and Revelations from Two Great Southern Cooks.* New York: Knopf, 2003.

Midda, Sara. *A Bowl of Olives: On Food and Memory.* New York: Workman, 2014.

Pinner, Patty. *Sweets: A Collection of Soul Food Desserts and Memories.* Berkeley, Calif.: Ten Speed Press, 2003.

Rogers, Amy. *Hungry for Home: Stories of Food from Across the Carolinas with More Than 200 Favorite Recipes.* Winston-Salem, N.C.: John F. Blair, 2004.

Wizenberg, Molly. *A Homemade Life: Stories and Recipes from My Kitchen Table.* New York: Simon & Schuster, 2009.

Cooking Basics

Beranbaum, Rose Levy. *The Cake Bible.* New York: William Morrow, 1988.

Bittman, Mark. *How to Cook Everything: 2000 Simple Recipes for Great Food.* Rev. ed. Hoboken, N.J.: Wiley, 2008.

Brown, Alton. *I'm Just Here for More Food: Food × Mixing + Heat = Baking.* New York: Stewart, Tabori & Chang, 2004.

———. *I'm Just Here for the Food: Food + Heat = Cooking.* Version 2.0. New York: Stewart, Tabori & Chang, 2006.

Corriher, Shirley O. *BakeWise: The Hows and Whys of Successful Baking.* New York: Scribner, 2008.

———. *CookWise: The Hows and Whys of Successful Cooking.* New York: William Morrow, 1997.

Daley, Regan. *In the Sweet Kitchen: The Definitive Baker's Companion.* New York: Artisan, 2001.

Figoni, Paula. *How Baking Works: Exploring the Fundamentals of Baking Science.* 3rd ed. Hoboken, N.J.: Wiley, 2014.

Flinn, Kathleen. *The Kitchen Counter Cooking School: How a Few Simple Lessons Transformed Nine Culinary Novices into Fearless Home Cooks.* New York: Viking, 2011.

McGee, Harold. *On Food and Cooking: The Science and Lore of the Kitchen.* Rev. ed. New York: Scribner, 2004.

Ostmann, Barbara Gibbs, and Jane L. Baker. *The Recipe Writer's Handbook*. Rev. ed. Hoboken, N.J.: Wiley, 2001.

Parsons, Russ. *How to Pick a Peach*. Boston: Houghton Mifflin, 2007.

Vileisis, Ann. *Kitchen Literacy: How We Lost Knowledge of Where Food Comes From and Why We Need to Get It Back*. Washington, D.C.: Island Press, 2008.

Whitman, Joan, and Dolores Simon. *Recipes into Type: A Handbook for Cookbook Writers and Editors*. New York: HarperCollins, 1993.

Folklore and Foodways

American Folklife Center. www.loc.gov/folklife.

American Folklore Society. www.afsnet.org.

Bartis, Peter. *Folklife and Fieldwork: A Layman's Introduction to Field Techniques*. Rev. ed. Washington, D.C.: Library of Congress, 2002.

Camp, Charles. *American Foodways: What, When, Why, and How We Eat in America*. Little Rock: August House, 1989.

Dabney, Joseph E. *Smokehouse Ham, Spoon Bread, and Scuppernong Wine: The Folklore and Art of Southern Appalachian Cooking*. Nashville: Cumberland House, 1998.

Edge, John T., ed. *Foodways*. Vol. 7 of *The New Encyclopedia of Southern Culture*. Chapel Hill: University of North Carolina Press, 2007.

Smithsonian Center for Folklife and Cultural Heritage. www.folklife.si.edu.

Food History

Allen, Brigid, ed. *Food: An Oxford Anthology*. Oxford: Oxford University Press, 1994.

Egerton, John. *Side Orders: Small Helpings of Southern Cookery and Culture*. Atlanta: Peachtree, 1990.

———. *Southern Food: At Home, on the Road, in History*. New York: Knopf, 1987.

Ferris, Marcie Cohen. *Matzoh Ball Gumbo: Culinary Tales of the Jewish South*. Chapel Hill: University of North Carolina Press, 2005.

Haber, Barbara. *From Hardtack to Home Fries: An Uncommon History of American Cooks and Meals*. New York: Free Press, 2002.

Kamp, David. *The United States of Arugula: How We Became a Gourmet Nation*. New York: Random House, 2006.

Kurlansky, Mark. *The Food of a Younger Land*. New York: Riverhead, 2009.

McWilliams, James E. *A Revolution in Eating: How the Quest for Food Shaped America*. New York: Columbia University Press, 2005.

Olver, Lynne. The Food Timeline. www.foodtimeline.org.

Root, Waverly, and Richard de Rochemont. *Eating in America: A History*. New York: William Morrow, 1976.

Schenone, Laura. *A Thousand Years over a Hot Stove: A History of American Women Told through Food, Recipes, and Remembrances.* New York: W. W. Norton, 2003.

Shephard, Sue. *Pickled, Potted, and Canned: How the Art and Science of Food Preserving Changed the World.* New York: Simon & Schuster, 2000.

Sitwell, William. *A History of Food in 100 Recipes.* Boston: Little, Brown, 2013.

Smith, Andrew F., ed. *The Oxford Companion to American Food and Drink.* New York: Oxford University Press, 2007.

Sokolov, Raymond. *Fading Feast: A Compendium of Disappearing American Regional Foods.* New York: Farrar, Straus & Giroux, 1981.

Symons, Michael. *A History of Cooks and Cooking.* Urbana: University of Illinois Press, 2000.

Theophano, Janet. *Eat My Words: Reading Women's Lives through the Cookbooks They Wrote.* New York: Palgrave, 2002.

Tye, Diane. *Baking as Biography: A Life Story in Recipes.* Montreal and Kingston: McGill-Queen's University Press, 2010.

Historical Research

Allen, Barbara, and William Lynwood Montell. *From Memory to History: Using Oral Sources in Local Historical Research.* Nashville: American Association for State and Local History, 1981.

Hunt, Marjorie. *The Smithsonian Folklife and Oral History Interviewing Guide.* Washington, D.C.: Smithsonian Institution Center for Folklife and Cultural Heritage, 2003.

Philibert-Ortega, Gena. *From the Family Kitchen: Discover Your Food Heritage and Preserve Favorite Recipes.* Cincinnati: Family Tree Books, 2012.

Ritchie, Donald A. *Doing Oral History.* 3rd ed. New York: Oxford University Press, 2014.

Sommer, Barbara W., and Mary Kay Quinlan. *The Oral History Manual.* 2nd ed. Lanham, Md.: AltaMira Press, 2009.

Sperry, Kip. *Abbreviations & Acronyms: A Guide for Family Historians.* Rev. 2nd ed. Provo, Utah: Ancestry, 2003.

———. *Reading Early American Handwriting.* Baltimore: Genealogical Publishing, 2008.

Stryker-Rodda, Harriet. *Understanding Colonial Handwriting.* Rev. ed. Baltimore: Genealogical Publishing, 2002.

Thornton, Tamara Plakins. *Handwriting in America: A Cultural History.* New Haven, Conn.: Yale University Press, 1996.

Veale, Sharon, and Kathleen Schilling. *Talking History: Oral History Guidelines.* Hurstville, Australia: New South Wales Department of Environment and Conservation, 2004.

Williams, Don, and Louisa Jaggar. *Saving Stuff: How to Care for and Preserve Your Collectibles, Heirlooms, and Other Prized Possessions.* New York: Fireside, 2005.

Working with Older Recipes

Anderson, Jean. *The American Century Cook-Book: The Most Popular Recipes of the 20th Century*. New York: Clarkson Potter, 1997.

Barchers, Suzanne I., and Patricia C. Marden. *Cooking Up U.S. History: Recipes and Research to Share with Children*. 2nd ed. Englewood, Colo.: Teacher Ideas Press, 1999.

Barile, Mary. *Cookbooks Worth Collecting*. Radnor, Pa.: Wallace-Homestead, 1994.

Brass, Marilynn, and Sheila Brass. *Heirloom Baking with the Brass Sisters*. New York: Black Dog & Leventhal, 2006.

Crump, Nancy Carter. *Hearthside Cooking*. McLean, Va.: EPM, 1986.

Donovan, Mary, Amy Hatrak, Frances Mills, and Elizabeth Shull. *The Thirteen Colonies Cookbook*. New York: Praeger, 1975.

Foxfire. "Foxfire's Book of Wood Stove Cookery." Special issue, vol. 15, no. 4 (1981).

Moss, Kay K. *Seeking the Historical Cook: Exploring Eighteenth-Century Southern Foodways*. Columbia: University of South Carolina Press, 2013.

Page, Linda Garland, and Elliot Wigginton, eds. *The Foxfire Book of Appalachian Cookery*. New York: Random House, 1984.

Shindler, Merrill. *American Dish: 100 Recipes from Ten Delicious Decades*. Santa Monica, Calif.: Angel City Press, 1996.

Spaulding, Lily May, and John Spaulding. *Civil War Recipes: Receipts from the Pages of Godey's Lady's Book*. Lexington: University Press of Kentucky, 1999.

Willard, Pat. *America Eats! On the Road with the WPA*. New York: Bloomsbury, 2008.

Bibliography

Abramson, Rudy, and Jean Haskell, eds. *Encyclopedia of Appalachia*. Knoxville:
    University of Tennessee Press, 2006.

Acton, Eliza. *Modern Cookery for Private Families*. London: Longmans, 1845.

Adnum, Heidi. *The Crafter's Guide to Taking Great Photos*. Loveland, Colo.: Interweave
    Press, 2011.

Allrecipes.com user ElizabethBH. "Best Big, Fat, Chewy Chocolate Chip Cookie."
    http://allrecipes.com/recipe/best-big-fat-chewy-chocolate-chip-cookie.

Anderson, Martha Lee. *Successful Baking for Flavor and Texture*, 5th ed. New York:
    Church & Dwight, 1936.

[Andrews, Julia C.] *Breakfast, Dinner, and Tea: Viewed Classically, Poetically, and
    Practically*. New York: D. Appleton, 1859.

Aulette, Judy Root. *Changing Families*. Belmont, Calif.: Wadsworth, 1994.

Barile, Mary. *Cookbooks Worth Collecting*. Radnor, Pa.: Wallace-Homestead, 1994.

Bartis, Peter. *Folklife and Fieldwork: A Layman's Introduction to Field Techniques*.
    Rev. ed. Washington, D.C.: Library of Congress, 2002.

Beard, James. *Delights and Prejudices*. New York: Atheneum, 1964.

Beecher, Catharine. *Miss Beecher's Domestic Receipt Book*. New York: Harper and
    Brothers, 1846.

Beeton, Mrs. [Isabella Mary]. *Mrs Beeton's Book of Household Management*. London:
    S. O. Beeton, 1861.

Beranbaum, Rose Levy. *The Cake Bible*. New York: William Morrow, 1988.

Bianchi, Suzanne M., John P. Robinson, and Melissa A. Milkie. *Changing Rhythms of American Family Life*. New York: American Sociological Association/Russell Sage Foundation, 2006.

Bird, Brad, screenwriter and director. *Ratatouille*. Pixar, 2007. DVD.

Bower, Anne L. "Our Sisters' Recipes: Exploring 'Community' in a Community Cookbook." *Journal of Popular Culture* 31, no. 3 (1997): 137–51.

Breckinridge, Issa Desha. Recipe Book, n.d. MS 997003, box 738, Breckinridge Family Papers. Manuscripts Division, Library of Congress.

Brillat-Savarin, Jean Anthelme. *The Physiology of Taste*. Translated and annotated by M. F. K. Fisher. 1949. New York: Knopf, 1971.

British Library. "Learning: Books for Cooks." www.bl.uk/learning/langlit/booksforcooks /booksforcooks.html.

——. "Learning: Dictionaries and Meanings." www.bl.uk/learning/langlit/dic/oed /receipt/recipe.html.

Brown, Alton. *I'm Just Here for More Food: Food × Mixing + Heat = Baking*. New York: Stewart, Tabori & Chang, 2004.

——. *I'm Just Here for the Food: Food + Heat = Cooking*. Version 2.0. New York: Stewart, Tabori & Chang, 2006.

Brown, Marion Lea. *The Southern Cook Book*. Chapel Hill: University of North Carolina Press, 1951.

Brunvand, Jan Harold, ed. *American Folklore: An Encyclopedia*. New York: Garland, 1996.

Bryan, Lettice. *The Kentucky Housewife*. Cincinnati: Shepard & Stearns, 1839.

Buchanan, David. *Taste, Memory: Forgotten Foods, Lost Flavors, and Why They Matter*. White River Junction, Vt.: Chelsea Green, 2012.

Bullock-Prado, Gesine. *Confections of a Closet Master Baker*. New York: Broadway Books, 2009.

Camp, Charles. *American Foodways: What, When, Why, and How We Eat in America*. Little Rock: August House, 1989.

Champion, Delia. *The Flying Biscuit Cafe Cookbook*. Salt Lake City: Gibbs Smith, 2007.

Child, Julia, and Jacques Pépin. *Julia and Jacques Cooking at Home*. New York: Knopf, 2000.

Child, Lydia Maria. *The American Frugal Housewife*. 29th ed. New York: Samuel S. & William Wood, 1844. Facsimile, Mineola, N.Y.: Dover, 1999.

Church & Dwight Company. *Arm & Hammer Bicarbonate of Soda Book of Valuable Recipes*. 64th ed. New York: Church & Dwight, 1900.

Claiborne, Craig. *Craig Claiborne's Southern Cooking*. New York: Times Books, 1987.

Cleveland County Home Demonstration Club Council. *Cookbook*. Rison, Ark.: CCHDCC, 1963.

Cleveland County Extension Home Makers Club. *Love Is Sharing Our Recipes*. Rison, Ark.: CCEHMC, 1975.

Cook, Lynnmarie P. "Mama Faye's Biscuits." *Southern Living*, March 1996, 234.

Cook's Country editors. *America's Best Lost Recipes*. Brookline, Mass.: America's Test Kitchen, 2007.

Cook's Illustrated. "The Art of Biscuit-Making." May 1993.

Corriher, Shirley O. *BakeWise: The Hows and Whys of Successful Baking*. New York: Scribner, 2008.

———. *CookWise: The Hows and Whys of Successful Cooking*. New York: HarperCollins, 1997.

Crossett Congress of Parent-Teachers. *Crossett Cook Book*. Crossett, Ark.: Oakhurst and Hastings, 1959.

Crump, Nancy Carter. *Hearthside Cooking*. McLean, Va.: EPM, 1986.

Dabney, Joseph E. *Smokehouse Ham, Spoon Bread, and Scuppernong Wine: The Folklore and Art of Southern Appalachian Cooking*. Nashville: Cumberland House, 1998.

Detroit Stove Works. *Detroit Jewel Recipes*. Detroit: Detroit Stove Works, [ca. 1920s].

Dewan, Shaila. "Biscuit Bakers' Treasured Mill Moves North." *New York Times*, June 18, 2008.

Dooley, Don, ed. *Better Homes and Gardens Heritage Cook Book*. New York: Meredith, 1975.

Dull, Mrs. S. R. *Southern Cooking*. 1928. Athens: University of Georgia Press, 2006.

Dupree, Nathalie. *Nathalie Dupree's Southern Memories: Recipes and Reminiscences*. New York: Clarkson Potter, 1993.

———. *New Southern Cooking*. New York: Knopf, 1986.

Dupree, Nathalie, and Cynthia Graubart. *Southern Biscuits*. Layton, Utah: Gibbs Smith, 2011.

Edge, John T., ed. *Foodways*. Vol. 7 of *The New Encyclopedia of Southern Culture*. Chapel Hill: University of North Carolina Press, 2007.

———. *A Gracious Plenty: Recipes and Recollections from the American South*. New York: G. P. Putnam's Sons, 1999.

Egerton, John. *Side Orders: Small Helpings of Southern Cookery and Culture*. Atlanta: Peachtree, 1990.

———. *Southern Food: At Home, on the Road, in History*. New York: Knopf, 1987.

Eubanks, Paula. "The Family Table." Unpublished manuscript, 2008.

Farmer, Fannie Merritt. *The Original Boston Cooking-School Cook Book, 1896: 100th Anniversary Edition; A Facsimile of the First Edition*. Westport, Conn.: Hugh Lauter Levin Associates, 1996.

Ferris, Marcie Cohen. *Matzoh Ball Gumbo: Culinary Tales of the Jewish South*. Chapel Hill: University of North Carolina Press, 2005.

Figoni, Paula. *How Baking Works: Exploring the Fundamentals of Baking Science*. 2nd ed. Hoboken, N.J.: Wiley, 2008.

Fischer, David Hackett. *Albion's Seed: Four British Folkways in America*. New York: Oxford University Press, 1989.

Fisher, Abby. *What Mrs. Fisher Knows about Old Southern Cooking*. San Francisco: Women's Cooperative Printing Office, 1881. Facsimile, Bedford, Mass.: Applewood Books, 1995.

Fleetwood, William C., Jr. *Tidecraft: The Boats of South Carolina, Georgia, and Northeastern Florida, 1550–1950*. Tybee Island, Ga.: WBG Marine Press, 1995.

Flinn, Kathleen. *The Kitchen Counter Cooking School: How a Few Simple Lessons Transformed Nine Culinary Novices into Fearless Home Cooks*. New York: Viking, 2011.

Fowler, Damon Lee, ed. *Classical Southern Cooking*. New York: Crown, 1995.

———. *Dining at Monticello: In Good Taste and Abundance*. Charlottesville, Va.: Thomas Jefferson Foundation, 2005.

Franklin, Linda Campbell. *300 Years of Kitchen Collectibles*. Iola, Wis.: Krause, 2003.

Frey, Eric. "Impressions of George Cowles." Unpublished manuscript, 2005.

Frey, Valerie. "Personal Information Systems: Journals and Diaries as Product and Process." Master's thesis, University of Tennessee, 1999.

Frey, Valerie, Kaye Kole, and Luciana Spracher, comps. *Voices of Savannah: Selections from the Oral History Collection of the Savannah Jewish Archives*. Savannah, Ga.: Savannah Jewish Archives, 2004.

General Foods. *Betty Crocker's Picture Cook Book, Revised and Enlarged*. New York: McGraw Hill, [1956].

———. *Favorite Recipes for Country Kitchens*. General Foods Corporation, 1945.

Glasse, Hannah. *The Art of Cookery Made Plain and Easy*. Facsimile of 1805 edition, with notes by Karen Hess. Bedford, Mass.: Applewood, 1997.

Goldberg, Natalie. *Writing Down the Bones: Freeing the Writer Within*. Boston: Shambhala, 1986.

Green, Thomas A., ed. *Folklore: An Encyclopedia of Beliefs, Customs, Tales, Music, and Art*. Santa Barbara: ABC-CLIO, 1997.

Greene, Jessica, and Ted Hafer. *The Grit Cookbook*. Athens, Ga.: Hill Street Press, 2001.

Grizzard, Lewis. *Don't Forget to Call Your Mama . . . I Wish I Could Call Mine*. Marietta, Ga.: Longstreet Press, 1991.

Harris, Jessica B. *The Welcome Table: African-American Heritage Cooking*. New York: Fireside/Simon & Schuster, 1995.

Hauser, Susan Carol. *You Can Write a Memoir*. Cincinnati: Writer's Digest Books, 2001.

Hearn, Lafcadio. *La Cuisine Creole: A Collection of Culinary Recipes, from Leading Chefs and Noted Creole Housewives, Who Have Made New Orleans Famous for Its Cuisine*. New Orleans: F. F. Hansell & Brothers, 1885.

Hess, John L., and Karen Hess. *The Taste of America*. 1977. Urbana: University of Illinois Press, 2000.

Hess, Karen, ed. *Martha Washington's Booke of Cookery*. New York: Columbia University Press, 1981. Manuscript held by the Historical Society of Pennsylvania.

Hill, Mrs. A. P. *Mrs. Hill's New Cook Book*. New York: James O'Kane, 1867. Facsimile of the 1872 edition, *Mrs. Hill's Southern Practical Cookery and Receipt Book*. Columbia: University of South Carolina Press, 1995.

Hopley, Claire. "American Cookery." *American History* 31, no. 2 (1996): 16–19.

Jacobsen, Rowan. *American Terroir: Savoring the Flavors of Our Woods, Waters, and Fields*. New York: Bloomsbury, 2010.

Junior League of Charleston. *Charleston Receipts*. 28th ed. Memphis: Wimmer Brothers, 1993.

Kamp, David. *The United States of Arugula: How We Became a Gourmet Nation*. New York: Random House, 2006.

Kander, Mrs. Simon. *The Settlement Cookbook*. Milwaukee: Milwaukee Public School Cooking Centers, 1901. Reprint, Mineola, N.Y.: Dover Publications, 2005.

Kivnick, Helen Q. "Remembering and Being Remembered: The Reciprocity of Psychosocial Legacy." *Generations* 20, no. 3 (1996): 49–53.

Koplin, Doris. *Cooking Drives Me Nuts, But I Love It*. Atlanta: privately published, 1992, 1994.

———. *The Quick Cook*. Atlanta: privately published, 2002.

Kummer, Corby. "Half a Loaf." *Atlantic* 302, no. 2 (October 2008): 122.

Kurlansky, Mark. *The Food of a Younger Land*. New York: Riverhead, 2009.

Lamott, Anne. *Bird by Bird: Some Instructions on Writing and Life*. New York: Pantheon, 1994.

Lauritzen, Georgia C. "Ingredient Substitution." Utah State University. http://digitalcommons.usu.edu/extension_histfood/17.

Leslie, Eliza. *Miss Leslie's New Cookery Book*. Philadelphia: T. B. Peterson and Brothers, 1857.

Lewis, Edna, and Scott Peacock. *The Gift of Southern Cooking: Recipes and Revelations from Two Great Southern Cooks*. New York: Knopf, 2003.

Lincoln, Mary J., et al. *Home Helps: A Pure Food Cook Book*. Chicago: N. K. Fairbank, 1910.

Long, Lucy M. "Culinary Tourism: A Folkloristic Perspective on Eating and Otherness." *Southern Folklore* 55, no. 3 (1998): 181–204.

Lupo, Margaret. *Southern Cooking from Mary Mac's Tea Room*. Rev. ed. New York: Dell, 1988.

Lynn, Kristie, and Robert W. Pelton. *The Early American Cookbook*. Georgetown, Del.: William H. McCauley, 1983.

Maclean, Norman. *A River Runs Through It, and Other Stories*. Chicago: University of Chicago Press, 1976.

Madenwald, A. Account Books of A. Madenwald (Medenwald), 1865–1910. Arkansas History Commission. Microfilm.

Major, Glenda. *Hollyhocks and Old Maid Aunts: A Book of Memories, Favorite Poems, Amusing Quotes, and Family Recipes*. Privately published, [2006].

Marks, Susan. *Finding Betty Crocker: The Secret Life of America's First Lady of Food.* New York: Simon & Schuster, 2005.

Maugham, W. Somerset. *The Summing Up.* Garden City, N.Y.: Doubleday, Doran, 1938.

McGahey, Marion. "Our Best Buttermilk Biscuits." *Southern Living*, November 2007, 166.

McGee, Harold. *On Food and Cooking: The Science and Lore of the Kitchen.* Rev. ed. New York: Scribner, 2004.

McNerney, Kathryn. *Kitchen Antiques, 1790–1940.* Paducah, Ky.: Collector Books, 1991.

McWilliams, James E. *A Revolution in Eating: How the Quest for Food Shaped America.* New York: Columbia University Press, 2005.

Moffat, Mary Jane. *The Times of Our Lives: A Guide to Writing Autobiography and Memoir.* 3rd ed. Santa Barbara, Calif.: John Daniel, 1996.

Moritz, Mrs. Chas. F. *Every Woman's Cook Book.* New York: Cuppies and Leon, 1926.

Moritz, Mrs. C. F., and Adèle Kahn. *The Twentieth Century Cook Book.* New York: G. W. Dillingham, 1897.

Moss, Kay K. *Seeking the Historical Cook: Exploring Eighteenth-Century Southern Foodways.* Columbia: University of South Carolina Press, 2013.

Neal, Bill. *Bill Neal's Southern Cooking.* Rev. ed. Chapel Hill: University of North Carolina Press, 1989.

Nelson, Don. "Cookies & Co. to Close in Downtown Athens." Online Athens, 4 September 2009. http://onlineathens.com/stories/090409/bre_489734226.shtml

Olver, Lynne. The Food Timeline. www.foodtimeline.org.

O'Neill, Molly. "Jam Session: A Breakfast Set with Biscuits and Scones." *New York Times Magazine*, May 31, 1998.

Oring, Elliott, ed. *Folk Groups and Folklore Genres: An Introduction.* Logan: Utah State University Press, 1986.

Ostmann, Barbara Gibbs, and Jane L. Baker. *The Recipe Writer's Handbook.* Rev. ed. Hoboken, N.J.: Wiley, 2001.

Page, Linda Garland, and Elliot Wigginton, eds. *The Foxfire Book of Appalachian Cookery.* New York: Random House, 1984.

Patridge, Tamara, and Mark Patridge. *Collard Greens and Sushi: A Diverse Collection of Favorite Recipes and Recollections from Those We Love.* Kearney, Nebr.: Morris Press Cookbooks, 2005.

Peacock, Scott. "Biscuits: Yep, They're Easy to Make." *Atlanta Journal and Constitution*, 3 April 2008, 3NC.

———. "Mini Prep Makes for Quick Biscuits." *Atlanta Journal and Constitution*, 20 March 2008, 7K.

Phaedrus. "Ask Uncle Phaedrus, Finder of Lost Recipes." www.hungrybrowser.com.

Pressfield, Steven. *The War of Art: Break Through the Blocks and Win Your Inner Creative Battles.* New York: Warner, 2002.

Proust, Marcel. *Swann's Way; Within a Budding Grove.* Vol. 1 of *Remembrance of Things*

Past. Translated by C. K. Scott Moncrieff and Terence Kilmartin. 1922. New York: Vintage, 1982.

Puckett, Susan. *A Cook's Tour of Mississippi*. Edited by Angela Meyers. Jackson, Miss.: *Clarion-Ledger*/Hederman Brothers, 1989.

Randolph, Mary. *The Virginia Housewife; or, Methodical Cook*. Philadelphia: E. H. Butler, 1860. Facsimile, New York: Dover, 1993.

Ritchie, Donald A. *Doing Oral History*. New York: Oxford University Press, 2003.

Roahen, Sara, and John T. Edge, eds. *The Southern Foodways Alliance Community Cookbook*. Athens: University of Georgia Press, 2010.

Roberts, Robert. *The House Servant's Directory; or, A Monitor for Private Families*. New York: Charles S. Francis, 1827.

Robinson, Sallie Ann. *Gullah Home Cooking the Daufuskie Way*. Chapel Hill: University of North Carolina Press, 2003.

Rogers, Amy. *Hungry for Home: Stories of Food from Across the Carolinas with More Than 200 Favorite Recipes*. Winston-Salem, N.C.: John F. Blair, 2004.

Rombauer, Irma S., and Marion Rombauer Becker. *Joy of Cooking*. 13th ed. Indianapolis: Bobbs-Merrill, 1975.

Royal Baking Powder Company. *Best War Time Recipes*. New York: Royal Baking Powder Company, 1918.

———. *Royal Baker and Pastry Cook*. New York: Royal Baking Powder Company, 1911.

Russell, Laura, and Marion L. Channing. *Laura Russell Remembers: An Old Plymouth Manuscript with Notes by Marion L. Channing*. New Bedford, Mass.: Reynolds-DeWalt Printing, 1970.

Rutledge, Sarah. *The Carolina Housewife; or House and Home by a Lady of Charleston*. Charleston: W. R. Babcock & Company, 1847. Facsimile, Columbia: University of South Carolina Press, 1979.

Sanders, Dori. *Dori Sanders' Country Cooking: Recipes and Stories from the Family Farm Stand*. Chapel Hill, N.C.: Algonquin, 1995.

Schenone, Laura. *A Thousand Years over a Hot Stove: A History of American Women Told through Food, Recipes, and Remembrances*. New York: W. W. Norton, 2003.

Shephard, Sue. *Pickled, Potted, and Canned: How the Art and Science of Food Preserving Changed the World*. New York: Simon & Schuster, 2000.

Shindler, Merrill. *American Dish: 100 Recipes from Ten Delicious Decades*. Santa Monica, Calif.: Angel City Press, 1996.

Shipley, Ina. Receipt Book, ca. 1851–1956. Unpublished manuscript. Collection of the author.

Simmons, Amelia. *American Cookery*. Hartford, Conn., 1796. Facsimile, *The First American Cookbook*. Kansas City: Andrews McMeel Publishing, 2012.

Smart-Grosvenor, Vertamae. *Vibration Cooking; or, The Travel Notes of a Geechee Girl*. Garden City, N.Y.: Doubleday, 1970.

Smith, Andrew F., ed. *The Oxford Companion to American Food and Drink*. New York: Oxford University Press, 2007.

Smith, E. *The Compleat Housewife; or, Accomplish'd Gentlewoman's Companion*. Williamsburg, Va.: William Parks, 1742.

Sokolov, Raymond. *Fading Feast: A Compendium of Disappearing American Regional Foods*. New York: Farrar, Straus & Giroux, 1981.

Sommer, Barbara W., and Mary Kay Quinlan. *The Oral History Manual*. 2nd ed. Lanham, Md.: AltaMira Press, 2009.

Southern Living. "Mississippi's Best Biscuits." July 2004, 47.

Spaulding, Lily May, and John Spaulding. *Civil War Recipes: Receipts from the Pages of Godey's Lady's Book*. Lexington: University Press of Kentucky, 1999.

Sperry, Kip. *Reading Early American Handwriting*. Baltimore: Genealogical Publishing, 2008.

Starr, Kathy. *The Soul of Southern Cooking*. Jackson: University Press of Mississippi, 1989.

Stewart, Martha. "Where to Find Martha: Radio." (Question and answer column.) *Martha Stewart Living*, no. 167 (October 2007): 164.

St. John, Robert. *Deep South Staples; or, How to Survive in a Southern Kitchen without a Can of Cream of Mushroom Soup*. New York: Hyperion, 2006.

Stryker-Rodda, Harriet. *Understanding Colonial Handwriting*. Rev. ed. Baltimore: Genealogical Publishing, 2002.

Sutherland, Amy. *Cookoff: Recipe Fever in America*. New York: Viking, 2003.

Taylor, John Martin. *The New Southern Cook: Two Hundred Recipes from the South's Best Chefs and Home Cooks*. New York: Bantam, 1995.

Theophano, Janet. *Eat My Words: Reading Women's Lives through the Cookbooks They Wrote*. New York: Palgrave Macmillan, 2002.

Thomas, George. "The Story of the Lives of Freida Miller and George Thomas." Unpublished manuscript, 2005.

Thornton, P. *The Southern Gardener and Receipt Book*. 1840. Birmingham, Ala.: Exmoor House, 1984.

Thornton, Tamara Plakins. *Handwriting in America: A Cultural History*. New Haven, Conn.: Yale University Press, 1996.

Times-Mirror. *Los Angeles Times Cook Book—No. 2*. Los Angeles: Times-Mirror Company, 1905?.

Tye, Diane. *Baking as Biography: A Life Story in Recipes*. Montreal and Kingston: McGill-Queen's University Press, 2010.

Van Dyke, Louis, and Billie Van Dyke. *The Blue Willow Inn Bible of Southern Cooking*. Nashville: Rutledge Hill Press, 2005.

Villas, James. *My Mother's Southern Kitchen*. New York: Macmillan, 1994.

Volo, James M., and Dorothy Denneen Volo. *Family Life in 17th- and 18th-Century America*. Westport, Conn.: Greenwood, 2006.

Webster, Mrs. A. L. *The Improved Housewife; or, Book of Receipts . . . By A Married Lady.* Hartford, Conn.: privately published, 1844.

White, Anna Mathews. Anna Mathews White Paper, 1828–1832. MS857, Georgia Historical Society.

White, Mrs. N. "Household Department: Domestic Receipts." *Southern Farm and Home* 1, no. 6 (1870): 214–16.

Whitman, Joan, and Dolores Simon. *Recipes into Type: A Handbook for Cookbook Writers and Editors.* New York: HarperCollins, 1993.

Wilcox, Estelle Woods. *Buckeye Cookery, and Practical Housekeeping: Compiled from Original Recipes.* Minneapolis, Minn.: Buckeye Publishing Company, 1877.

Wilkes, Sema. *Mrs. Wilkes' Boardinghouse Cookbook.* With a history by John T. Edge. Berkeley, Calif.: Ten Speed Press, 2001.

Willard, Pat. *America Eats! On the Road with the WPA.* New York: Bloomsbury, 2008.

Williams, Don, and Louisa Jaggar. *Saving Stuff: How to Care for and Preserve Your Collectibles, Heirlooms, and Other Prized Possessions.* New York: Fireside, 2005.

Williams, Thomas L., ed. *You Say Cuisine; I Say Vittles: The Southern Chapter Compendium of Recipes and Reminiscences.* Southern Chapter of the Medical Library Association. Collierville, Tenn.: Fundcraft Publishing, 2004.

Wilson, Bee. *Consider the Fork: A History of How We Cook and Eat.* New York: Basic Books, 2012.

Wilson, Mary A., ed. *Rumford Southern Recipes.* Providence, R.I.: Rumford, 1926.

Wilson, Mrs. Henry Lumpkin, comp. *Tested Recipe Cook Book.* Atlanta: Foote & Davies, 1895.

Winegardner, Mark, ed. *We Are What We Ate: 24 Memories of Food.* San Diego: Harcourt Brace, 1998.

Wizenberg, Molly. *A Homemade Life: Stories and Recipes from My Kitchen Table.* New York: Simon & Schuster, 2009.

Zafar, Rafia. "The Signifying Dish: Autobiography and History in Two Black Women's Cookbooks." *Feminist Studies* 25, no. 2 (1999): 449–69.

Ziemann, Hugo, and F. L. Gillette. *White House Cookbook.* Revised and updated by Patti Bazel Geil and Tami Ross. Boston: Houghton Mifflin Harcourt, 1996.

Zimmer, Anne Carter. *The Robert E. Lee Family Cooking and Housekeeping Book.* Chapel Hill: University of North Carolina Press, 1997.

Zinsser, William. *Writing about Your Life: A Journey into the Past.* New York: Marlowe, 2004.

———. "Writing Family History." *Writer* 119, no. 7 (July 2006): 14.

Interviews with the Author

(Names appear in the format preferred by the interviewee, along with the interviewee's
town of residence or workplace at the time of the interview.)

Altieri, Marylène, Schlesinger Library, Boston, Mass. 25 September 2008.

Ashley, Bertha Schulze (1908–2013). Manchester, Tenn. 22 May 2008.

Bennett, Eddie. Decatur, Ga. 25 July 2007.

Bridges, Jane. Savannah, Ga. 13 February 2008.

Boswell, Rochelle O'Neal. Middlesex, N.C. 23 June 2007.

Carter, Constance. Science, Technology, and Business Division, Library of Congress,
Washington, D.C. 26 February 2008.

Cotner, Dennis. Colonial Williamsburg Foundation, Williamsburg, Va. 25 July 2007.

Couch, Dale. Sparta, Ga. 28 April 2008.

Crowley, Bonnie Esco (1923–2014). Athens, Ga. 27 March 2008, 9 October 2008.

Curry, Robert. Sparta, Ga. 28 April 2008.

Curry, Susie. Sparta, Ga. 28 April 2008.

Debeerst, Birgit. Ellenwood, Ga. 13 May 2008.

Dirksen, Jean. Augusta, Ga. 10 August 2007.

Eubanks, Martha. Macon, Ga. 2 December 2007.

Eubanks, Paula. Little Cumberland Island, Ga. 2 December 2007, 26 April 2008.

Gres, Dusty. Vidalia, Ga. 4 August 2007.

Hall, Carolyn Wade. Arabi, Ga. 24 March 2007.

Hensley, Norma Jean Thompson. New Edinburg, Ark. 9 September 2007.

Higginbotham, Maryellen. Root House Historic Site, Marietta, Ga. 14 May 2008.

Holland, Robynn. Locust Grove, Ga. 12 May 2008.

Ihrie, John (1922–2008). Louisburg, N.C. 23 June 2007.

Jarboe, Graham. Athens, Ga. 23 June 2007.

Jarrell, Greg. Sparta, Ga. 28 April 2008.

Koplin, Doris. Atlanta, Ga. 12 July 2007.

Major, Glenda. LaGrange, Ga. 31 January 2008.

McClellan, Joe Robert. Warren, Ark. 25 April 2005.

McClellan, Sue Reaves (1935–2007). Warren, Ark. 8 September 2007.

McCoy, Norma Faye Reaves. New Edinburg, Ark. 8–9 September 2007.

McCoy, Tully. New Edinburg, Ark. 2 July 2008.

McDonald, Gillie (1919–2013). Arabi, Ga. 24 March 2007.

Morgan, Martha Jean (1923–2013). Knoxville, Tenn. 23 May 2008.

Oliver, Hoyt. Oxford, Ga. 12 August 2007.

O'Neal, Rachel. Bishop, Ga. 8 October 2008.

O'Neal, Willene England. Athens, Ga. 19 June 2008.

Patridge, Tamara Welborn. Morrow, Ga. 18 July 2007.

Pourreau, Leslie Browning. Kennesaw, Ga. 1 August 2008.

Puckett, Susan. Atlanta, Ga. 12 May 2008.

Reaves, Lloyd "Buddy" (1937–2011). New Edinburg, Ark. 2 July 2008.

Reaves, Michelle. New Edinburg, Ark. 8–9 September 2007.

Robinson, Anna Santiago. Atlanta, Ga. 13 May 2008.

Stone, Carl. Kennesaw, Ga. 24 March 2007.

Sullivan, Eleanor O'Neal. Greenville, N.C. 23 June 2007.

Sullivan, Luann. Greenville, N.C. 23 June 2007.

Thomas, Brian. Washington, D.C. 28 February 2008.

Thomas, Dominic. Atlanta, Ga. 17 January 2008.

Thomas, George. Athens, Ga. 27 March 2008.

Thomas, Heidi Anne. Antioch, Tenn. 25 January 2008.

Thomas, Janie Knott. Antioch, Tenn. 25 January 2008.

Thomas, Zack. Seattle, Wash. 8 March 2008.

Thompson, LouElla Huddleston (1916–2014). New Edinburg, Ark. 9 September 2007.

Thompson, Marcia Martin. Savannah, Ga. 13 February 2008.

Vessels, Christian. Chattanooga, Tenn. 23 May 2008.

Vessels, Karen. Chattanooga, Tenn. 23 May 2008.

Winkler, Micha. Washington, D.C. 28 February 2008.

Index

Locator numbers in *italics* indicate an illustration

book publishing procedures, 25–26, 30, 33, 171–75

cookbooks: comparison of foreign/ domestic, 100–101; earliest American (1796), 215; suggested reading, 272–75

cooking mentors, 230–51

cooking utensils: biscuit brake, 216–17; biscuit cutters, 197–98, *199*, 199–200, 203, 225–26; for biscuit making, 222–27; biscuit tables, 222; candy thermometer, 110; canning jars, *64*; care and conservation of, 61–64; cast iron, 61, 206, 244–45; for cleanup, 204–5; cookie cutters, *61*; copper bowl, 76; dinner horn, *62*; dough bowl, 222, *223*; egg beaters, 85; grater, *63*; gridiron, 215; knives, *63*; for measuring, *71*, 86–87, 121–22; ovens/microwaves, 81, 85, 213; paddle, *62*; pasta maker, 217;

pastry blender, 202; pastry mat, 225; pestle, 215; quality of, 244–45; rolling pin, 203, 225; scales, 122; sifter/sieve, *201*, 222; tube pan, 23

cooking visits. *See under* interviews

Cooperative Extension services, 80, 156, 260–61

family anecdotes: breakfast pound cake, 22; Eric's Four-Wheeling Spaghetti, 20; Grandpa's ice cream, 160; mulligan stew, 3–4; orange slices, 20; about pralines, 246–47; recipes in coffin sketches, 37; secret cobbler recipe, 128

family history: and biscuit evolution, 211–27; and cooking lessons, 241–51; and cooking mentors, 229–40; and foreign ingredients, 101–5; and legacy, 240–51; and personal tastes, 190–91; in recipes, 3–6, 97–105, 139–41, 149; resources for, 211–13; in scrapbooks/ journals, 15, 145–53, 233–34, 243;

supplemental material for, 140–41; and traditions, 245–46. *See also* foodways; recipe collections

foods:

—apples, 75, 207

—bacon, 10, 197

—Bitter-Mandel Aroma, 101–2

—catsup/ketchup, 84

—cheese, 105

—chicken, 2, 10–11, 82, 92, 237

—corn, 10, 99, 231

—crawfish, 238–40

—eggs, 83, 107, 109–10, 136, 218

—fats, 191–92, 195–96; bacon grease, 192, 195; butter, 195, 202; lard, 137, 194–96, 199, 224, 226; margarine, 137, 158, 193, 195–209; oil, 75, 82, 192, 195, 202; shortening, *67, 82*, 85, 95, 137, 192–93, 195, 199, 201, 209

—flours, *82*, 84, 102, 193–94, 197

—gluten (protein), 74, 193, 200, 203

—leavenings, 191, 215–20; baking powder, 194, 213, 219–20; baking soda,

foods (*continued*)
194, 213, 218–20; cream of tartar, 194, 219–20, 251; saleratus, 218–20; yeast, 197, 218
—liquids, 85, 163, 196–97, 201, 203
—meat, 11, 99, 104–5
—milk/buttermilk/cream, 84, 105, 123, 191, 195
—nutmeg/mace, 164, 264n39
—onions, 10, 93
—oysters, 84
—pasta, 10, 131
—peaches, 127–28, 231
—potatoes, 10, 81
—salt, 195
—spices, 231–32
—sucre vanillé, 101
—sugar, 137, 196–97
—tomatoes, 10, 207
—zucchini squash, 104
foodways: biscuit sidekicks, 205; Cajun, 24, 233–34, 237–39, 241, 243, 246–47; defined, 29; evolution of, 221; legacy of, 240–51; meat varieties, 1–4, 99; mulligan stew, 3–4, 10; one-pot dishes, 4; recipe research and, 212–13, 221; regional/worldwide, 99–105; rejection of mediocrity, 242–44; roux rite of passage, 241–42; socialization and, 244; veganism, 245–46

heirloom recipes. *See* recipes
history. *See* family history

ingredient considerations: acid-alkali balance, 219–20; adaptability techniques, 244–45; additives, 81, 220; age of chicken, 237; availability, 83–84; barometric pressure, 85; community culture, 91–92, 238; cooking styles, 238; cost, 213; dating, 140; dough handling, 203; flavor, 202; flour protein (gluten), 193; foreign, 100–105; impurities, 194; for pies, 84–

85; Pure Food and Drug Act and, 220–21; quality, 92–93, 237–38; recheck for reformulations, 85; sources, 101, 103; storage, 93; substitution lists, 91; sugar types, 80; texture, 202; variants, 85, 248–49. *See also* measurements; recipe ingredients
interviews: checklist of questions for, 24–25, 251; cooking visits, 120–23, 126–28, 224–25; for exploring legacy, 234–51; note taking at, 17–18, 111–12; preparation for and conduct of, 111–18; transcription of, 123–25

measurements: during cooking visits, 121–22; in foreign recipes, 100; guides for older measures, 164–65; in heirloom recipes, 71–73, 86–87, 136, 138–39. *See also* temperatures
mentors, cooking, 230–51
methods/techniques: adaptability of, 244–45; for adding liquids, 197, 203; for baking, 188; for beating, 215–16; bench tolerance and, 200; for biscuits, 191–92, 199–200, 202–4, 206, 226; for chicken gumbo, 237; cleanup tricks, 204–5; for clove orange pomander, 232; for cutting in shortening, 201; for dough handling, 192, 203–4; for freezing leftovers, 239–40; for hand-shaping, 204; instructional sources for, 80; for kneading, 200, 203, 225; for mixing, 194, 202–3, 223–25; older versus newer, 84–85, 164; refrigeration after mixing, 202–3; resting dough, 199–200; for roux, 241–42; sifting, 200–201; skills and, 234, 236–40, 243–44; stirring, 203; temperature/heat and, 204; with wooden dough bowl, 222–24. *See also* recipe modification

recipe collections: acknowledgments in, 46; as artifacts, 151; authentication

challenges, 1–43, 139–41; biscuit quest, 190–91; care and handling of, 40, 85, 110, 144–45; cooks' legacies and, 229–33; copyright and, 45–46, 258n11; damage management of, 15, 50–55, *54*, 61, *62*, 88–89, 91, 259n13; digital media and, 41, 57–60, 91–92; etiquette for, 47; evolution of, 93–94, 221; expansion of, 43–47; on file cards, 233–34; filing system for, 38–40; food history and, 212–13; forms of, 37; gathering of, 43–47; goals for, 13–14, 16–18, 30–33; as group project, 27–33; handwriting challenges and, 141–44; indexes for, 36, 40; as inspiration, 94–95; as legacy, 28, 89–90, 93, 230–32; locations of, 142, 145–53; memories and, 94; note taking and, 16–18; organization of, 35–41; origins of, 44–48; pitfalls of, 30–33, 81–87, 92–93; preservation of, 15, 50–55, *54*, 61, *62*, 88–89, 91, 259n13; printed cookbooks and, 151–53; regional variants and, 190–91; release forms for, 49; remembered dish and, 90–92; sketchy/unwritten recipes and, 89–90, 133–34; software upgrades and, 41; as solo project, 25–27; sources of, 38, 97–105; storage containers for, 55–56; supplemental material for, 14–16; supplies for, 38, 40–41; and *terroir* (taste of place), 93; translation of, 98–99. *See also* family history; interviews; recipe modification; recipes
recipe ingredients:
—almonds, in cucumber sandwiches, 249
—apples, in lazy gal pie, 207
—bacon grease, in biscuits, 192
—baking powder: in biscuits, 209; in cake, 106; in pound cake, 23; in teacakes, 68
—baking soda: in sweetbread, 95; in teacakes, 68
—basil, in clam sauce, 131

—beer, in crepes, 103
—bell peppers, in crawfish stew, 250
—biscuits: in cake in a bowl, 208; in Cush, 207; in lazy gal pie, 208
—bitter almond flavoring, in cake, 106
—black pepper: in clam sauce, 131; in cucumber sandwiches, 249
—brown sugar: in chess tarts, 18; in pralines, 251
—butter: in biscuits, 209, 215–16; in cake, 125; in chess tarts, 18; in crepes, 103; in cucumber sandwiches, 249; in pound cake, 23; in pralines, 251
—buttermilk: in biscuits, 209; in sweetbread, 95
—celery, in crawfish stew, 250
—cheese, in cheese straws, 18
—cherries, in glaze, 106
—cherry liqueur, in frosting, 106
—cinnamon: in cake, 106; in lazy gal pie, 208; in sweetbread, 95
—clam juice, in clam sauce, 131
—clams, in clam sauce, 131
—cloves, in cake, 106
—cocoa: in cake, 106; in lazy gal pie, 208; in pound cake, 23
—cooking spray, for biscuit baking, 192
—corn syrup, in divinity, 110
—crawfish/shrimp/crab fingers, in crawfish stew, 250
—cream: in pound cake, 23; in pralines, 251
—cream of tartar, in pralines, 251
—Creole seasoning, in cucumber sandwiches, 249
—crushed pineapple, in pineapple sauce, 125
—cucumbers, in cucumber sandwiches, 249
—dark chocolate, in frosting, 106
—eggs: in biscuits, 215; in cake, 106, 125; in chess tarts, 18; in crepes, 103; in pound cake, 23; in sweetbread, 95; in teacakes, 68

—egg whites, in divinity, 110
—flavored extract/emulsion, 68
—flour (all-purpose): in biscuits, 215–16; in cake, 106; in cheese straws, 18; in chess tarts, 18; in crawfish stew, 250; in crepes, 103; in pound cake, 23; in teacakes, 68
—flour (cake), in cake, 106
—flour (self-rising): in biscuits, 192, 209; in cake, 125; in pound cake, 23; in sweet bread, 95
—garlic, in clam sauce, 131
—ginger, in sweetbread, 95
—green onions, in cucumber sandwiches, 249
—herbs/spices, in Cush (leftovers), 207
—Maizena, in cake, 106
—margarine: in biscuits, 209; in cheese straws, 18
—mayonnaise, in cucumber sandwiches, 249
—milk: in biscuits, 192, 209, 215; in cake, 125; in chess tarts, 18; in crepes, 103; in lazy gal pie, 208; in pound cake, 23; in pralines, 251
—molasses, in sweetbread, 95
—oil: in biscuits, 192; in clam sauce, 131; in crawfish stew, 250
—onions, in crawfish stew, 250
—parsley, in clam sauce, 131
—pecans: in chess tarts, 18; in divinity, 110; in pralines, 251
—raspberry jam, in frosting, 106
—red pepper, in crawfish stew, 250
—salt: in biscuits, 215; in cake, 106; in cheese straws, 18; in crawfish stew, 250; in cucumber sandwiches, 249; in Cush (leftovers), 207; in divinity, 110; in pound cake, 23
—seafood seasoning, in crawfish stew, 250
—sesame seeds, in cheese straws, 18
—shortening: in biscuits, 209; in sweetbread, 95; in teacakes, 68

—shrimp, in crawfish stew, 250
—soy milk, in pound cake, 23
—*sucre vanillé*, in cake, 106
—sugar (confectioner's/powdered): in cake, 125; in frosting, 107
—sugar (granulated): in biscuits, 209; in cake, 125; in chess tarts, 18; in crepes, 103; in Cush (leftovers), 207; in divinity, 110; in lazy gal pie, 208; in pound cake, 23; in sweetbread, 95; in teacakes, 68
—Tabasco sauce, in crawfish stew, 250
—tomatoes: in clam sauce, 131; in Cush (leftovers), 207
—vanilla extract; in chess tarts, 18; in creamy pralines, 251; in crepes, 103; in divinity, 110; in lazy gal pie, 208; in pound cake, 23; in teacakes, 68
—walnuts, in chess tarts, 18
—water: in biscuits, 209; in cake, 106; in cheese straws, 18; in crawfish stew, 250; in divinity, 110; in teacakes, 68
—whipping cream, in frosting, 106
—white bread, in cucumber sandwiches, 249
—white wine, in clam sauce, 131
recipe modification: advice for, 65–66, 70, 259n3; for biscuits, 187–210; checklists for, 75–80, 164; clarification of, 70–78, 194; examples of, 110, 134–39, 187–210; of family recipes, 246–47; for foreign/regional/world sources, 99–105; ladder for, 89; listing of ingredients, 75, 79, 82–83; measuring accuracy and, 70–73, 86–87, 110, 136, 164, 259n3; multiple versions, 66–70, 139–41; from other cooks, 87–88; pitfalls of, 81–87; problem words in, 143; re-creating a remembered dish, 90–92; standardizing weights/measures for, 71–73, 86–87, 164–65; technology and, 20, 58–61, 221; tips/tools for, 71–73, 78–80

recipes:

—complete: Apoquiniminc Cakes, 215–16; apple crisp, *93*; apple tapioca, *93*; Aunt Mabel's Pecan Divinity, 110; beaten biscuits, 215; Belgian Beer Pancakes (crepes), 103; Berry-Marble Cobbler, 39; biscuit sidekicks, 205; Black Forest Cake, 106–7; boardinghouse-style biscuits, 209; cheese straws, 18; chess tarts, 18; chicken mulligan, 10; chocolate cake in a bowl, 207–8; crawfish stew (handwritten), *250*; creamy pralines, 251; Cush (leftovers), 206–7; Ellen Moseley Teacakes, 68; Freida's Cucumber Sandwiches, 249; lazy gal pie, 207; Lemon Pie, 141; Mama Ralston's Sweet Bread, 95; Mrs. Bonnie Crowley's 1-2-3-4 Cake, 125; mulligan stew, 3; Norma Reaves McCoy's Quick Biscuits, 192; pineapple pourover cake/sauce, 125; pineapple sauce, 125; pound cakes and toppings, 23; red clam sauce for pasta, 131; steamed clams, 131; teacakes, 68

—discussed: biscuits, 188–209, 215–16, 225–26; Black Forest Cake, 101–2; chess tarts, 86; foundational, 192; for leftovers, 20, 207, 239–40; mulligan stew, 4; orange almond chicken, 92; origins of, 44–47; roux, 241–42; teacakes, 67–70, 134–39

research: cooks' legacies and, 229–33; example (biscuits), 213–27; expanding sources, 43; exploring a legacy, 234–51; family recipes and, 44; for heirloom recipes, 134–51, 214–15; identification of foods, 105; note taking, 17–18, 111–12; questions to consider, 146–51; recipe adjustment example, 134–39; recipe origins, 43–47; resources for, 211–13

seafood, 84, 209, 250

techniques. *See* methods/techniques.

technology, and recipe collecting, 20, 58–61, 111–14, 221

temperatures: air/moisture conditions and, 85; baking time and, 204; for biscuits, 197, 224; for cooking, 137–38, 164, 197, 224; effect of, on ingredients, 199, 201; guides to older measurements, 164; measurement of, 137–38, 164, 197, 224. *See also* measurements

utensils. *See* cooking utensils

writing aids: finding one's voice, 20–21, 24; *Recipe Writer's Handbook* (Baker/ Ostman), 46, 74; tips for writing, 69–70